Using Fireworks

macromedia

Acknowledgments

Writing: Lynn Flink, Stephanie Gowin, Sarah Hanily, Robin Hunt-Smith, Gavan Murphy, and Pamela Lu

Editing: Gary White.

Project management: Erick Vera and Stuart Manning

Production: Sherri Harte and Rocky Angelucci

First Edition: November 2000

Macromedia, Inc.
600 Townsend St.
San Francisco, CA 94103

CONTENTS

CHAPTER 7

CHAPTER 8

CHAPTER 15
Creating Rollovers 271

CHAPTER 16
Creating Animation 289

CHAPTER 17
Optimizing Graphics 307

CHAPTER 18

Exporting 329

CHAPTER 19

Using Dreamweaver and
Fireworks Together 349

CHAPTER 20

Automating Repetitive Tasks 365

CHAPTER 21

Fireworks for Photoshop Users 385

CHAPTER 22

Fireworks HTML. 403

INDEX 409

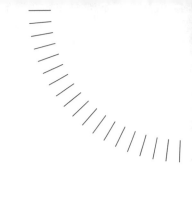

INTRODUCTION
Getting Started

Fireworks 4 is the solution for professional Web graphics design and production. It is the first production environment to overcome the special challenges facing Web graphic designers and developers.

Use Fireworks® to create, edit, and animate Web graphics, add advanced interactivity, and optimize images in a professional environment. Fireworks combines both bitmap and vector editing tools. In Fireworks, everything is editable, all the time. And you can automate the workflow to meet the demands of updates and changes.

Fireworks integrates with other Macromedia products such as FreeHand, Director, Dreamweaver™, and Macromedia Flash™, as well as other favorite graphics applications and HTML editors, to provide a true integrated Web solution. You can easily export Fireworks graphics with HTML and JavaScript™ code customized for the HTML editor you're using.

System requirements

The following hardware and software is required to run Fireworks:

- For Microsoft Windows™: An Intel Pentium® processor (Pentium II recommended) running Windows 95, 98, ME, 2000, or NT 4 (with Service Pack 5) or later; 64 MB of RAM plus 100 MB of available disk space; 800 x 600 pixel resolution, 256-color display (1024 x 768 resolution, millions of colors recommended); a mouse or digitizing tablet; and a CD-ROM drive.

- For the Macintosh®: A Power Macintosh (G3 or higher recommended), running System 8.6 or 9.x; 64 MB of RAM plus 100 MB of available disk space; Adobe Type Manager® 4 or later for using Type 1 fonts; a color monitor (1024 x 768 resolution, millions of colors recommended); a mouse or digitizing tablet; and a CD-ROM drive.

Installing Fireworks

Before installing Fireworks, make sure your computer is equipped as listed in "System requirements" on page 11. Read the ReadMe document on the Fireworks CD-ROM for late-breaking information.

To install Fireworks on Windows:

1 Insert the Fireworks 4 CD into your computer's CD-ROM drive.

2 Begin installing:

• In Windows, the Fireworks installation program starts automatically. If it doesn't, choose Start > Run. Click Browse and choose the file Setup.exe on the Fireworks 4 CD. Click OK in the Run dialog box.

• On the Macintosh, double-click the Fireworks 4 Installer icon.

3 Follow the onscreen instructions. The installation program prompts you to enter required information.

4 If prompted, restart your computer.

Learning Fireworks

A variety of resources are available for learning Fireworks, including a printed manual, a help system you can launch from the application, onscreen interactive lessons, and several Web-based information sources.

Fireworks Help is available whenever the Fireworks application is active. It contains the same material as this guide, plus some additional information.

Fireworks tutorial is an interactive introduction to the key features in Fireworks, and it can be completed in about an hour. It includes common Fireworks tasks such as optimizing GIFs and JPEGs, and creating animations and rollovers. If you are new to Fireworks, start with the lessons in the Help menu, then perform the tutorial.

Fireworks lessons are a series of short, onscreen lessons that focus on specific Fireworks features, from the basics of animation to creating rollovers and pop-up menus. The steps in each lesson can be performed in about 10 minutes. If you are new to Fireworks, start learning by completing the lessons and then proceed to the tutorial.

The **Fireworks application** contains many dialog boxes and ToolTips designed to assist you in using the program. ToolTips appear when your pointer pauses over a user interface element.

Using Fireworks includes information about basic and advanced Fireworks features. If you have used Photoshop but are new to Fireworks, read "Fireworks for Photoshop Users" on page 385 to help you make the transition. If you plan to take advantage of Fireworks and Dreamweaver integration, read "Using Dreamweaver and Fireworks Together" on page 349.

Extending Fireworks includes information about writing JavaScript to automate Fireworks tasks. Every command or setting in Fireworks can be controlled using special JavaScript commands that Fireworks can interpret. A PDF version of Extending Fireworks is available for download from http://www.macromedia.com/support/fireworks/extend.html.

The **Fireworks Support Center Web site** is updated regularly with the latest information on Fireworks, plus advice from expert users, advanced topics, examples, tips, and updates. Check the Support Center for news on Fireworks and how to get the most out of the program at http://www.macromedia.com/support/fireworks/.

The **Fireworks discussion group** provides a lively exchange for Fireworks users, technical support representatives, and the Fireworks development team. Use a newsgroup reader to go to news://forums.macromedia.com/macromedia.fireworks.

What's new in Fireworks 4

Fireworks 4 offers many new features to enhance your Web design experience.

Macromedia user interface

A consistent, familiar user interface helps designers work smoothly in Macromedia Flash, Dreamweaver, Dreamweaver UltraDev, and Fireworks. Whichever Macromedia Web design product you are using, you'll see the same icons, tools, toolbars, and terms wherever possible.

The Macromedia user interface has customizable keyboard shortcuts. You can install keyboard shortcuts that you use in other Macromedia or non-Macromedia graphics applications, or set up your own favorite shortcuts.

A Mini-Launcher along the bottom of the document window gives you quick access to common Fireworks panels.

For more on the new user interface, see "Fireworks Basics" on page 43.

Dreamweaver compatibility

Fireworks and Dreamweaver work together better than ever!

Round-trip table editing lets you edit and update HTML and JavaScript code and graphics from Dreamweaver while maintaining edits to the table. It updates HTML table images placed in Dreamweaver while preserving changes made to the HTML itself outside of Fireworks. If you change behaviors, enter new text, change the link, or make other edits, you can update graphic changes without overwriting HTML in Dreamweaver.

The enhanced Launch and Edit window brings you into Fireworks from a host application such as Dreamweaver or Macromedia Flash. You can take care of edits to documents you created in Fireworks, then click Done and go back to work in the host application.

When you launch and edit Fireworks images placed in Dreamweaver, the Dreamweaver Property inspector lets you know whether you are editing an image or a table. Click the Edit button on the Property inspector and the source PNG file is tracked.

For more on Fireworks and Dreamweaver compatibility, see "Using Dreamweaver and Fireworks Together" on page 349.

Drag-and-drop behaviors

Creating swap image and disjoint rollovers is as easy as dragging from trigger to target with drag-and-drop behaviors. Each slice and hotspot now contains a behavior control that you simply drag to assign behaviors. After you drag the control, a dialog box automatically opens so you can assign the behavior to a frame.

When you view them in the Web Layer, drag-and-drop behaviors show you what's linked to what. Click a behavior control and add more behaviors to a slice or hotspot from a context menu. Drag-and-drop behaviors are the same as traditionally assigned Fireworks behaviors, but they're easier to apply and manage. You can still view, edit, and assign behaviors in the Behaviors panel. For more information see "Applying drag-and-drop behaviors to hotspots" on page 253.

Pop-up menus

You've probably seen run-time navigation menus in lots of innovative Web sites, but either you didn't know how they did it or you didn't have time to do it. Fireworks has added the Fireworks Pop-Up Menu command to its growing arsenal of time-saving features.

You can create a pop-up menu using stylized text, or get creative by using graphics for your pop-up menu items. Either way, the Pop-Up Menu command turns a very difficult task into an easy one. You can use the same font families as in Dreamweaver. For more information, see "Creating Rollovers" on page 271.

Masking, Layers panel, and Frames panel enhancements

The new Layers panel displays a thumbnail view of each layer's objects, including slices and hotspots in the Web Layer. You can create a vector or bitmap mask in the Layers panel using thumbnails and the Add Mask button, or you can use the traditional paste-inside technique.

You can quickly and easily select, name, move, and delete individual objects right from the Layers panel. You can hide, show, lock, or unlock multiple layers by dragging down the hide/show and lock/unlock columns in the Layers panel. Opacity and blending mode settings are in an intuitive location on the Layers panel.

You can also name individual frames in the Frames panel to better manage frames in rollovers and animations and to import layers as frames (see "Layers and Masking" on page 203, and "Creating Animation" on page 289).

Reorganized and expanded export and import options

The Fireworks 4 Export dialog box is easier to use. The layout is more logical, and inapplicable options for the current export format are dimmed or hidden. The Export Special options are now located on the Export dialog box.

Fireworks has improved its export and import capabilities for a variety of file formats:

Photoshop PSD export lets you choose whether to maintain editability over appearance or maintain Fireworks appearance quality, or to flatten layers into a fully rendered image. You can also decide whether to maintain editability of effects and text.

Photoshop PSD import is enhanced by the new Fireworks layers and frames functionality. For example, when you import layers as frames, Photoshop layer names become Fireworks frame names. Each Photoshop layer translates to an object on a layer in Fireworks. Photoshop layer masks import intact into Fireworks as image object masks.

FreeHand 9 import allows separate control over anti-aliasing for text and anti-aliasing for objects. The same is true for other vector import formats such as Illustrator and CorelDRAW.

Director export lets you export layers or slices, as well as HTML, into Director if you have the Import Xtra for Director installed. When you choose Insert > Fireworks > Fireworks HTML, your graphics import both to the stage and to the score, keeping registration points intact. To download the Xtra, go to www.macromedia.com/support/director/xtras.html.

EPS import is now available in Fireworks. The file is rendered as a bitmap image.

WBMP import and export is also available in Fireworks 4. The WBMP file format is optimized for wireless computing devices.

For more on exporting from Fireworks, see "Exporting with the Export Wizard" on page 332.

User experience enhancements

Fireworks has improved the way many features work to create a better user experience.

- When you create a button, it resides on a regular layer, like other vector objects.

- If slices accidentally overlap, the topmost slice in the stacking order is active in the overlapping area. Fireworks slices files upon export based on the perimeter of the topmost slice; it does not export extraneous files from the overlapping area.

- The pointer displays the size and shape of the brush or eraser as you draw when you choose the Brush-Size Painting Cursor preference.

- You can easily switch between original and previews using convenient menus in 2-up and 4-up views.

- You can view transformation information in the Info panel as you transform objects.

- You can hide the striped border that appears when you are in bitmap mode by deselecting the Show Striped Border preference.

- When you drag the pointer past the document window, documents that continue beyond the window will scroll in the direction of the pointer position. Also, you can scroll past the document canvas so you can zoom in and work along the edges of your artwork.

- Marquee selecting is smoother and more precise.

- Fill handles appear by default, so you can quickly edit the pattern or gradient fill of a vector object. Also, a new Edit button on the Fill panel makes it easier to edit gradients.

- When you drag an endpoint of a path near the endpoint of a path with similar stroke characteristics, the two paths snap together.

Selective JPEG compression

Using the marquee tools and the Set Selective JPEG feature, you can identify important parts of a JPEG image that you want to display as a high-quality image. Then you can make the overall image file size smaller by compressing the less important parts of the image.

Pen tool improvements

The Pen tool has been enhanced for greater control when drawing and editing vector graphics. New smart pointers indicate what you're about to do when using the tool. Holding down Control (Windows) or Command (Macintosh) temporarily switches from the Pen tool to the Subselection tool for greater pointer control.

Rectangles with rounded corners

With the new Rounded Rectangle tool, you set a corner radius before you draw a rectangle. Also, you can change the corner radius of a selected rectangle drawn with the Rounded Rectangle tool.

Live animation controls in the workspace

Fireworks now has a live animation user interface that lets you set the start and end location directly on screen, similar to Director and Macromedia Flash. Fireworks uses animation symbols and an animation line with clear starting and ending points and intermediate points representing frames in the animation.

When you select an animation symbol, the Object panel displays animation properties such as number of frames, scaling, opacity, and rotation. You can edit the selected animation by changing values in the Object panel.

Animated GIFs now import as animation symbols. See "Creating Animation" on page 289.

Batch processing

Fireworks has a redesigned batch processing user interface that logically presents the processing options. You now can determine the location and name of the output folder as you set up your batch process tasks.

Options are in plain view on panels instead of hidden in pop-up menus. First, you select the files to batch process in the Open Files to Batch dialog box. Then you enter information on the panels, which are organized to lead you through the setup process.

The first panel lets you choose actions to perform in the batch process and the order in which to perform them. The second panel lets you select how processed files are saved and backed up.

For more on the subject, see "Batch processing" on page 371.

Reorganized HTML Setup dialog box

HTML options are easy to find and choose with the new HTML Setup dialog box. The options are organized in four tabbed panels: General, which sets global preferences; File Name, which sets file name conventions, associations (Macintosh), and extensions; Table, which sets how HTML tables are exported; and Document Specific, which sets options for the current document, such as manual or automatic slice naming.

The HTML Setup dialog box lets you precisely control many variables of HTML, JavaScript, and image output.

By customizing setup and export variables, you can make the Fireworks output fit within specific work methods, style guidelines, and server application requirements. You can specify HTML style (generic, Dreamweaver, GoLive™, FrontPage®, or custom) and extensions (.htm, .html, .HTML, .asp, .jsp, .php, .shtml, or custom).

You can include HTML comments, force lowercase file names, and set a spacer style (none, 1-pixel transparent, or from image). You can set empty cell color and contents. Macintosh users can specify File and Creator settings for the exported files.

Fireworks 4 simplifies the task of setting up a slice naming convention. You can choose each part of your naming convention from a series of pop-up menus on the Document Specific tab of the HTML Setup dialog box.

Text improvements

Fireworks 4 keeps track of text color and fill color independently. If you select a text color, Fireworks continues using the same color for the next text block you create.

Also, if you choose another drawing tool and change the stroke or fill, and then return to the Text tool, the text color you last used is restored to the Text tool.

You can now reposition a text block in the workspace while the Text Editor is open.

CHAPTER 1
Tutorial

This tutorial lets you experience the versatility of Fireworks 4 firsthand. By taking the tutorial, you'll discover how Fireworks consolidates the features of a variety of task-specific applications in one easy-to-use solution. Additionally, Fireworks offers unique features that automate the more demanding tasks of creating Web objects, entire Web pages, and text and graphics with Live Effects.

What you'll learn

By taking the tutorial, in less than two hours you'll replicate a typical Fireworks production workflow for designing a Web page. The workflow includes the following tasks:

- Creating vector shapes and text
- Importing and editing bitmap images
- Aligning objects in a document
- Creating JavaScript buttons
- Adding links to buttons
- Using the History panel
- Creating simple and disjoint rollovers
- Exporting the file into HTML

What you should know

Although the tutorial is designed for beginning Fireworks users, you should possess the basic skills covered in the Fireworks lessons. These interactive lessons offer hands-on practice on the following topics:

- Introducing Fireworks
- Creating animation
- Creating slices
- Creating rollovers with drag-and-drop behaviors
- Creating a pop-up menu
- Automating repetitive tasks

To take a lesson, choose Help > Lessons, and select from the list. Be sure you're comfortable with the concepts presented in the lessons before starting the tutorial.

View the completed Web page

Additionally, before you begin the tutorial, view the completed tutorial file to see how your finished project will appear after you export it as an HTML file.

1   In your Fireworks 4 application folder, open Tutorial\Complete.

2   Select the Final.htm file and drag it to an open browser window.

   For the tutorial, you will complete a partially finished version of this page for Compass, an adventure travel agency. You'll also add links from the button bar to two additional Web pages that comprise the Compass site.

3   Move your pointer across the button bar along the top of the Web page and notice the rollover effect—how a button appears to change as the pointer rolls over it.

   Also notice the disjoint rollover—how the large graphic image changes in response to the pointer rolling over a button.

4   Click the Travel Log button to test the link, and then use your browser's back button to return to the Final.htm page.

5   When you finish viewing the Web page, you can either close it or leave it open for reference as you take the tutorial.

Note: Your Tutorial folder also includes the Fireworks document from which the HTML file is generated. To view this document, open it at Fireworks 4\Tutorial \Complete\Final.png.

Open the Start file

You've taken the lessons and viewed the Final.htm file in a browser; you're ready to begin your project.

1   In Fireworks, choose File > Open. Navigate to the Fireworks 4 application folder and open Tutorial\Start\Start.png.

    Fireworks documents in the authoring environment have a PNG extension. When you complete a Fireworks document, you can export it into a variety of formats.

2   Choose File > Save As and name the file MyFile.png. Save MyFile.png in the same Start folder.

    By making a copy of the file, you save the results of your work while letting others do the tutorial at a later time.

Note: While completing the tutorial, you may find it useful to undo a change you've made. Fireworks can undo several of your recent changes, depending on the number of undo levels you have set in Preferences. To undo, choose Edit > Undo.

As you complete the tutorial, remember to save your work frequently.

Add vector shapes

A vector shape is a mathematical description of a geometric form, whereas a bitmap defines an image as a grid of colored pixels. Both types of graphics offer advantages: vector shapes, for example, are often easy to edit while bitmap images are appropriate for artwork with complex color variations, such as photographs.

While many applications offer tools to edit either vector shapes or bitmap images, Fireworks lets you work with both types of graphics. By default, Fireworks opens in vector mode. You'll use vector mode now to create a shape that you'll soon transform into a button.

Create a vector shape

The Tools panel, which you use to create a vector shape, has both vector and bitmap tools, as well as tools whose function changes depending on the mode you're in.

1 Choose View > Guides and verify that Show Guides and Snap to Guides are selected. If not, select them both.

Notice the guides, green by default, in your document. They assist you in aligning objects on the canvas.

2 If the Layers panel is not visible, choose Window > Layers, and select the Buttons layer by using the Pointer tool to click the layer title.

You'll learn more about the Layers panel and its benefits later in the tutorial. For now, you simply need to know that the Layers panel offers, among its many features, a way to organize sets of objects. Selecting the Buttons layer will place the buttons you create on the same layer as other buttons in the document.

3 If the Tools panel is not visible, choose Window > Tools. In the Tools panel, select the Rectangle tool. Position the cross-hair pointer in the upper left corner of the cell shown in the following illustration, and drag to the opposite corner of the cell, so that the rectangle snaps into alignment against the guides.

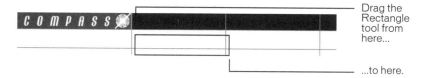

Drag the Rectangle tool from here...

...to here.

Add a gradient fill

A few more creative touches will make your vector shape look more like a button. First you'll add gradient colors, then Live Effects. A gradient displays subtle variations of a color or transitions between two or more colors. You'll add a linear gradient to your vector shape.

1 If the Fill panel is not visible, choose Window > Fill, and verify that your vector shape is still selected. In the Fill panel, use the Fill Category pop-up menu to select Linear.

Note: In vector mode, the mode you're in now, you use the Pointer tool to select an object. A selection path (light blue by default) outlining the object indicates that the object is selected.

2 In the Fill name pop-up menu, select Black, White.

3 Click Edit and drag the left color swatch to the right to make the gradient slightly darker.

When you add light text to the button, it will be most legible over the slightly darker fill color.

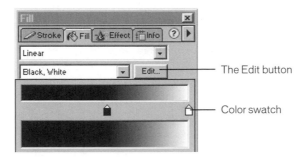

The Edit button

Color swatch

Apply Live Effects

Using Fireworks Live Effects, you can add a variety of special effects, such as beveling and embossing, to both text and graphics.

1 If the Effect panel is not visible, choose Window > Effect, and verify that your vector shape is still selected.

2 In the Effect panel's Add Effect pop-up menu at the top of the panel, choose Bevel and Emboss > Inner Bevel.

Additional fields appear on the Effect panel.

3 In the Bevel edge shape pop-up menu, choose Sloped.

4 To decrease the width of the bevel, move the pop-up Width slider to 4, or type 4 in the Width field and press Enter.

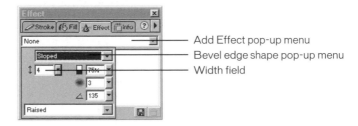

Add Effect pop-up menu

Bevel edge shape pop-up menu

Width field

Note: After you've added a Live Effect, if you wish to modify it, click the Info button on the Effect panel.

Create buttons

You're ready to turn your vector shape into a button by converting it into a button symbol. (A *symbol* is a reusable media element stored in your document's library.) Then you will create additional button states, for the rollover effect, in the Button Editor. In Fireworks, you can determine the object that will appear during a rollover for as many as four different button states (see "Creating Buttons and Navigation Bars" on page 235). Here, you'll create a button rollover that swaps shapes when the pointer rolls over the button.

Convert the shape into a button symbol

To create a button, you first create a symbol.

1　With your vector shape selected, choose Insert > Convert to Symbol.

2　In the Symbol Properties dialog box, name the symbol MyButton.

3　Select Button as the type, and click OK.

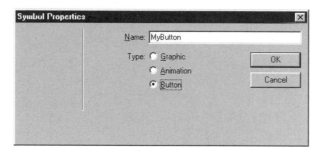

On the canvas, note how the vector shape has changed. The button has an overlay, indicating it's a slice, which won't appear in the exported file. The small arrow in the lower left corner of the button indicates the object is an instance of the MyButton symbol that appears in the Library. Later, you'll use the circular behavior control to create a disjoint rollover.

 Behavior control

4 To see the button symbol in the Library, choose Window > Library.

Your new button appears in the Library

Add text to the button

You add text to the button by first opening the button in the Button Editor and then opening the Text Editor.

1 With the Pointer tool, double-click the MyButton instance on the canvas.

The Button Editor appears.

2 In the Tools panel, select the Text tool and click the left side of the button in the Button Editor.

3 In the Text Editor, choose Impact as the font, 16-point as the font size, and Center Alignment.

4 Verify that the style attributes, such as bold and italics, are not selected.

5 Use the font color box to select a shade of orange, or you can type a hexadecimal value in the edit field.

The Final.png file uses a shade of orange with the hexidecimal value of #FF9900.

6 Verify that Smooth Anti-Alias is selected in the Anti-aliasing level field and Auto Kern is selected.

Anti-Alias smooths text edges, and kerning adjusts the spacing between certain letter combinations to improve the way the letters look next to each other.

7 Also verify that the Auto-apply check box (not the Apply button) is selected so you can view the text on the button as you type it.

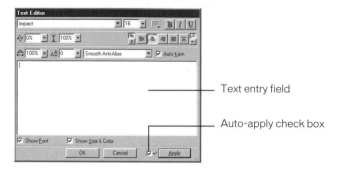

Text entry field

Auto-apply check box

8 In the text entry field, type **Adventure Planner** and click OK.

Align the text

To align the text within the button, you use menu commands.

1 With the Pointer tool, select the button and Shift-click to select the text.

2 Choose Modify > Align > Center Vertical.

3 Choose Modify > Align > Center Horizontal.

Note: If the gradient is too light for the text, slide the color swatch on the left of the button to the right to make the gradient darker.

Color swatch

Create a rollover

You've designed the way the button appears during its Up state, when the user's pointer has not touched the button. Now you'll use the Button Editor to design the button's Over state—the way the button appears when the pointer is over the button.

1 Click the Over tab in the Button Editor, and then click Copy Up Graphic on the lower right side of the window.

The Copy Up Graphic feature saves you from having to create another similar button from scratch.

2 Use the Pointer tool to select the button. Go to the Fill panel's Preset gradient color sets pop-up menu and select White, Black.

Note that the gradient colors are now reversed to transition from white to black.

3 With the Pointer tool, click the text on the button. In the Fill panel, use the color box to select a shade of red, such as #FF3300.

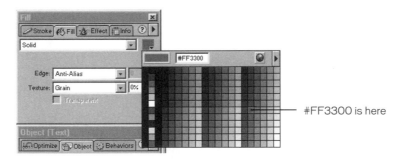

#FF3300 is here

4 Select the button and slide the color swatch on the right of the button toward the left until the gradient is just dark enough for the text to be legible.

Slide the color swatch toward the left

5 Close the Button Editor by clicking its Close box.

6 Use the Pointer tool to move the button back within the guide line.

Remember to save your work frequently.

By using the Button Editor, you have created a rollover button without writing JavaScript. When you export the file into HTML, the JavaScript for your rollover is included in the HTML file.

View the button behavior

The Behaviors panel lets you view and attach JavaScript behaviors to buttons, slices, and hotspots. If you look at the Behaviors panel now, you see that it includes the rollover behavior.

Choose Window > Behaviors to view the Behaviors panel.

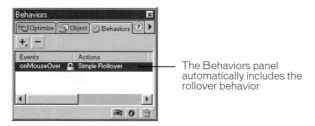 The Behaviors panel automatically includes the rollover behavior

Preview the button

The Preview tab, along the upper left side of your document window, shows how your document will appear in a Web browser. While the Original tab does not display the rollover, you can see the action in Preview.

1 In the Tools panel, click the Hide Slices icon along the bottom of the panel to hide the green overlay.

 Hide Slices icon

2 Click the Preview tab.

3 Move your pointer over the Adventure Travel button to view the rollover effect.

Note: In addition to using the Preview tab, you can choose File > Preview in Browser, and then choose a browser. The browser displays a temporary version of your file.

Create multiple instances of a single symbol

You'll now see the advantage of having reusable symbols stored in the Library: you won't have to repeat the steps to create two more rollover buttons. Instead, you'll drag two instances of the button symbol from the Library to the canvas. Then you will modify the text for the two instances without affecting the original symbol.

1 To exit Preview, click the Original tab.

2 In the Library panel, select MyButton and drag the button instance onto the canvas, placing it next to the existing Adventure Planner button so that it snaps against the guides.

3 Drag another instance of the same button and place it next to the second button. (Be sure not to drag the circular behavior control). Again, use the guides to align the button with the other two.

4 With the second MyButton instance selected, go to the Object panel (Choose Window > Object if the panel is not visible). Select the text in the Button Text field and replace it with **Check Conditions**. Then press Enter.

5 A dialog box asks if you want to edit all of the button instances or just the current one. Click Current.

6 Repeat steps 4 and 5 with the last button, this time changing the text to **Travel Log**.

7 Use the Preview tab to view your rollover buttons. When you finish, return to the Original tab.

Assign URLs to the buttons

Buttons generally provide a method of navigation. To specify the links for each of your buttons, you use the Link Wizard.

1 On the canvas, select the Adventure Planner button, then click Link Wizard in the Object panel.

2 In the Link tab of the Link Wizard dialog box, type **compasssite/ adventureplanner/index.html** in the top pop-up menu and click OK.

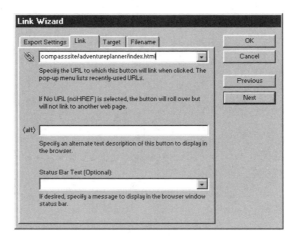

3 Select the Check Conditions button on the canvas and use the Link Wizard to assign it the URL **compasssite/checkconditions/index.html**.

4 Select the travellog button on the canvas and assign it the URL **compasssite/ travelog/index.html**.

You can test the links later in the tutorial after you export your document.

Import and modify bitmap images

Until now, you've been working in vector mode. Fireworks also offers features to create, import, and modify bitmap images. You can add Live Effects to bitmap graphics just as you would to vector shapes. Additionally, you can correct and delete colors in the bitmap image.

In this tutorial, you'll take bitmap images that you import and modify and use them to create disjoint rollovers—where an image changes in one area of the document in response to the pointer rolling over another area.

Add a layer

Layers offer a way to arrange sets of objects within a document on planes that are analogous to transparent overlays.

Note: If you're familiar with Photoshop, keep in mind that the term *layer* has a different meaning in Fireworks. In Fireworks, an object is anything that you create or import, such as a vector shape or bitmap image, and you place objects onto layers.

By using layers, you can easily modify objects on one layer without affecting objects on another layer. Layers also offer a way to organize media, such as by putting all buttons on one layer (as you did earlier in the tutorial) and all bitmap images on another.

Now you will add a new layer, name the layer, and then import two bitmaps onto the layer in preparation for creating a disjoint rollover.

1   If the Layers panel is not visible, choose Window > Layers, or click the Show Layers icon on the Launcher along the lower right side of your application window.

Show Layers icon

Note that the tutorial has five layers, including a default Web Layer for Web objects. You can use the expand and collapse buttons to show or hide the list of objects on a layer. You can hide a layer on the canvas by clicking the Show/Hide icon.

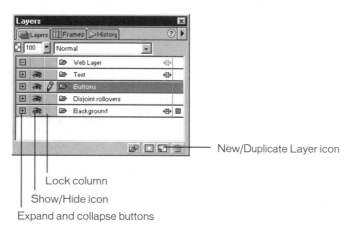

New/Duplicate Layer icon

Lock column

Show/Hide icon

Expand and collapse buttons

2   Choose Insert > Layer, or click the New/Duplicate Layer icon along the bottom of the panel.

3   To rename the new layer, double-click the existing name in the Layers panel.

4 In the Layer Name field of the pop-up menu that appears, type **Disjoint Rollover Art**. Verify that Share Across Frames is not selected, then click anywhere else in the application to close the pop-up menu.

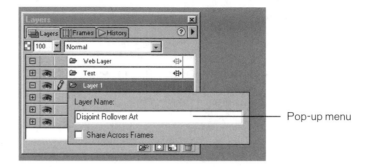 ——— Pop-up menu

5 In the Layers panel, verify that the layers icon for the Web layer is not visible and that the green slice overlays do not appear on the canvas. If necessary, click the Show/Hide icon to hide the Web Layer.

Note: Once you have configured all objects on a layer as desired, you can lock the layer by clicking the layer's Lock/Unlock icon to prevent inadvertent changes.

Add frames

In a Web browser, a rollover quickly swaps one image with another. To create a rollover, Fireworks uses frames, like frames in cell animation, to hold the rollover content.

When disjoint rollovers swap images that all occupy the same canvas area and replace one another, you must create a separate frame for each image that is being swapped. Later in this tutorial, you'll use drag-and-drop behaviors to specify that the frames you add appear during the disjoint rollover.

To create a disjoint rollover, you'll add two new frames, then import a bitmap image onto each of the frames.

1 With the Disjoint Rollover Art layer still selected, open the Frames panel (choose Window > Frames, if necessary).

Note: You might question why the Frames panel indicates your document has only one frame, yet your simple rollover for your buttons requires two frames: one for the up state and one for the over state. Frames for buttons appear in the Frames panel only when the Button Editor is active.

2 Choose Insert > Frame, or click the New/Duplicate Frame icon in the Frames panel.

3 In the Frames panel, double-click Frame 2, the new frame that you added, and name it **Check Conditions**.

4 Choose Insert > Frame and name this frame **Travel Log**.

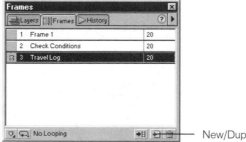

New/Duplicate Frame icon

Import the first bitmap image

Fireworks offers several different ways to add an existing image to a document, including cutting and pasting, dragging and dropping, and using the Import command—the method that you'll use now.

1 With the Disjoint Rollover Art layer selected in the Layers panel and the Check Conditions frame selected in the Frames panel, choose File > Import.

Note: The canvas displays only the objects in Check Conditions, the second frame.

2 In the Import dialog box, browse to Tutorial\Start\Assets within your Fireworks application folder, and double-click Check_Cond.png.

3 Move the Import pointer to the corner where the third horizontal guide from the top meets the left edge of the canvas, as shown in the following illustration, and click to import the new image.

Click the Import
pointer here

Import the second bitmap image

Now, on the third frame, you'll import the bitmap image associated with the Travel Log button.

1 With the Disjoint Rollover Art layer selected in the Layers panel, and the Travel Log frame selected in the Frames panel, choose File > Import.

2 In the Import dialog box, browse to Tutorial\Start\Assets within your Fireworks application folder, and double-click Trav_Log.png.

3 Move the import pointer to the same corner where you imported the previous bitmap, and click to import the new image.

Delete similarly colored pixels and add color correction

When you imported the bitmap image associated with the Check Conditions button, you might have noticed that the colors are bright in comparison to the other colors in your document. Because a sepia-toned image would be more consistent with the existing artwork, you'll delete the white space on the bitmap, then use color correction to give the image a sepia tint. The Magic Wand tool lets you delete an area of similarly colored pixels.

1 In the Frames panel, select the Check Conditions frame.

The Disjoint Rollover Art layer should still be selected in the Layers panel.

2 Double-click the Magic Wand tool to open the Tool Options panel.

3 Use the Tolerance slider to select 15, and select Anti-Alias from the Edge pop-up menu.

Lower tolerance settings instruct the Magic Wand to select adjacent colors that closely match the color of the selected pixel. Anti-aliasing smooths jagged lines.

4 With the Magic Wand, click anywhere in the white space on the right of the bitmap on the canvas.

The striped border that appears around the canvas indicates you're in bitmap mode. The area of white pixels in the bitmap is selected.

Area of white pixels

5 Press Backspace (Windows) or Delete (Macintosh), or choose Edit > Cut to delete the white pixels.

6 Choose Modify > Exit Bitmap Mode.

7 With the Pointer tool, click to select the bitmap image if necessary.

Do not double-click or you will return to bitmap mode.

8 In the Effect panel, choose Adjust Color > Color Fill from the Effect pop-up menu.

9 In the Effect panel's color box, select a medium-brown shade (the Final.png file uses brown with a hexidecimal value of #CC6600).

10 Move the Tint Level slider to 35% and press Enter.

Note that the bitmap image now has a soft sepia tint.

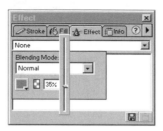

Add a drop shadow

1 In the Effect panel, with the bitmap still selected, choose Shadow and Glow > Drop Shadow from the Effect pop-up menu.

2 Move the Distance slider to 10 and click outside the panel.

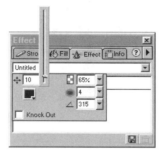

The Distance slider lets you indicate the width and placement of the shadow.

Automate tasks with the History panel

With the bitmap image you imported for the Travel Log button, you also need to add color correction and a drop shadow. Rather than repeating the steps to add these effects, you'll use the History panel to automate repetitive tasks.

1 In the Frames panel, select the Travel Log frame.

2 With the Pointer tool, select the Travel Log image (the image of the pen and map that you imported) on the canvas.

3 Choose Window > History.

4 On the list of commands in the History panel, click the last time Set Effects appears, and Shift-click the Set Effects command prior to the last one.

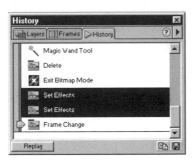

5 Click Replay in the History panel and notice how Fireworks executes the commands to modify your bitmap image on the canvas.

Remember to save your work frequently.

Create a disjoint rollover

To create a disjoint rollover, each object that comprises the rollover must have an associated slice object. Slice objects appear on your document's Web Layer. You'll create a slice object for the bitmap images, then add drag-and-drop behaviors to create the disjoint rollover.

Insert a slice

Because both objects in a rollover must be slice objects, you will add a slice to an image.

1 In the Frames panel, select the Check Conditions frame.

2 On the canvas, use the Pointer tool to select the image of the woman holding binoculars and choose Insert > Slice.

On the canvas, a green overlay, indicating a slice object, appears on the bitmap image. The Layers panel now includes the slice in the Web Layer.

Drag and drop to create the disjoint rollover

To associate the image with the button, you will simply drag the pointer from the behavior control for the button to the slice over the image that will appear during the disjoint rollover.

1 With the Pointer tool, select the Check Conditions button.

2 Click the behavior control in the center of the Check Conditions button and drag to the slice over the images that you imported.

A blue line, the behavior line, snaps to the slice, indicating that the two slices are associated. The Swap Image dialog box appears.

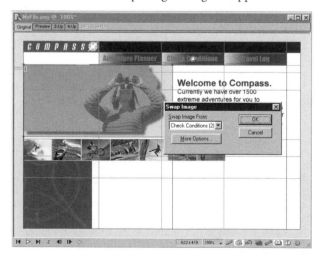

3 In the dialog box, verify that you're swapping the image from the Check Conditions frame, and click OK.

That quickly, you have created a disjoint rollover.

Remember to save your work frequently.

Add the final disjoint rollover

You'll complete similar steps to create a disjoint rollover for the Travel Log button.

1 On the canvas, select the Travel Log button, and drag the button's behavior control to the bitmap image slice area on the canvas.

2 In the dialog box, select Travel Log (Frame 3) as the swap image, and click OK.

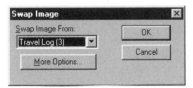

3 Click the Preview tab and roll over the buttons to view your disjoint rollover. When you finish viewing the preview, click the Original tab.

Export your Fireworks file into HTML

Congratulations on completing your Fireworks document. Next in the process, you'll export your document to display in a browser. Fireworks supports export into a variety of different Web and print formats; you will export your document into HTML. Note that the export process does not modify your PNG file—you'll still have the PNG file available to modify and export again if you wish.

Export your file

To export, you use the Export dialog box.

1 Save your file and choose File > Export.

2 In the Export dialog box, browse to Tutorial\Start\Export in your Fireworks application folder.

In the File name field, note that the name of your HTM file, by default, will be the same as the name of your PNG file.

3 In the Slices pop-up menu, verify that Export Slices is selected.

Selecting Export Slices ensures your buttons will work in the HTM file.

4 Select Put Images in Subfolder.

Fireworks will create an images subfolder within your Export folder that will contain all your images.

5 Click Options and verify that Dreamweaver appears in the HTML Style pop-up menu, then click OK.

6 In the Export dialog box, click Save.

View your exported document in a browser

The new files created during the export process appear in your Export folder.

1 Browse to your Tutorial\Start\Export folder and open it.

2 Notice that Fireworks created the HTM file. If you open the Images subfolder, you see that Fireworks also created graphics files for all of your art. Each slice in Fireworks exports as its own separate graphics file.

3 From the Export folder, drag the MyFile.htm file that you created to an open Web browser.

4 In the browser, click the buttons you added to test the links, then use the browser's Back button to return to the MyFile.htm file.

5 Test the other features that you added.

6 Most Web browsers let you view the source code with a command such as View > Source. Find and execute the command that lets you view the code.

7 Scroll through the source. If you know JavaScript, you will recognize the JavaScript that Fireworks created for you. If you don't know JavaScript, you can appreciate that Fireworks gives you no compelling reason to have to learn it.

Use Fireworks with Dreamweaver

If you're interested in learning how to use Fireworks and Dreamweaver together, be sure to take the Fireworks and Dreamweaver tutorial. It introduces you to the basics of using Dreamweaver with Fireworks to edit, optimize, and place Web graphics in HTML pages. You'll learn how to import a Fireworks image or table file into a Dreamweaver document, where you can continue to modify the file using Dreamweaver's many editing tools. You'll also learn how to use the unique launch-and-edit feature, which lets you use Fireworks to edit or optimize a Fireworks image or slice table placed in Dreamweaver, and then return to Dreamweaver with all your updates intact. To take the Fireworks and Dreamweaver tutorial, go to http://www.macromedia.com/support/dreamweaver/programs.html.

Take the next steps

You've now accomplished major tasks in the production workflow to create a Web page with Fireworks. These tasks included the following:

- Creating vector shapes and text
- Importing and editing bitmap images
- Aligning objects in a document
- Creating JavaScript buttons
- Adding links to buttons
- Using the History panel
- Creating simple and disjoint rollovers
- Exporting the file into HTML

For detailed information about any of the features covered in the tutorial, and for information on additional Fireworks features, refer to the index in this user guide or search the Fireworks Help topics. Also, be sure to visit Macromedia's award-winning Support Center at http://www.macromedia.com/support/fireworks.

CHAPTER 2
Fireworks Basics

Fireworks is a state-of-the-art application for designing graphics for use on the Web. Its innovative solutions tackle the major problems facing graphic designers and Web masters.

Fireworks is an incredibly versatile drawing tool for graphic and Web designers. Its wide range of tools lets you create graphics using some of the best features of both vector and bitmap graphic applications in a single application. You can edit with vector-object flexibility and apply bitmap effects—including bevels, glows, drop shadows, and Photoshop filters—that redraw automatically as you edit.

The advent of Fireworks freed Web designers from having to jump back and forth among as many as a dozen task-specific applications. Its nondestructive Live Effects eliminate the frustration of having to recreate Web graphics from scratch after any simple edit. Fireworks generates JavaScript, making rollovers easy to create. Its optimization features shrink the file size of Web graphics without sacrificing quality.

About vector and bitmap graphics

Computers display graphics in either vector or bitmap format. Understanding the difference between the two formats can help you work more efficiently. Fireworks lets you create images using vector or bitmap drawing tools, and lets you import and manipulate vector and bitmap graphics that have been created in other applications.

Vector graphics

Vector graphics describe images using lines and curves, called vectors, that also include color and position information. For example, the image of a leaf may be described by a series of points, all connected by lines of varying shapes and thicknesses, the result of which is the leaf's outline. The leaf's color is determined by the color of the outline and the color of the area enclosed by the outline.

When you edit a vector graphic, you modify the properties of the lines and curves that describe its shape. You can move, resize, reshape, and change the color of a vector graphic without changing the quality of its appearance. You can overlap objects so that they are partly hidden and alter transparency. Vector graphics are resolution independent, meaning they can be displayed on output devices of varying resolutions without losing any quality.

Bitmap graphics

Bitmap graphics describe images using dots, called *pixels*, arranged in a grid. Your computer screen itself consists of a large grid of pixels. In a bitmap graphic, the above image of a leaf would be determined by the location and color value of each pixel in the grid. Each dot is assigned a color, and when viewed at the correct resolution, the dots go together like tiles in a mosaic to form the image.

When you edit a bitmap graphic, you modify pixels, rather than lines and curves. These bitmap graphics are resolution dependent, because the data describing the image is fixed to a grid of a particular size. Enlarging a bitmap graphic can make the image's edges ragged, as pixels are redistributed within the grid. Displaying a bitmap graphic on an output device with a lower resolution than the image itself also degrades the image's quality.

About the Fireworks workflow

When you design graphics with Fireworks, you can create bitmap and vector images, design Web effects such as rollovers and pop-up menus, manipulate graphics to reduce their file size, and avoid repetition by automating frequent tasks.

When the document is complete, you can export it as an HTML file, if you intend to use it on the Web, or as a Photoshop or Illustrator file if you need to do further work.

Creating graphics

Fireworks lets you draw in both vector mode and bitmap mode. In vector mode you draw and edit paths; in bitmap mode you edit pixels.

You can create new vector and bitmap images in Fireworks by selecting the appropriate tools from the Tools panel and applying them to the canvas. Each drawing mode has its own set of tools. Some are specific to only one mode; other tools work in both modes, although they may operate differently between the two. For more information, see "Working with Objects" on page 85 and "Working with Bitmaps" on page 125.

Creating Web objects

Web objects are the basic building blocks Fireworks uses to make a Web page interactive. A Web object is either a slice or a hotspot. Slices cut an image into different sections and enable you to apply behaviors, animation, and Uniform Resource Locator (URL) links to parts of the overall image. Slices allow you export the sections using different settings. Hotspots simply let you assign a URL link to all or part of a graphic. You can also assign certain behaviors to hotspots. For more information, see "Using Hotspots and Slices" on page 249.

Optimizing

You can optimize Web graphics in Fireworks to minimize file size for fast-loading Web sites. Fireworks offers powerful optimization techniques that help you achieve smaller document sizes without degrading the quality of the information you want to convey.

For example, you can select background information in a photograph and reduce the number of colors in this specific part. Or you can cut up an image into smaller parts and then convert each part into the format that best suits the content.

Exporting documents

When you have finished optimizing your work, the next step is to export it to a file that is viewable on a Web browser or that is compatible with another graphics or Web application. Regardless what export settings you choose, the original Fireworks PNG file remains unchanged. This way, you can export to a variety of Web and print formats using the same source file.

You can also optimize your graphic as part of the export process. All optimization options are available during export.

About the Fireworks work environment

Opening Fireworks 4 for the first time displays a menu bar across the top of the screen, a Tools panel on the left side of the screen, and several multitab panels on the right. When you open a document, Fireworks places a document window in the middle.

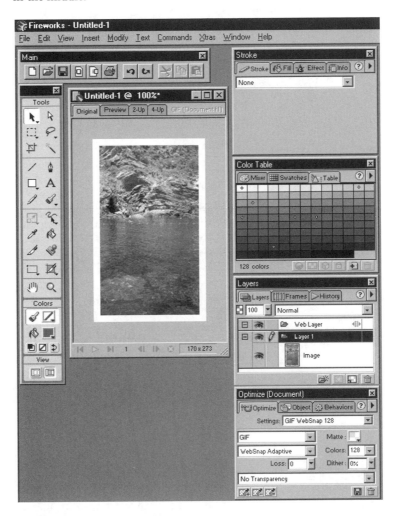

Displaying a Fireworks document

In the document window, the title bar displays the document name and the current magnification percentage. You also see four tabs. Each tab represents a different view of the document. The Original tab displays the current Fireworks PNG document. The three remaining tabs are for previewing export versions of the document.

The Original tab and three preview tabs are at the top left corner of the workspace.

To display the original PNG document:

Click the Original tab in the document window.

Previewing documents

The Preview tab displays the graphic as it would appear in a Web browser, based on current export settings. The 2-Up and 4-Up views compare export previews based on variable export settings. In 2-Up and 4-Up views, you can compare optimized versions to the original document.

To display an export preview:

Click the Preview, 2-Up, or 4-Up tab in the document window.

Use the Optimize panel and Color Table panel to change export settings. These panels and the Preview replicate the Export Preview dialog box in previous versions of Fireworks, bringing optimization into the workspace.

You can check rollover and navigation behaviors, as well as animation, in Preview.

Displaying and choosing tools

The Tools panel contains the tools you use to create, select, and edit objects. In Windows, the Main and Modify toolbars provide easy access to many commands. If you are a Macintosh user, you can choose these commands from menus.

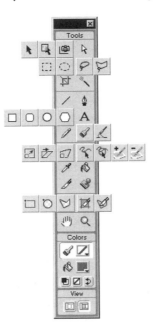

The Tools panel includes dozens of tools, some of which are arranged in tool groups, as shown. A tool group is indicated by the small triangle in a tool's lower right corner.

Click a tool to choose it. Or press shortcut keys to switch quickly from one tool to another. For more information about shortcut keys, see "Changing keyboard shortcut sets" on page 57.

Note: You can see the shortcut key for a tool by holding the pointer over the tool icon in the Tools panel until the Tooltip displays. The shortcut is the letter after the tool name.

To choose an alternative tool from a tool group:

1 Click and hold any tool with a triangle in the lower right corner.

2 Drag the pointer to the alternative tool you want and release the mouse button. The tool you choose displays in the Tools panel.

Note: The function of some tools changes depending on whether you are editing bitmap or vector objects. For more information on Fireworks tools, see "Working with Vector Objects" on page 99 and "Working with Bitmaps" on page 125.

Rearranging toolbars (Windows only)

You can show and hide toolbars, undock them, or move them to the top or bottom.

To show or hide the Tools panel or a toolbar:

Choose Window > Tools or choose a toolbar from the Window > Toolbars submenu.

If a toolbar is undocked, you can click the Close button at the top right of the title bar.

To undock a toolbar:

Drag the toolbar by its title bar away from its docked location. The toolbar becomes a floating panel.

To dock a toolbar:

1 Move the current tool onto the title bar.

2 Drag the toolbar onto a docking area at the top or bottom of the application window.

Changing tool options

The Tool Options panel displays options related to the active tool. For example, the Pointer tool options include Mouse Highlight, Preview Drag, and Show Fill Handles. For information about specific tool options, see the sections throughout the manual that introduce the various tools.

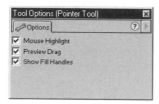

To show or hide the tool Options panel:

• Double-click a tool in the Tools panel.

• Choose Window > Tool Options.

Using panels

Panels are floating controls that help you edit different aspects of a selected object. Panels let you work on frames, layers, symbols, color swatches, and more. For example, you can use the Effect panel to select an effect to apply to an object.

Each panel is draggable, so you can group controls together in custom arrangements.

The Mini-Launcher contains icons for opening and closing your most frequently used panels, including the Stroke, Layers, Behaviors, and Optimize panels. The Mini-Launcher is located at the bottom of each document window.

The Object, Stroke, Fill, and Effect panels control a wide range of object characteristics.

The Color Mixer and Swatches panel manage the current document's color palette.

The Layers and Frames panels organize a document's structure and contain options for creating, deleting, and manipulating layers and frames. The Frames panel includes options for creating animation.

The Behaviors panel manages behaviors, which determine what hotspots and slices do in response to mouse movement.

The History panel lists commands you have recently used so that you can quickly undo and redo them. You also can choose commands to repeat, and save command sequences to reuse as a single command.

The Library panel contains graphic symbols, button symbols, and animation symbols. You can easily drag instances of these symbols from the Library onto your document. You can make global changes to all instances by modifying only the symbol.

The Optimize and Color panels let you manage the settings that control an object's size and file type.

The Project Log lets you export selected files using their last export settings and select files for batch processing.

The Info panel provides information about the dimensions of selected objects and the exact coordinates of the pointer as you move it across the canvas.

The Tool Options panel lets you edit the settings of the current pointer tool.

The Styles panel lets you modify the appearance of an object or text. Fireworks comes with a number of styles for you to choose from.

To show or hide a panel:

Choose the panel from the Window menu.

All panels have an Options pop-up menu.

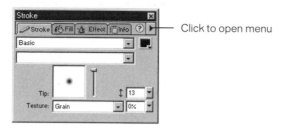
Click to open menu

To choose an option from a panel Options pop-up menu:

1 Click the right-arrow button near the top right corner of the panel. The Options pop-up menu appears.

2 Choose an Options pop-up menu command.

Some controls on panels have a pop-up menu, color palettes, slider, or dial.

To use an option pop-up menu:

1 Click the down arrow next to the box.

2 Change the value:

• Choose an option or color swatch.

• Drag the slider or dial.

• Type the first letter of the option you want to choose (Windows). Press the letter repeatedly to cycle through all options beginning with that letter.

To enter information in a panel text box:

1 Click in the text box.

2 Type a value.

3 Press Enter.

To combine two or more panels:

1 Drag one floating panel over another floating panel. When the highlighted border appears on the panel underneath, release the mouse button.

2 Click any tab in the panel to bring it forward.

To remove a panel from a tabbed panel:

Drag the panel away from the tabbed panel by its tab.

To hide a panel or a tabbed panel group:

Click the Close button at the top of the panel or panel group window.

To hide all panels or view hidden panels:

- Choose View > Hide Panels.

    Note: Panels that were hidden when you chose Hide Panels remain hidden when you deselect it.

To return panels to their default positions:

- Choose Commands > Panel Layout Sets > 1024 x 768.

To reset application-level preferences:

1 Quit Fireworks.

2 Delete the preferences file named Fireworks 4 Preferences in the Fireworks folder (Windows) or the System\Preferences folder (Macintosh).

3 Relaunch Fireworks.

Using Context menus

Context menus let you quickly access commands that are relevant to the current selection.

To display a context menu:

Right-click (Windows) or Control-click (Macintosh) a selected item in the document window.

Setting preferences

Fireworks preference settings control the general appearance of the user interface, as well as editing and folder aspects.

To set preferences:

1 Choose Edit > Preferences.

2 Select the group of preferences you wish to modify. (See following sections for details on those preference groups.)

3 Make your changes and choose OK.

Setting General preferences

The number of undo steps and color defaults are General preferences.

Undo Steps sets undo/redo steps to a number between 0 and 100. This setting applies to both the Edit > Undo command and the History panel.

A large number of undos can increase the amount of memory Fireworks requires.

Color Defaults sets the default colors for brush strokes, fills, and highlight paths.

Interpolation sets one of four different scaling methods that Fireworks uses to interpolate pixels when images are scaled:

- Bicubic interpolation gives the sharpest and highest quality most of the time and is the default scaling method.

- Bilinear interpolation gives sharper results than Soft interpolation but not as sharp as Bicubic.

- Soft interpolation, which was used in Fireworks 1, gives a soft blur and eliminates sharp details. This method is useful when others produce unwanted artifacts.

- Nearest Neighbor interpolation results in jagged edges and sharp contrasts with no blurring. The effect is similar to zooming in or out on an image with the Zoom tool.

Setting Editing preferences

The Editing preferences control pointer appearance and visual cues for working in bitmap mode.

Precise cursors replaces tool icon pointers with the cross-hair pointer.

Delete Objects when Cropping permanently deletes pixels or objects that are outside the bounding box of a selection when you choose Edit > Crop Document or Modify > Canvas Size.

Brush Size Painting Cursors sets the size and shape of the Brush tool and Eraser tool pointers to accurately reflect what you are about to draw or erase.

Note: For certain large multitipped brushes, the cursor will default to cross hairs.

Expand to Fill Document expands the striped border to surround the entire canvas when you switch to bitmap mode, allowing pixel editing within the entire document. When it is deselected, only the pixels within a selected bitmap object's border are editable.

Open in Bitmap Mode opens any image file directly in bitmap mode. Deselect it to open all files in vector mode.

Turn Off "Hide Edges" automatically disables Hide Edges when entering or leaving bitmap mode.

Display Striped Border automatically turns on a striped border around a bitmap image when in bitmap mode.

Pick Distance lets you specify how close to an object the pointer must be before you can select it. Pick distance can be between 1 and 10 pixels.

Snap Distance lets you specify how close the object you are moving must be before it snaps to a grid or guide line. Snap distance works when Snap to Grid or Snap to Guides is turned on. You can set Snap distance to from 1 to 10 pixels.

Setting Launch and Edit preferences

You can set whether the Fireworks source PNG file opens when you edit and optimize from Dreamweaver.

When Editing from External Application determines whether the original Fireworks PNG file opens when you use Fireworks to edit images from within Dreamweaver or another HTML editor.

When Optimizing from External Application determines whether the original Fireworks PNG file opens when you optimize a graphic using the Optimize Image in Fireworks command in Dreamweaver.

For more information on working with Fireworks objects within Dreamweaver, see "Editing Fireworks files placed in Dreamweaver" on page 356.

Managing external folders and scratch disks

The preferences in Folders give you access to additional Photoshop plug-ins, texture files, and pattern files from external sources. Also, you can specify where you want Fireworks to store temporary cache files.

Additional Materials (Photoshop Plug-Ins, Textures, and Patterns) targets folders containing plug-ins, textures, and patterns. The folders can be in another folder on your hard drive, on a CD-ROM or other external drive, or on a network volume.

- Photoshop plug-ins appear in the Fireworks Xtras menu and the Effects panel.

- Textures or patterns stored as PNG files appear as options in the Pattern and Texture pop-up menus in the Fill panel and the Textures pop-up menu in the Stroke panel.

For more information about textures and patterns, see "Using Fireworks Xtras as Live Effects" on page 194, "Using Photoshop plug-ins as Live Effects" on page 195, and "Applying Colors, Strokes, and Fills" on page 157

Scratch Disks (Primary and Secondary) specify where Fireworks stores temporary cache files, which can sometimes grow very large. If you have more than one hard disk in your computer, target the disk with the most free space as your primary scratch disk. You can specify a secondary hard disk in case the primary disk runs out of free space.

Setting Photoshop file import preferences

The preferences under Import manage several file conversion issues for importing Photoshop files.

For more information on the Import preferences, see "Importing Photoshop files into Fireworks" on page 386.

Changing keyboard shortcut sets

Fireworks lets you use keyboard shortcuts to select menu commands, choose tools from the Tools panel, and speed up miscellaneous tasks that do not exist as menu commands. Using shortcuts increases your productivity by allowing you to quickly perform simple actions. If you are used to using shortcuts from other applications such as FreeHand, Illustrator, Photoshop, or products that use the Macromedia standard, you can switch to the shortcut system you prefer.

To change the current shortcut set:

1 Select Keyboard Shortcuts from the Edit Menu.

2 Select the set you prefer from Current Set.

Keyboard Shortcuts dialog box

Creating custom shortcuts

You can create your own custom keyboard shortcuts. To do this, duplicate any of the preinstalled sets, and then modify the copy appropriately. A custom shortcut set is always based on a preinstalled set. Shortcut sets follow a few general rules:

• Menu commands must include the Control key (Windows) or Command key (Macintosh).

   Note: The only exception to this rule is that you can assign available function keys (F2 to F12) to menu commands.

• In Fireworks, tool shortcuts cannot include modifier keys (Control, Shift, Alt in Windows, and Command, Shift, Option, and Control in Macintosh). Tool shortcuts consist of a single letter or number key.

To create a custom shortcut for a menu command, tool, or miscellaneous action:

1 Open the Keyboard Shortcuts dialog.

2 Click the Duplicate Set button.

3 Enter a name for the custom set in the Duplicate Set dialog and click OK.

   The name of the new custom menu appears in the Current Set field.

4 Select the appropriate shortcut category from the Commands list.

• Choose Menu Commands to create a custom shortcut for any command accessed through the menu bar.

• Choose Tools to create a custom shortcut for any tool on the Tools panel.

• Choose Miscellaneous to create a custom shortcut for a range of predefined actions.

   Once selected, all possible shortcuts in the particular category appear in the Commands scroll list.

5 Select the command whose shortcut you want to modify from the Commands list.

   The shortcut is displayed in the Shortcuts list.

6 Enter the new shortcut in the Press Key field.

7 Click Change.

Creating secondary shortcuts

You can create secondary shortcuts if you need to have several different ways to perform an action. Secondary shortcuts appear in the Shortcuts list, beneath the existing shortcut. You can also create a shortcut where no shortcut currently exists.

To create a secondary shortcut or a shortcut where no shortcut currently exists:

1 Follow steps 1 through 6 of the previous procedure.

2 Click the Add Shortcut (+) button.

3 Enter the shortcut.

Deleting custom shortcuts and custom shortcut sets

You can delete any custom shortcut or any custom shortcut set.

To delete a custom shortcut set:

1 Open the Keyboard Shortcuts dialog box.

2 Click the Delete Set button.

3 Select the shortcut set you want to delete from the Delete Set dialog box.

4 Click the Delete button.

5 Select the set you want to delete from the list displayed in the Delete Set dialog box.

To delete a custom shortcut:

1 Select the custom shortcut from the Shortcut list.

2 Click the Remove Shortcut button (-).

Creating a reference sheet for the current shortcut set

A reference sheet is a record of the current shortcut set stored in HTML table format. You can view the reference sheet in a Web browser or print it.

To create a reference sheet:

1 Open the Keyboard Shortcuts dialog box.

2 Click the Export Set as HTML button beside the Current Set field.

   The Save dialog box is displayed.

3 Enter the name for the reference sheet, and select the appropriate location for the file.

4 Click Save.

Undoing and repeating multiple actions

With the History panel, you can view, modify, and repeat the actions taken to create the document. The History panel lists the most recent actions you have performed in Fireworks, up to the number specified in the Number of Undo's Preference. With the History panel, you can do any of the following:

- Quickly undo and redo recent actions using the History panel Undo Marker.

- Choose recently performed actions from the History panel and click Replay to repeat them.

- Save a group of recently performed actions as a custom command, and then choose it from the Command menu to reuse the group as a single command. For more information about creating commands using the History panel, see "Scripting" on page 380.

To undo and redo actions:

1 Choose Window > History to open the History panel.

2 Drag the marker up or down with the pointer.

To repeat actions:

1 If the commands are to affect objects, select the objects.

2 In the History panel, highlight the commands to be repeated. Shift-click to highlight a continuous range of commands.

3 Click the Replay button at the bottom of the History panel.

To save actions for reuse:

1 Highlight the actions to be saved in the History panel.

2 Click the Save button at the bottom of the panel.

3 Enter a command name and click OK to add the command to the Modify > Command submenu.

To use the saved custom command:

Choose the command name from the Command submenu.

CHAPTER 3
Setting up a Fireworks Document

When you choose File > New to create a new document in Fireworks, you create a Portable Network Graphic, or PNG document. PNG is the native file format for Fireworks. After you create graphics in Fireworks, you can export them in other familiar Web graphic formats, such as JPEG, GIF, and animated GIF. When you export a graphic in another file format, the original Fireworks PNG file remains unchanged, so you can use it again and again.

While your PNG document is open, you can zoom in and zoom out on graphics. You can change the size and resolution of the document. You can also rotate the canvas to rearrange an upside-down or sideways imported image. Switching the Gamma view shows you what your graphic would look like on either Macintosh or Windows monitors.

You can open Photoshop, FreeHand, Illustrator, uncompressed CorelDRAW®, WBMP, EPS, and animated GIF files. In addition, you can import images from a digital camera or scanner. You can also export to other file formats.

Creating a new document

To create a Web graphic in Fireworks, you must first set up a new document or open an existing one. With a new document, it is more efficient to set it up properly at first than to make a lot of changes to the setup later.

If you want to base the size of a new document on another graphic, you can copy the graphic to the Clipboard first. For a list of the applications you can copy data from, see "Pasting into Fireworks" on page 70.

To create a new document:

1 Choose File > New. The New Document dialog box opens.

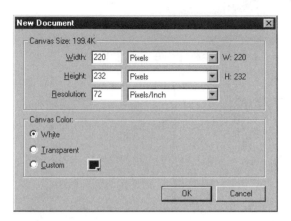

2 Enter the canvas width and height measurements in pixels, inches, or centimeters.

Any graphic you create must be able to fit inside the canvas.

3 Enter a resolution in pixels per inch or pixels per centimeter.

4 Select white, transparent, or a custom color for the canvas.

Use the Custom color box pop-up window to choose a custom canvas color.

5 Click OK to open the new document.

To create a new document the same size as an existing object:

1 Copy an object to the Clipboard from any of following:

• Another Fireworks document

• A Web browser

• Any of the applications listed in "Pasting into Fireworks" on page 70.

2 Choose File > New. The New Document dialog box opens with the width and height dimensions of the object on the Clipboard.

3 Set resolution and canvas color and click OK.

4 Choose Edit > Paste to paste the object from the Clipboard into the new document.

To open an existing document:

1 Choose File > Open. The Open dialog box appears.

2 Select the file and click Open.

Opening graphics from other applications

With Fireworks, you can open files of other applications or file formats, including Photoshop, FreeHand, Illustrator, uncompressed CorelDRAW, WBMP, EPS, and animated GIF files.

When you open a file format other than PNG using File > Open, a new Fireworks document is created. While the new document is a PNG file, the original file remains unchanged.

Opening Fireworks 1 files

In Fireworks 1, the background layer is a permanent image stretching across the entire canvas, under which no objects or layers can be placed. Fireworks 4 documents do not have a permanent background layer.

When you open Fireworks 1 documents in Fireworks 4, the background layer from the Fireworks 1 document is converted into a bitmap object and is placed as a shared layer on the bottom of the document. Also, the URL overlay in the Fireworks 1 document is converted to the Web Layer.

For more information about layers, see "Layers and Masking" on page 203.

Opening Photoshop files

When you open a Photoshop file in Fireworks, by default text layers remain fully editable and Photoshop layers are converted to Fireworks objects. You can modify Photoshop import settings so that Photoshop layers are converted to Fireworks frames and text layers to bitmap images. For information on changing Photoshop file options, see "Importing Photoshop files into Fireworks" on page 386.

Note: In Windows, Photoshop file names must include a PSD extension for Fireworks to recognize the Photoshop file type.

To open Photoshop files:

1 Choose File > Open.

2 Choose the file and click Open.

Opening FreeHand, Illustrator, or CorelDRAW files

You can open a vector drawing from FreeHand, Illustrator, or CorelDRAW and then apply Fireworks edits such as brush strokes and textured fills to the drawing.

Fireworks can import uncompressed CDR files created with CorelDRAW 7 or 8 for Windows. Fireworks cannot open or import CMX files or compressed CDR files.

Because CorelDRAW supports a different set of features than Fireworks, these changes occur when importing CDR files:

- Master page contents are repeated in each Fireworks frame.

- Only the two end objects of a CorelDRAW blend are imported. The objects are grouped after import.

- Dimensions convert to vector objects.

- Basic text is imported. Most character and paragraph parameters are unsupported.

- Colors are converted to RGB.

To open FreeHand, Illustrator, or CorelDRAW files:

1 Choose File > Open.

2 Choose the desired options in the Vector File Options dialog box:

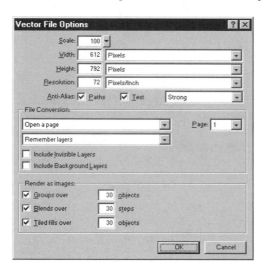

Scale specifies the scale percentage for the imported file.

Width and Height specify in pixels the width and height of the imported file.

Resolution specifies the resolution of the imported file.

Anti-Alias smooths imported objects to avoid jagged edges.

Note: To change selected objects to Anti-Alias or Hard Edge, use Modify > Alter > Hardfill, Anti-Alias Fill, and Feather Fill after importing.

File Conversion specifies how multipage documents are handled when imported:

- Open a page imports only the specified page.

- Open pages as frames imports all the pages from the document and places each in a separate frame.

- Remember layers maintains the layer structure of the imported file.

- Convert layers to frames places each layer of the imported document into a separate frame.

Include Invisible Layers imports objects on layers that have been turned off. Otherwise, invisible layers are ignored.

Include Background Layers imports objects from the document's background layer. Otherwise, the background layer is ignored.

Render as images rasterizes complex groups, blends, or tiled fills and places each as a single bitmap object in a Fireworks document. Enter a number in the text box to determine how many objects a group, blend, or tiled fill can contain before it is rasterized during import.

Opening animated GIFs

You can bring animated GIF files into Fireworks in two ways:

- You can import an animated GIF as an animation symbol. A symbol enables you to edit and move all the elements of the animation as a single unit. It also lets you use the Library panel to create new instances of the symbol.

   Note: When you import an animated GIF, the frame delay setting defaults to 0.20 seconds. If necessary, use the Frames panel to restore to the original timing.

- You can open an animated GIF as you would a normal GIF file. Each element of the GIF is placed as a separate image on its own Fireworks frame. You can still convert the graphic to an animation symbol if you wish.

Opening EPS files

Fireworks opens EPS files as flattened bitmap images if it cannot open the file as a vector.

When you import an EPS file into an existing document, the EPS File Options dialog box opens.

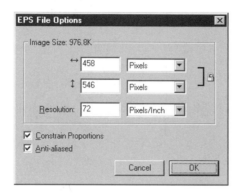

Units of measure determines the units in which the image's proportions are displayed. You can choose from pixels, percent, inches, and centimeters.

Resolution indicates the pixels per unit you want as the resolution.

Constrain Proportions opens the file in the same size proportion as the original.

Anti-aliased anti-aliases the opened EPS file.

Opening WBMP files

Fireworks can open WBMP files, which are 1-bit (monochrome) files optimized for mobile computing devices. This format is for use on Wireless Application Protocol (WAP) pages.

Importing from a scanner or digital camera

To import images from scanners or digital cameras, you use TWAIN modules or Photoshop Acquire plug-ins (Macintosh). Images imported into Fireworks from a scanner or digital camera open as new documents.

Note: Fireworks cannot scan images unless the appropriate software drivers, modules, and plug-ins have been installed. For specific instructions about installation, settings, and options, consult your documentation for the TWAIN module or Photoshop Acquire plug-in.

On the Macintosh, Fireworks automatically looks for the Photoshop Acquire plug-ins in the Fireworks 4\Output\Xtras folder. If you do not want to put the plug-ins here, you must point Fireworks to the alternative location.

To tell Fireworks where to look for the Photoshop Acquire plug-ins:

1 In Fireworks, choose Edit > Preferences.

2 Select the Folders tab.

3 Choose Photoshop Plug-Ins.

4 Click Browse, and navigate to the folder containing the Photoshop plug-ins.

To import an image from a scanner or digital camera:

1 Connect the scanner or camera to your computer.

2 Install the software that accompanies the scanner or camera.

3 In Fireworks, choose File > Scan and choose a TWAIN module or Photoshop Acquire plug-in that corresponds to the device from which you are importing an image.

For most TWAIN modules or Photoshop Acquire plug-ins, additional dialog boxes prompt you to set other options.

4 Follow instructions and apply settings.

The imported image is opened as a new Fireworks document.

Inserting objects into a Fireworks document

You can import, drag and drop, or copy and paste vector objects, bitmap images, or text created in other applications, as well as images from a digital camera or scanner, into a Fireworks document.

Dragging and dropping

You can drag vector objects, bitmap images, or text into Fireworks from any application that supports drag and drop:

- FreeHand 7 or later
- Flash 3 or later
- Photoshop 4 or later
- Illustrator 7 or later
- Microsoft Office 97 or later
- Microsoft Internet Explorer 3 or later
- Netscape Navigator 3 or later
- CorelDRAW 7 or later

To drag and drop into Fireworks:

Drag a graphic from another application to an open Fireworks document.

Pasting into Fireworks

You can copy and paste any of these formats from the Clipboard:

- FreeHand 7 or later
- Illustrator
- PNG
- PICT (Macintosh)
- DIB (Windows)
- BMP (Windows)
- ASCII text
- EPS
- WBMP

When you paste an object copied from another application into Fireworks, the object is centered in the active document.

Each edit mode handles pasted data differently:

- In vector mode, pasting a pixel selection yields a rectangular bitmap object that uses alpha transparency to maintain the appearance of the selection. Vector objects retain vector attributes.

- In bitmap mode, pasting a vector graphic or bitmap object pastes a pixel selection that remains floating until it is deselected. When deselected, the selection becomes part of the current image.

Resampling pasted objects

When pasting a bitmap with a resolution that differs from the destination Fireworks document, Fireworks displays a message asking if you want the bitmap to be resampled.

Resampling adds pixels to or subtracts them from a resized bitmap to match the appearance of the original bitmap as closely as possible. Resampling a bitmap to a higher resolution typically causes little data or quality loss. Resampling to a lower resolution always causes data loss and a drop in quality.

- To maintain the pasted data's original width and height, adding or subtracting pixels as necessary, choose Resample.

- To keep all the original pixels, which may make the relative size of the pasted image larger or smaller than expected, choose Don't Resample.

Importing PNG files

You can import Fireworks PNG files onto the current drawing layer. Hotspot objects and slice objects are placed on the document's Web Layer. For more information, see "Viewing and naming slices in the Layers panel" on page 262.

To import a PNG file into a Fireworks document:

1   Choose File > Import to open the Import dialog box.

2   Navigate to the file and click Open.

3   Move the import pointer where you want the top left corner of the image to be:

- Click to import the full-size image.

- Drag the import pointer to resize the image as you import. Fireworks retains the proportions of the image.

Navigating and viewing the document

You can control your document's magnification, the number of views, and the display mode. In addition, you can easily pan the view of a document. This is helpful if you zoom in and can no longer see the entire graphic.

Zooming in and out on a document

The zoom range in Fireworks is from 6% to 6400%. When zoomed in, you can scroll past the edge of the canvas into the gray area.

Choose a zoom setting from the
pop-up menu

The Zoom pop-up menu in the document window and the Zoom tool and Hand tool in the Tools panel.

To zoom in on a document:

- Choose the Zoom tool and click inside a document window where you want the new center point.

- Choose a zoom setting from the Zoom pop-up menu.

- Choose View > Zoom and choose a Zoom option.

To zoom out on a document:

- Choose a zoom setting from the Zoom pop-up menu.

- Choose View > Zoom and choose a zoom option.

To zoom in on a specific area:

Drag a selection area with the Zoom tool.

To zoom out based on a selection area:

Hold down Alt (Windows) or Option (Macintosh) and drag a selection area with the Zoom tool.

To return to 100% size:

Double-click the Zoom tool in the Tools panel.

To pan around your document:

1   Choose the Hand tool. The Hand cursor appears.

2   Drag the Hand cursor.

> *Note:* While panning, when you reach the edge of a document, the view continues to scroll a few pixels into the gray area.

To fit the document in the current view:

Double-click the Hand tool.

Displaying multiple document views

Use multiple views to see one document at different magnifications simultaneously. Changes you make in one view automatically appear at different magnifications in different views.

To open an additional document view at a different zoom setting:

1   Choose Window > New Window.

2   Select a zoom setting for the new window.

To tile document views:

Choose Window > Tile Horizontal or Window > Tile Vertical.

To close a document view window:

Click the window's Close button.

Controlling document redraw

Display modes affect a document's onscreen representation, but not its object data or output quality.

- Full Display mode displays the document in all available colors with full detail.

- Draft Display mode displays paths as 1 pixel wide with no fill and displays images with an X through them.

- Macintosh Gamma (Windows) or Windows Gamma (Macintosh) modifies Full Display to show how a graphic looks on another computer platform. When working on the Windows platform, you can use this command to view how a graphic looks on the Macintosh platform, and vice versa.

To switch to another display mode:

Select Full display from the View menu.

Changing the canvas

You set up canvas characteristics when you first create a new Fireworks document. But afterwards, you can still go back and modify the size and color of the canvas and change the image's resolution. As you work with the document, you can also rotate the canvas and trim away unwanted parts of it.

Changing document size, color, and resolution

Fireworks makes it easy to change to the canvas size, canvas color, and image resolution characteristics.

To change canvas size:

1 Choose Modify > Canvas Size.

2 Click an Anchor button to specify which sides of the canvas Fireworks will add to or delete from, and click OK.

   Note: By default, the center anchor is selected, indicating that changes to the size of the canvas are made on all sides.

3 Enter the new dimensions in the Width and Height fields.

To change canvas color:

1 Choose Modify > Canvas Color.

2 Select from the following options:

• White

• Transparent

• Custom

   If you choose Custom, click the color box to pick a color from the color box pop-up window.

3 Click OK.

To resize a document and all of its contents:

1 Choose Modify > Image Size. The Image Size dialog box opens.

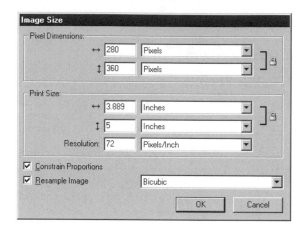

2 In the Pixel Dimensions text boxes, enter new horizontal and vertical dimensions.

   You can also change the units of measure. If Resample Image is deselected, you can change the Resolution or Print Size but not Pixel Dimensions.

3 In the Print Size text boxes, enter horizontal and vertical dimensions for the image size for printing. You can also change the units of measure.

4 In the Resolution text box, enter a new resolution for the image.

   You can also choose between pixels/inch and pixels/cm as the units, or choose Resample Image. Changing Resolution also changes the pixel dimensions.

5 To maintain the same ratio between the document's horizontal and vertical dimensions, choose Constrain Proportions. Deselect Constrain Proportions to resize width and height independently.

6 Select Resample Image to add or remove pixels when resizing the image to approximate the same appearance at a different size.

7 Click OK.

About resizing in Fireworks

Resampling in Fireworks differs from that in most image editing applications. Fireworks contains pixel-based bitmap image objects and path-based vector objects.

- When a bitmap object is resampled, pixels are added to or removed from the image to make it larger or smaller.

- When a vector object is resampled, little quality loss occurs because the path is redrawn mathematically at a larger or smaller size.

However, since the attributes of vector objects in Fireworks are visible as pixels, some strokes or fills may appear slightly different after resampling because the pixels that compose the stroke or fill must be redrawn.

Note: Guides, hotspot objects, and slice objects are resized when an image is resized.

Resizing bitmap objects always presents a unique problem—do you add or remove pixels to resize the image, or do you change the number of pixels per inch or centimeter?

You can alter the size of a bitmap image by adjusting the resolution or by resampling the image. When adjusting the resolution, you in effect change the size of the pixels in the image so that more or fewer pixels fit in a given space. Adjusting the resolution without resampling does not result in data loss.

- Downsampling, or removing pixels to make the image smaller, always causes quality loss because pixels are discarded to resize the image.

- Resampling up, or adding pixels to make the image larger, may result in quality loss because some pixels are being added to make the image larger, and the pixels being added do not always correspond to the original image.

Original and after downsampling an image

Rotating the canvas

Rotating the canvas is helpful when an image is imported upside down or sideways. You can rotate the canvas 180 degrees, 90 degrees clockwise, or 90 degrees counterclockwise.

When you rotate the canvas, all objects in the document rotate.

Original and rotated 180 degrees

To rotate the canvas:

1   Choose Modify > Rotate Canvas.

2   Choose a rotation option.

Trimming the canvas

If your document contains extra empty space around an image, you can trim the canvas. You can also remove empty canvas space by cropping the image. For more information, see "Cropping a path" on page 121 or "Cropping a bitmap image" on page 140.

Original

Trimmed canvas

To trim the canvas:

Choose Modify > Trim Canvas to automatically remove excess pixels from around the edge of the document.

Each edge of the canvas is cropped to the edges of the object or objects in the document.

If the document has more than one frame, Trim Canvas crops to include all objects in all frames, not just the current frame.

You can also trim the canvas using Modify > Fit Canvas. This command lets you expand the canvas to fit objects that extend beyond its boundary, as well as trimming the canvas like the normal Trim Canvas command.

Using rulers, guides, and the grid

To lay out objects as precisely as possible and to help you draw, use rulers and guides. You can place guides in the document and snap objects to those guides, or turn on the Fireworks grid and snap objects to the grid.

Using rulers

Rulers help you to organize and plan the layout of your work. Rulers measure in pixels at all times, regardless of the unit of measurement you used when creating the document.

To show and hide rulers:

Choose View > Ruler.

Vertical and horizontal rulers appear along the margins of the document window.

Working with guides

Guides are lines that you drag onto the document canvas from the rulers. They serve as drawing aids to help you place and align objects. Use guides to set off or mark important parts of your document, such as the margins, the document center point, and areas where you want to carry out precise work. You can also export the image as an HTML table that is sliced along the guides.

To help you align objects, Fireworks lets you snap objects to guides.

You can prevent guides from being accidentally moved by locking them.

Note: Guides do not reside on a layer or export with a document. They are merely design tools.

Guides are different from slice guides. For information on slice guides, see "Using Hotspots and Slices" on page 249.

To create a horizontal or vertical guide:

1 Click and then drag from the corresponding ruler.

2 Position the guide on the canvas and release the mouse button.

You can reposition the guide by dragging it again.

To move a guide to a specific position:

1 Double-click the guide.

2 Enter the new position in the Move Guide dialog box.

3 Click OK.

To show or hide guides:

Choose View > Guides > Show Guides.

To snap objects to guides:

Choose View > Guides > Snap to Guides.

To change guide colors:

1 Choose View > Guides > Edit Guides.

2 From the color box pop-up window, select the new guide color and click OK.

To lock or unlock all guides:

Choose View > Guides > Lock Guides.

To remove a guide:

Drag the guide off the canvas.

Using the grid

Use the grid to display a system of horizontal and vertical lines on the canvas. The grid is useful for precisely placing objects. You can view, edit, resize, and change the color of the grid.

Note: The grid does not reside on a layer or export with a document. It is merely a design tool.

To show and hide the grid:

Choose View > Grid > Show Grid.

To snap objects to the grid:

Choose View > Grid > Snap to Grid.

To change the grid color:

1 Choose View > Grid > Edit Grid.

2 From the color box pop-up window, select the new grid color and click OK.

To change the size of the grid's cells:

1 Choose View > Grid > Edit Grid.

2 Enter the appropriate values in the horizontal and vertical spacing fields and click OK.

CHAPTER 4
Working with Objects

As you work in vector mode in Fireworks, you will need to manipulate vector objects, text blocks, symbols, slices and hotspots, and bitmap graphics. Anything you may want to do with an existing object in vector mode requires that you select it first.

Once you select an object, you can move, copy, delete, or edit it. Also, you can use the transformation tools in vector mode to rotate, scale, and skew objects without losing resolution quality. In documents that have multiple objects, you can organize the objects by stacking, grouping, and aligning them.

Selecting objects in vector mode

Fireworks has several tools for selecting vector objects. You can also use these tools to select text blocks, symbols, Web objects, and bitmap graphics while in vector mode. "Selecting pixel areas" on page 127 describes methods for selecting pixels in bitmap mode.

You can choose from these selection options:

- To select a vector object, use the Pointer tool (see "Using the Pointer tool" on page 86).

- To select an object and individual points, use the Subselection tool (see "Using the Subselection tool" on page 87).

- To select an object that is behind another object, use the Select Behind tool (see "Using the Select Behind tool" on page 87).

- To select an area to be exported as a separate file, use the Export Area tool.

Using the Object panel

Whenever you select an object, the Object panel identifies the selection. When a single object is selected, the Object panel title bar describes it by object type, such as rectangle, slice, path, or text. When more than one object is selected, the Object panel title bar and status bar display the number.

Note: Selected objects are also identified in the status bar at the bottom of the document window in Windows.

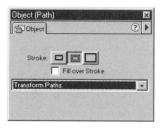

The Objects panel also displays information and settings for some selected objects. For example, when you select a vector path, the Object panel displays buttons for setting the location of the path's stroke in relation to the vector path. It also displays a pop-up menu containing options for what happens to the vector object when it is transformed.

Select a slice, for instance, and you can set the slice to be an image or text slice in the Object panel. You can also assign a URL, enter alt text, specify a link target, and set a naming convention for exported sliced images. You can even change the color of the slice.

Information on specific settings on the Object panel is discussed throughout the manual in the context of other information about the various objects that you can select in Fireworks.

Using the Pointer tool

The Pointer tool selects objects when you click them or when you drag a selection area around all or part of the objects. You cannot select individual points using the Pointer tool; use the Subselection tool for this (see "Selecting points" on page 113).

To select an object by clicking:

Move the Pointer tool over the object's stroke and click.

If the object has a fill, you can click the fill to select it.

To preview what you would select if you were to click, choose the Mouse Highlight option on the Tool Options panel. A red line highlights the object's path when the pointer is in position to select it.

To select objects by dragging:

Drag the Pointer tool over one or more objects.

Using the Subselection tool

As with the Pointer tool, you can use the Subselection tool to select objects by clicking them or dragging a selection area around them, but the Subselection tool has several additional capabilities:

- You can select and move points.

- You can edit the paths adjacent to points by dragging the point handles (see "Reshaping paths using vector mode editing tools" on page 114).

- You can select and modify an object within a group or composite path (see "Grouping objects" on page 94).

To easily switch back and forth between the Pointer tool and the Subselection tool, press Alt (Windows) or Option (Macintosh).

Using the Select Behind tool

When working with graphics that contain multiple objects, you can use the Select Behind tool to select an object that is hidden or obscured by other objects.

To select an object behind other objects:

Click the Select Behind tool repeatedly over the stacked objects, progressing through the objects one by one until you have selected the object you want.

Note: You also can select a hard-to-reach object by clicking its thumbnail view in the Layers panel.

Using the Layers panel to select objects

The Layers panel contains a named thumbnail of each object on each layer in a document. Each object is listed in the Layers panel under the layer on which it is placed. When an object is selected, a small blue selection indicator appears to the right of the layer name in the Layers panel.

To select an object from the Layers panel:

Click the thumbnail or the name of the object.

To move selected objects from one layer to another:

- Drag an object's thumbnail view onto another layer name in the Layers panel.

- Drag the small blue selection indicator from one layer to another in the Layers panel.

Modifying a selection

After you have selected a single object, you can add objects to the selection and deselect selected objects. You can select or deselect everything on every layer in a document by choosing a single command. You can hide the selection path so you can edit a selected object while viewing it as it will appear on the Web or in print.

To add to a selection:

Hold down Shift while clicking additional objects with the Pointer, Subselection, or Select Behind tool.

To deselect an object while leaving other objects selected:

Hold down Shift while clicking the selected object.

To select everything on every layer in the document:

Choose Edit > Select All. To deselect all selected objects, choose Edit > Deselect.

Select All does not select hidden objects.

Also, you must deselect the Single Layer Editing preference to select all unhidden objects on all layers in a document. When the Single Layer Editing preference is chosen, only objects on the current layer are selected (see "Using the Layers panel to select objects" on page 87).

To hide the path of a selected object:

Choose View > Hide Edges.

Note: To identify the selected object when the outline and points are hidden, look at the Status bar (Windows) or Object panel.

To hide selected objects:

Choose View > Hide Selection. To show them again, choose View > Show All.

To hide objects whether they are selected or not, you can click or drag along the show/hide layer/object column in the Layers panel.

Note: Hidden objects are not exported.

Moving, copying, cloning, and deleting objects

You can move selected objects by dragging them on the canvas, cutting and pasting them, pressing the arrow keys, or entering location coordinates in the Info panel. You can move selected objects between Fireworks and other applications using the Clipboard. You can copy objects by pasting them from the Clipboard or by dragging them. If you no longer want an object on the canvas, you can delete it.

To move a selection:

- Drag it with the Pointer, Subselection, or Select Behind tool.

- Press any arrow key to move the selection by 1-pixel increments. Hold down Shift to move it in 10-pixel increments.

- In the Info panel, enter the X and Y coordinates for the location of the top left corner of the selection. The coordinates for the top left corner of the canvas are X=0 and Y=0. Coordinates are expressed in pixels.

To move or copy selected objects by pasting:

1 Select an object or multiple objects.

2 Choose Edit > Cut or Edit > Copy. The object is cut or copied to the Clipboard.

3 Choose Edit > Paste.

Note: If you create a new document in Fireworks with a selection on the Clipboard, the canvas size defaults to the dimensions of the selection.

To duplicate a selection:

Choose Edit > Duplicate.

Duplicates of the selection appear in a cascading arrangement from the original; each new duplicate becomes the selected object.

To clone a selection:

Choose Edit > Clone.

The clone of the selection is stacked precisely in front of the original and becomes the selected object.

To move a selected clone away from the original with pixel-by-pixel precision, use the arrow keys. This is handy if you want to maintain specific distances between clones or maintain the alignment of the clones.

To delete selected objects:

- Press Delete or Backspace.

- Right-click (Windows) or Control-click (Macintosh) the object and choose Edit > Cut from the context menu.

- Choose Edit > Clear.

- Choose Edit > Cut.

Transforming and distorting objects

You can scale, rotate, flip, distort, or skew an object or group in vector mode using the Transform tools and menu commands.

Transform tools

Choosing any Transform tool or menu command displays the transform handles around selected objects.

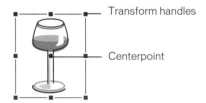

Transform handles

Centerpoint

Original object

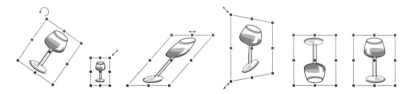

Rotated, scaled, skewed, distorted, and flipped vertically and horizontally

To edit selected objects using the transform handles:

1   Choose a Transform tool. As you move the pointer toward the selection, it changes to indicate the current transformation.

2   Drag to transform the objects.

Viewing transformation information on the Info panel

The Info panel lets you view numerical transformation information for the currently selected object. The information updates as you edit the object.

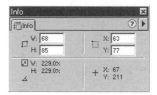

- For scaling and free transformations, the Info panel shows the width (W) and height (H) of the original object before transformation and the percentage increase or decrease in width and height during the transformation.

- For skewing and distorting, the Info panel shows the X and Y grid coordinates of the original object before transformation and the new X and Y coordinates during the transformation.

When you release the mouse button and move the pointer away from the object, color information replaces the transformation information.

To view transformation information as you transform a selection:

Choose Window > Info.

Resizing (scaling) objects

Scaling an object enlarges or reduces it horizontally, vertically, or in both directions.

To scale a selected object:

1 Display the transform handles:

- Choose the Scale Transform tool.

- Choose Modify > Transform > Scale.

2 Drag the transform handles:

- To scale the object both horizontally and vertically, drag one of the corner handles. Proportions are constrained as you scale.

- To scale the object horizontally or vertically, drag a side handle.

You can also scale selected objects by entering new width (W) and height (H) dimensions in the Info panel.

Rotating objects

When rotated, an object pivots on its center point. You can rotate an object by dragging its transform handles or by choosing a preset angle.

To rotate a selected object 90 or 180 degrees:

Choose Modify > Transform and choose a Rotation command from the submenu.

To rotate a selected object by dragging:

1 Choose any Transform tool.

2 Move the pointer outside the object until the rotation pointer appears.

3 Drag to rotate the object.

To constrain rotation to 15-degree increments relative to the horizon, hold down Shift and move the pointer beyond the handles.

To relocate the axis of rotation:

Drag the center point away from the center.

To reset the axis of rotation to the center of the selection, double-click the center point.

Flipping objects

You can flip an object across its vertical or horizontal axis without moving its relative position on the canvas.

To flip a selected object:

Choose Modify > Transform > Flip Horizontal or Flip Vertical.

Skewing objects

Skewing an object transforms it by slanting it along the horizontal or vertical axis, or both axes. You can skew an object by dragging.

To skew a selected object:

1 Display the transform handles:

 • Choose the Skew Transform tool.

• Choose Modify > Transform > Skew.

2 Drag a handle to skew the object.

To achieve the illusion of perspective:

Drag a corner point.

Note: To drag a corner point of a rectangle—which is a group when drawn using the Rectangle tool—ungroup it first.

Distorting objects

Distorting an object moves its sides or corners in the direction in which you drag the Distortion tool.

To distort a selected object:

1 Display the transform handles:

• Choose the Distortion Transform tool.

• Choose Modify > Transform > Distort.

2 Drag a handle to distort the object.

Numeric transformations

Instead of dragging to scale, resize, or rotate an object, you can transform it by entering specific values.

To scale or rotate selected objects by specific values:

1   Choose Modify > Transform > Numeric Transform.

   The Numeric Transform dialog box opens.

2   From the pop-up menu, choose the type of transformation to perform on the current selection:

- Scale

- Resize

- Rotate

3   Choose Constrain Proportions to maintain horizontal and vertical proportions when scaling or resizing a selection.

4   Choose Scale Attributes to transform the fill, stroke, and effects of the object along with the object itself. Deselect Scale Attributes to transform the path only.

5   Type numeric values to transform the selection and click OK.

Organizing objects

When working with multiple objects within a single document, you can use different techniques to organize the document:

- You can group individual objects to treat them as one or protect each object's relationship to the others in the group.

- You can arrange objects behind or in front of other objects. The way objects are arranged is called the *stacking order*.

- You can align selected objects to an area of the canvas or to a vertical or horizontal axis.

Grouping objects

You can group individual selected objects and then manipulate them as if they were a single object. For example, after drawing the petals of a flower as individual objects, you can group them to easily select and move the entire flower as a single object.

You can edit groups without ungrouping them. You can select an individual object in a group for editing without ungrouping the objects. You can also ungroup the objects anytime.

Group selected objects as a single object.

To group two or more selected objects:

Choose Modify > Group.

To ungroup a selected group, choose Modify > Ungroup.

Selecting objects within groups

To work with individual objects within a group, you can either ungroup the objects or use the Subselection tool to subselect individual objects while leaving the group intact.

Subselection tool

Modifying the attributes of a subselected object changes only the subselected object, not the entire group. Moving a subselected object to another layer removes the object from the group.

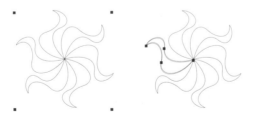

Subselect an object within a group.

To select an object that is part of a group:

Choose the Subselection tool and click the object or drag a selection area around it. To add objects to or deselect them from the selection, hold down Shift as you click or drag.

To select the group that contains a subselected object:

• Right-click (Windows) or Control-click (Macintosh) anywhere on the group and choose Select > Superselect from the context menu.

• Choose Edit > Superselect.

To select all objects within a selected group:

• Right-click (Windows) or Control-click (Macintosh) anywhere on the group and choose Select > Superselect from the context menu.

• Choose Edit > Subselect.

Stacking objects

Within a layer, Fireworks stacks objects based on the order in which they were created, placing the most recently created object on the top of the stack. The stacking order of objects determines how they appear when they overlap.

Note that layers also affect the stacking order. For example, if a document has two layers named Layer 1 and Layer 2, and Layer 1 is listed below Layer 2 on the Layers panel, then everything on Layer 2 appears in front of everything on Layer 1. To change the order of layers, drag the layer in the Layers panel to a new position (see "Layers and Masking" on page 203).

To change the stacking order of a selected object or group within a layer:

• Choose Modify > Arrange > Bring to Front or Send to Back to move the object or group to the top or bottom of the stacking order.

• Choose Modify > Arrange > Bring Forward or Send Backward to move the object or group up or down one position in the stacking order.

If more than one group is selected, the groups move in front of or behind all unselected groups while maintaining their order relative to each other.

Aligning objects

The Align commands on the Modify menu enable you to align objects along a horizontal or vertical axis. You can align selected objects vertically along their right edge, center, or left edge, or horizontally along their top edge, center, or bottom edge. Edges are determined by the bounding boxes enclosing each selected object.

Using the Align commands, you can distribute selected objects so that their centers or edges are evenly spaced. You can resize selected objects so that the horizontal or vertical dimensions of all objects match those of the largest selected object. You can also align selected objects to the canvas. You can apply one or more Align commands to selected objects.

To align selected objects:

- Choose Modify > Align > Left to align the objects to the leftmost selected object.

- Choose Modify > Align > Center Vertical to align the center points of the objects along a vertical axis.

- Choose Modify > Align > Right to align the objects to the rightmost selected object.

- Choose Modify > Align > Top to align the objects to the topmost selected object.

- Choose Modify > Align > Center Horizontal to align the center points of the objects along a horizontal axis.

- Choose Modify > Align > Bottom to align the objects to the bottommost selected object.

To evenly distribute the widths or heights of three or more selected objects:

Choose Modify > Align > Distribute Widths or Modify > Align > Distribute Heights.

Arranging objects among layers

The Layers panel offers another dimension of organizational control. You can move selected objects from one layer to another by dragging the object thumbnail or the blue selection indicator in the Layers panel to another layer (see "Layers and Masking" on page 203).

CHAPTER 5
Working with Vector Objects

A vector object is a computer graphic whose shape is defined by a series of lines and curves, called *vectors*, connected by points that form a path. A vector object's stroke color follows the path. Its fill occupies the area inside the path. The stroke and fill typically determine how the graphic looks when published in print or on the Web.

Fireworks has many tools for drawing and editing vector objects using a variety of techniques. With the basic shape tools, you can quickly draw straight lines, circles and ellipses, squares and rectangles, stars, and any equilateral polygon with 3 to 360 sides.

You can draw freeform vector paths with the Pencil, Brush, and Pen tools. The Pen tool enables you to draw complex shapes with smooth curves and straight lines by plotting points one by one.

After you have drawn vector objects, Fireworks offers several methods for editing them. You can change an object's shape by moving, adding, or deleting points. You can use point handles to change the shape of adjacent path segments. Freeform tools let you alter the shape of objects by editing paths directly.

Commands on the Modify menu give you more options for editing objects, including combining objects to create a single object, creating an object from the intersection of several objects, and expanding the stroke of an object. You can also import bitmap and vector images and manipulate them in vector mode.

Entering vector mode

Fireworks has two drawing modes—vector mode and bitmap mode. You must be in vector mode to draw vector objects.

Note: In previous versions of Fireworks, vector mode was called object mode.

When Fireworks is in bitmap mode, by default a striped border surrounds the canvas.

To switch from bitmap mode to vector mode:

Do one of the following:

- Click the Exit Bitmap Mode button at the bottom of the document window.

Exit Bitmap Mode button

- Choose Modify > Exit Bitmap Mode.
- Press the Esc key.
- Choose a tool that works only in vector mode, such as the Pen tool.

Drawing basic shapes

Squares, rectangles, circles, ovals, stars and other polygons are easy to draw when you use the basic shape tools. You can draw rectangles with rounded corners and adjust the corner radius after you draw the rectangle. You can also draw a variety of stars, from narrow and pointy to wide and stubby.

The basic shape drawing tools are in the drawing tool section of the Tools panel. When you use any drawing or painting tool to create an object, the tool applies the current stroke and fill attributes to the object. To change the current stroke and fill attributes, as well as the stroke and fill attributes of existing objects, see "Applying Colors, Strokes, and Fills" on page 157.

All the shape drawing tools

Note: You can paint pixels using the basic shape tools in bitmap mode. See "Painting in bitmap mode" on page 135.

Drawing lines, rectangles, and ellipses

Use the Line, Rectangle or Ellipse tool to quickly draw basic shapes. The Rectangle tool draws rectangles as grouped objects. To move a rectangle corner point independently, you must ungroup the rectangle or use the Subselection tool. To draw rectangles with rounded corners, see "Drawing rectangles with rounded corners" on page 101.

To draw a line, rectangle, or ellipse:

1 Choose the Line, Rectangle, or Ellipse tool.

2 Optionally, set the stroke and fill attributes (see "Applying Colors, Strokes, and Fills" on page 157).

3 Drag on the canvas to draw the shape.

For the Line tool, Shift-drag to constrain lines to 45-degree increments from horizontal.

For the Rectangle or Ellipse tool, Shift-drag to constrain shapes to squares or circles.

To draw a line, rectangle, or ellipse from a specific center point:

Position the pointer at the intended center point and Alt-drag (Windows) or Option-drag (Macintosh) the drawing tool.

To both constrain a shape and draw from the center point:

Position the pointer at the intended center point and Shift+Alt-drag (Windows) or Shift+Option-drag (Macintosh) the drawing tool.

To resize a selected line, rectangle, or ellipse:

- Drag a point.

- Enter new width (W) or height (H) values in the Info panel.

- Choose Transform > Scale and drag a control handle.

Drawing rectangles with rounded corners

You can draw rectangles with rounded corners by using the Rounded Rectangle tool and specifying a corner radius from 0% to 100% before you draw, or by using the Object panel to adjust the corner roundness of selected rectangles. The Rounded Rectangle tool draws rectangles as grouped objects. To move rounded rectangle points independently, you must ungroup the rectangle or use the Subselection tool.

To draw a rectangle with rounded corners:

1 Double-click the Rounded Rectangle tool to open the Tool Options panel.

2 Specify the corner roundness by typing a number from 0 to 100 or by dragging the slider:

You can adjust the corner roundness as you draw by pressing the Up or Down arrow key repeatedly.

To round the corners of a selected rectangle:

Enter a value in the Roundness field in the Object panel and press Enter.

Drawing polygons

With the Polygon tool, you can draw any equilateral polygon, from a triangle to a polygon with 360 sides.

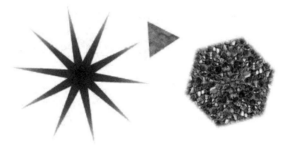

To draw a polygon:

1 Double-click the Polygon tool to open the Polygon tool Options panel.

2 Choose Polygon from the Shape pop-up menu.

3 Enter the number of sides for the polygon:

• Use the slider to choose 3 to 25 sides.

• Enter a number from 3 to 360 in the Sides text box.

4 Drag to draw the polygon.

To constrain a polygon's orientation to increments of 45 degrees, hold down Shift as you draw. The Polygon tool always draws from a center point.

Drawing stars

Using the Polygon tool's Star option, you can draw stars with 3 to 360 points and the full range of point angles.

To draw a star:

1 Double-click the Polygon tool to open the Options panel.

2 Choose Star from the Shape pop-up menu.

3 Enter the number of points for the star.

4 Choose Automatic Acuteness or enter an angle. Values closer to 0 result in long, thin points; values closer to 100 result in short, stubby points.

5 Drag on the canvas to draw the star.

   To constrain a star's orientation to increments of 45 degrees, hold down Shift as you drag. The Polygon tool always draws from a center point.

Drawing and painting freeform paths

You can draw freeform vector paths with the Pencil or Brush tool, much the same way you would use a real pencil or paintbrush.

Pencil tool and Brush tool

You can change the stroke and fill attributes of paths drawn with the Pencil or Brush tool. See "Applying Colors, Strokes, and Fills" on page 157. Also, you can use the Pencil and Brush tools in bitmap mode (see "Working with Bitmaps" on page 125).

Using the Pencil tool

In vector mode, the Pencil tool draws a vector path with a 1-pixel stroke. You can modify existing Pencil strokes and add fills to selected objects you have drawn with the Pencil tool, but the Pencil tool reverts to a 1-pixel path each time you use it to draw another object.

To draw a vector object with a 1-pixel Pencil stroke:

1 Double-click the Pencil tool to open the Options panel and choose or deselect Pencil tool options:

   Anti-Aliased puts a smooth edge on the lines you draw.

   Auto Erase draws the fill color over the stroke.

   Preserve Transparency restricts the Pencil tool to draw paths only into existing pixels, not into transparent areas of a graphic. This option only works in bitmap mode.

2 Optionally, change the stroke name to 1-Pixel Soft, Colored Pencil, or Graphite in the Stroke panel. You can also change the stroke color using any stroke color box (see "Drawing and painting freeform paths" on page 103).

3 Drag to draw. To constrain the path to a horizontal or vertical line, hold down Shift while dragging.

4 Release the mouse button to end the path. To close the path, release the mouse button when you have returned the pointer to the point at the beginning of the path.

Note: You can paint pixels using the Pencil tool in bitmap mode (see "Painting in bitmap mode" on page 135).

Using the Brush tool

The Brush tool has a wide variety of brush stroke categories, including air brush, spray paint, calligraphy, crayon, and unnatural. Within each category are dozens of strokes, including light and dark felt tips, splattered oil, bamboo, ribbon, confetti, 3D, toothpaste, and viscous alien paint.

Although the strokes may look like paint or ink, they all have points just like any other vector objact. That means that you can change the shape of the stroke by moving its points. After you reshape the path, the stroke is redrawn. In this way you can edit an entire painting without ever having to erase and redraw strokes.

A painting edited by moving vector points

You can also modify existing brush strokes and add fills to selected objects you have drawn with the Brush tool. The new stroke and fill settings are retained for subsequent use of the Brush tool within the current document. However, if you change the stroke category to Pencil while the Brush tool is active, it reverts to the default Basic stroke category the next time you use it.

To paint a freeform vector path:

1   Click the Brush tool.

    The options for this tool only work in Bitmap mode.

2   Optionally, set stroke and fill attributes (see "Applying Colors, Strokes, and Fills" on page 157).

3   Drag to draw. To constrain the path to a horizontal or vertical line, hold down Shift while dragging.

4   Release the mouse button to end the path. To close the path, release the mouse button when you have returned the pointer to the point at the beginning of the path.

Note: You can paint pixels using the Brush tool in bitmap mode (see "Painting in bitmap mode" on page 135).

Using the Pen tool

One way to draw and edit vector objects in Fireworks is to plot points as if drawing a connect-the-dots picture. When you click each point with the Pen tool, the path of the vector object draws automatically from the last point you clicked.

In addition to connecting the points with only straight segments, the Pen tool can draw smooth, mathematically derived curve segments known as Bezier curves. Each point's type—corner point or curve point—determines whether the adjacent curves are straight lines or curves.

- A corner point designates at least one adjacent segment as straight.

- A curve point designates at least one adjacent segment as curved.

Whether drawn with the Pen tool or with another Fireworks drawing tool, all points on all vector objects have control handles. The position of each point's control handles determines the shape of the adjacent segments. You can edit the shape of a vector object by dragging control handles with the Pen or Subselection tools. You can also change the shape of an object by changing a point from straight to curved.

Pen tool

Drawing straight path segments

Drawing straight line segments with the Pen tool is a simple matter of clicking to place the points. Each click with the Pen tool plots a corner point.

To draw a path with straight line segments:

1 Choose the Pen tool.

2 Enable any of the following options in the Options panel if desired:

• Show Pen Preview to preview the line segment that would result from the next click.

• Show Solid Points to draw solid points.

3 Click to place the first corner point.

4 Move the pointer and click to place the next point. A straight line segment joins the two points.

5 Continue plotting points. Straight segments bridge each gap between points.

6 End the path, either open or closed:

• Double-click the last point to end the path as an open path.

• Choose another tool to end the path as an open path. When you choose certain tools and then return to the Pen tool, your next click resumes drawing the object.

• To close the path, click the first point you plotted. A closed path's beginning and end points are the same.

Note: Loops formed by a path overlapping itself are not closed paths. Only paths that begin and end on the same point are closed paths.

Drawing curved path segments

To draw curved path segments, you need only click and drag as you plot points. As you draw, the current point shows control handles.

To draw an object with curved segments:

 1 Choose the Pen tool.

2 Click to place the first corner point.

3 Move to the location of the next point, then click and drag to produce a curve point. Each time you click and drag, Fireworks extends the line segment to the new point.

4 Continue plotting points. If you click and drag a new point, you produce a curve point; if you just click, you produce a corner point.

5 End the path, either open or closed:

• Double-click the last point to end the path as an open path.

• Choose another tool to end the path as an open path. When you choose certain tools and then return to the Pen tool, your next click resumes drawing the object.

• Click the first point you had plotted to close the path. A closed path's beginning and ending points are the same.

Adjusting the shape of a straight path segment

To adjust a straight path segment:

1   Select the path with the Pointer or Subselection tool.

2   Click a point with the Subselection tool to select it.

Selected corner points appear as solid blue squares.

3   Drag the point to a new location.

Adjusting the shape of a curved path segment

To adjust the Bezier curve of a path segment:

1   Select the path with the Pointer or Subselection tool.

2   Click a curve point with the Subselection tool to select it.

A selected curve point appears as a solid blue circle. The control handles extend from the point.

3 Drag the point or one of its handles to a new location. The blue path preview shows where the new path will be drawn if you release the mouse button.

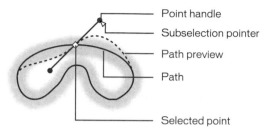

For example, drag the left control handle downward. Notice that the right control handle goes up.

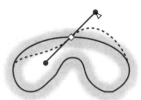

To constrain handle movement to 45-degree angles:

Press Shift while dragging.

Converting path segments to straight or curved

Straight path segments are intersected by corner points. Curved path segments contain curve points.

You can convert a straight segment to a curved segment and vice versa by converting its point.

To convert a corner point on a selected path to a curve point:

 1 Choose the Pen tool.

2 Click a corner point and drag away from it.

The handles extend, curving the adjacent segments.

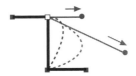

To convert a curve point on a selected path to a corner point:

 1 Choose the Pen tool.

2 Click a curve point to convert it.

The handles retract and the adjacent segments straighten.

To move a point:

Drag it with the Subselection tool.

The path redraws to reflect the point's new position.

To change the shape of a path segment:

Drag a point handle.

Continuing an existing path

To resume drawing an existing open path:

 1 Choose the Pen tool.

2 Click the ending point and continue the path.

3 The pen tool cursor changes to indicate that you are adding to a path.

Merging two open paths

You can connect two open paths to form one continuous path. When connecting two paths, the topmost path's stroke, fill, and effect attributes become the attributes of the newly merged path.

To merge two open paths:

1 Click the end point of one of the paths.

2 Move the pointer to the end point of the other path and click.

Auto-joining similar open paths

You can easily join one open path with another that has similar stroke and fill characteristics.

To auto-join two open paths:

1 Select an open path.

2 Choose the Subselection tool and drag an end point of the path within a few pixels of the end of the similar path. The end point snaps to the other path, and the two become a single path.

Inserting and deleting points on a path

You can add points to a path and delete points from a path. Adding points to a path gives you control over a specific segment within the path. Deleting points from the path reshapes it or simplifies editing.

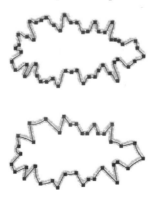

To insert a point on a selected path:

Using the Pen tool, click anywhere on the path that does not contain a point.

To convert a curve point to a corner point:

Click a curve point with the Pen tool.

To delete a point from a selected path segment:

- Click a corner point on a selected object with the Pen tool.

- Double-click a curve point on a selected object with the Pen tool.

- Select a point with the Subselection tool and press Delete or Backspace.

Selecting points

You can select only one point with the Pen tool. To select multiple points, use the Subselection tool and Shift-click each point. Or, using the Subselection tool, drag around the points to be selected.

Before selecting a point with the Pen tool, select the path using the Pointer tool. Otherwise, the Pen tool draws a new path rather than selecting a point on the existing path.

To select specific points:

 1   Choose the Subselection tool.

2   Click a point, or hold down Shift and click multiple points one by one.

To display a curve point's handles:

Click it with the Subselection tool. If either point nearest the clicked point is a curve point, the near handle is also displayed.

To display the near handles of curve points on either side of a corner point:

1 Alt-drag (Windows) or Option-drag (Macintosh) from the point with the Subselection tool.

2 To display the second point handle, repeat the previous step.

The path preview shows where the new path will be drawn if you release the mouse button.

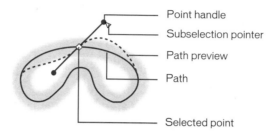

Drag a point handle with the Subselection tool to edit adjacent path segments.

To bend a segment adjacent to a corner point:

 1 Choose the Subselection tool.

2 Select a corner point.

3 Alt-drag (Windows) or Option-drag (Macintosh) a point handle to bend the adjacent segment.

Reshaping paths using vector mode editing tools

In addition to dragging points and point handles, you can use several Fireworks tools to edit vector objects directly.

Vector mode editing tools: Freeform, Reshape Area, Path Scrubber, Redraw Path, and Knife tools

Bending and reshaping vector objects

Use the Freeform tool to bend and reshape vector objects directly instead of manipulating points. You can push or pull any part of a path, regardless of where the points are located. Fireworks automatically adds, moves, or deletes points along the path as you change the vector object's shape.

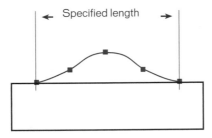

Freeform tool pulling a path segment

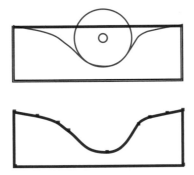

Freeform tool pushing a path segment, and path redrawn to reflect the push

As you move the pointer over a selected path, it changes to the push or pull pointer, depending on its location relative to the selected path.

This pointer	Indicates
⬐₀	The Freeform tool is in use.
⬐⌇	The Freeform tool is in use, and the pull pointer is in position to pull the selected path.
⌄⬐	The Freeform tool is in use, and the pull pointer is pulling the selected path.
◯	The Freeform tool is in use, and the push pointer is active.
◎	The Reshape Area tool is in use, and the reshape area pointer is active. The area from the inner circle to the outer circle represents reduced strength.

When the pointer is directly over the path, you can pull the path. When the pointer is not directly over the path, you can push the path. You can change the size of the push pointer.

To pull selected paths:

1 Choose the Freeform tool.

2 Move the pointer directly over the selected path.

The pointer changes to the pull pointer.

3 Drag the path.

To push selected paths:

1 Choose the Freeform tool.

The pointer changes to the push pointer.

2 Point slightly away from the path.

3 Drag toward the path to push it. Nudge the selected path to reshape it.

To change the size of the push pointer, do one of the following:

• Press Right Arrow or 2 to increase the width of the pointer.

• Press Left Arrow or 1 to decrease the width of the pointer.

• To set the size of the pointer and set the length of the path segment that it affects, enter a value from 1 to 500 in the Size text box of the Options panel. The value indicates the size of the pointer in pixels.

Note: The Freeform tool also responds to pressure from a Wacom or other compatible tablet.

Distorting paths

Use the Reshape Area tool to pull the area of all selected paths within the outer circle of the reshape area pointer.

The pointer's inner circle is the boundary of the tool at full strength. The area between the inner and outer circle reshapes paths at less than full strength. The pointer's outer circle determines the gravitational pull of the pointer. You can set its strength.

Note: The Reshape Area tool also responds to pressure from a Wacom or other compatible tablet.

To distort selected paths:

1 Choose the Reshape Area tool.

2 Drag across the paths to redraw them.

To change the size of the reshape area pointer:

- Click and hold and then press Right Arrow or 2 to increase the size of the pointer.

- Click and hold and then press Left Arrow or 1 to decrease the width of the pointer.

- To set the size of the pointer and set the length of the path segment that it affects, enter a value from 1 to 500 in the Size text box of the Options panel. The value indicates the size of the pointer in pixels.

To set the strength of the inner circle of the reshape area pointer:

Enter a value from 1 to 100 in the Strength text box of the Options panel. The value indicates the percentage of the pointer's potential strength. The higher the percentage, the greater the strength.

Redrawing paths

Use the Redraw Path tool to redraw a segment of a selected path while retaining the path's stroke, fill, and effect characteristics.

To redraw a segment of a selected path:

 1 Choose the Redraw Path tool.

2 Move the pointer directly over a path.

   The pointer changes to the redraw path pointer.

3 Drag to redraw a path segment. The portion of the path to be redrawn is highlighted in red.

4 Release the mouse button to replace the path segment.

Cutting paths into multiple objects

 Use the Knife tool to slice a path into two or more paths.

Note: If you select a bitmap image, the Knife tool becomes the Eraser tool.

To cut a selected path:

1   Choose the Knife tool.

2   Do one of the following:

• Drag the pointer across the path.

• Click the path.

3   Deselect the path.

Reshaping vector objects using path operations

You can use path operations on the Modify menu to create new shapes by combining or altering existing paths. For some path operations, the stacking order of selected path objects defines how the operation works. For information on arranging the stacking order of selected objects, see "Stacking objects" on page 96.

Note: Using a path operation removes all pressure and speed information from the affected paths.

Combining path objects

You can combine path objects into a single path object.

To create one continuous path from two open paths:

1   Choose the Subselection tool.

2   Select two end points on two open paths.

3   Choose Modify > Join.

To create a composite path:

1 Select two or more open or closed paths.

2 Choose Modify > Join.

To break apart a composite path:

1 Select a composite path.

2 Choose Modify > Split.

To combine closed paths into one path enclosing the entire area of the original paths:

Choose Modify > Combine > Union. The resulting path assumes the stroke and fill attributes of the back object.

Creating an object from the intersection of other objects

You can create an object from the intersection of two or more objects.

To create a closed path that encloses the area common to all selected closed paths:

Choose Modify > Combine > Intersect. The resulting path assumes the stroke and fill attributes of the back path object.

Removing portions of a path object

You can remove portions of a selected path object as defined by the overlapping portions of another selected path object arranged in front of it.

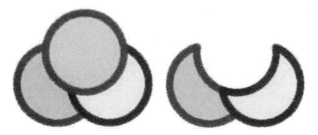

To remove portions of a path object:

1 Select the path object that defines the area to be removed.

2 Choose Modify > Arrange > Bring to Front.

3 Hold down Shift and add to the selection the path object from which the portions are to be removed.

4 Choose Modify > Combine > Punch.

Stroke and fill attributes remain unchanged.

Cropping a path

You can remove portions of a selected path outside the area defined by another selected path that is arranged in front of it.

To crop a selected path:

1 Select the path object that defines the area to be cropped.

2 Choose Modify > Arrange > Bring to Front.

3 Hold down Shift and add to the selection the path object to be cropped.

4 Choose Modify > Combine > Crop.

The resulting path object retains the stroke and fill attributes of the back path object.

Simplifying a path

You can remove points from a path while maintaining the same overall shape.

To simplify a selected path:

Choose Modify > Alter Path > Simplify.

Expanding a stroke

You can convert the perimeter of the stroke of a selected path into a closed path. The resulting path creates the illusion of a path with no fill and a stroke that is the same as the original path object's fill.

To expand a selected object's stroke:

1   Choose Modify > Alter Path > Expand Stroke to open the Expand Stroke dialog box.

2   Set the width of the resulting closed path.

3   Specify a corner type: miter, round, or beveled.

4   If you chose miter, set the miter limit, the point at which a miter corner automatically becomes a beveled corner. The miter limit is the ratio of miter corner length to stroke width.

5   Choose an end cap option: butt, square, or round, and click OK.

    A closed path in the shape of the original and with the same stroke and fill attributes replaces the original path.

Contracting or expanding a path

You can contract or expand the path of a selected object by a specific amount.

To expand or contract a selected path:

1 Choose Modify > Alter Path > Inset Path to open the Inset Path dialog box.

2 Choose a direction to contract or expand the path:

• Inside contracts the path.

• Outside expands the path.

3 Set the width between the original path and the contracting or expanding path.

4 Specify a corner type: miter, round, or beveled.

5 If you chose miter, set the miter limit, the point at which a miter corner automatically becomes a beveled corner. The miter limit is the ratio of miter corner length to stroke width.

6 Click OK.

A smaller or larger path object with the same stroke and fill attributes replaces the original path object.

CHAPTER 6
Working with Bitmaps

Bitmap images are made up of pixels, which are tiny squares that combine like the tiles of a mosaic to create an image. An example of a bitmap image is a scan of a color photograph. In addition to vector drawing and editing tools, Fireworks offers a wide range of tools for manipulating bitmap images.

Bitmap editing options include painting and drawing with traditional bitmap-application tools, changing the color of pixels, erasing pixels, replicating bitmap image elements with the Rubber Stamp tool, feathering edges of bitmap images, cropping bitmap images, and transforming bitmap images.

Entering bitmap mode

When you choose a bitmap-mode tool such as the Lasso tool, double-click a bitmap image, or select a bitmap image in the Layers panel, Fireworks changes to *bitmap mode*. When Fireworks is in bitmap mode, a striped border appears around the entire document. The border reminds you that bitmap mode is active and that you are currently editing pixels.

Note: In previous versions of Fireworks, bitmap mode was called image edit mode.

A striped border outlines the canvas in bitmap mode.

Drawing and editing in bitmap mode paints individual pixels on the bitmap image. Unlike with drawing objects in vector mode, whatever you draw in bitmap mode changes the pixels, erasing whatever was on those pixels before.

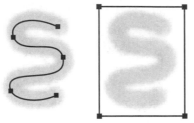

A vector object with a path and points, and a bitmap image composed entirely of pixels

Switching to and from bitmap mode

To edit pixels in the bitmap you import, open, or create, you must switch from vector mode to bitmap mode.

To switch to bitmap mode:

- Select a bitmap image object with any of these tools: Marquee, Ellipse Marquee, Lasso, Polygon Lasso, Magic Wand, Eraser, or Rubber Stamp.
- Double-click a bitmap image using the Pointer tool.
- Click the thumbnail view of a bitmap image in the Layers panel.
- Select a bitmap image object and choose Modify > Edit Bitmap.

To return to vector mode from bitmap mode:

- Click the Stop button located at the bottom of the document window.
- Double-click beyond the canvas with any selection tool.
- Double-click an area of the document window beyond the canvas with any selection tool.

Stop button

- Select a vector object in the Layers panel.
- Choose Modify > Exit Bitmap Mode.
- Press Esc.

To temporarily hide the striped border:

Choose View > Hide Edges. Leaving bitmap mode turns off Hide Edges.

To set the preference that hides the striped border:

1 Choose Edit > Preferences.

2 In the Preferences dialog box, choose the Editing topic.

3 Deselect Display Striped Border and click OK.

To prevent the striped border from surrounding the entire document:

1 Choose Edit > Preferences.

2 In the Preferences dialog box, choose the Editing topic.

3 Deselect Expand to Fill Document and click OK.

This is helpful if a document contains small bitmap images and you want the striped border to surround only the selected bitmap image.

Selecting pixel areas

In bitmap mode, the primary selection tools are the Marquee and Ellipse Marquee tools, the Lasso and Polygon Lasso tools, and the Magic Wand tool.

Marquee tools

Lasso and Magic Wand tools

The pixel selection tools define the area of pixels you want to select. After you draw the selection marquee, you can click or drag to select the pixels using the Pointer tool:

- You can move or resize the pixels within the marquee by dragging.

- You can create a floating selection of pixels that you can edit, move, cut, or copy by clicking inside the marquee.

When a marquee tool is active, you can hold down Control (Windows) or Command (Macintosh) to temporarily switch to the Pointer tool and then drag the marquee to create a floating selection of pixels.

Choosing marquee tool options

When you double-click the Marquee, Lasso, or Magic Wand tool, the Tool Options panel displays tool-specific options. Edge options are available for all pixel selection tools:

Hard creates a marquee selection with a defined edge.

Anti-alias prevents jagged edges in the marquee selection.

Feather lets you soften the edge of the pixel selection.

Style options are available for the Marquee tools only:

Normal lets you create a marquee in which the height and width are independent.

Fixed Ratio constrains the height and width to defined ratios.

Fixed Size constrains the height and width to a set dimension.

To select a rectangular or elliptical area of pixels:

1 Double-click the Marquee or Ellipse Marquee tool to open the Tool Options panel.

2 Choose Style and Edge options.

3 Drag to select pixels.

Note: Hold down Shift to draw square or circular marquees. Hold down Alt (Windows) or Option (Macintosh) to draw from the center.

To select a freeform area of pixels:

1 Double-click the Lasso tool to open the Tool Options panel.

2 Choose an Edge option.

3 Drag the pointer around the pixels you want to select.

To select a polygon area of pixels:

1 Double-click the Polygon Lasso to open the Tool Options panel, and choose an Edge option.

2 Click to outline the selection.

3 Close the polygon:

• Click the starting point.

• Double-click in the workspace.

Note: Hold down Shift to constrain Polygon Lasso marquee segments to 45-degree increments.

To select an area of pixels of similar colors:

1 Double-click the Magic Wand tool to open the Tool Options panel.

2 Choose an Edge option and set the tolerance level by dragging the tolerance slider.

Tolerance sets the range of colors that are selected when you click a pixel with the Magic Wand. If you enter 0 and click a pixel, only adjacent pixels of the exact same color are selected. If you enter 65, a wide range of related colors is selected.

3 Click the area of color you want to select. A marquee appears around the selected range of pixels.

Pixels selected with tolerance set to 87

To select similar colors:

1 Select an area of color with a marquee or lasso tool.

2 Choose Edit > Select Similar. A marquee appears around the selected range of pixels.

The current tolerance setting in the Tool Options panel determines the range of similar colors that is selected.

To remove a marquee:

• Draw another marquee, or click outside the current selection with a marquee or lasso tool.

• Choose Edit > Deselect.

• Exit bitmap mode.

Adjusting a selection marquee

After selecting pixels with a marquee or lasso tool, you can move a marquee border without affecting the pixels beneath it and you can edit the marquee border. You can manually add or delete pixels from a marquee border using modifier keys.

You can also expand or contract the marquee border by a specified amount, select an additional area of pixels around the existing marquee, smooth the border of the marquee, or create a floating selection of pixels. A floating selection allows you to edit, move, cut, or copy a selected area of pixels.

Moving a marquee

You can move a marquee without affecting the pixels beneath it.

To move the marquee:

• Drag it with a marquee or lasso tool.

• Use the arrow keys to nudge the marquee in 1-pixel increments.

• Press Shift and use the arrow keys to move in 10-pixel increments.

Adding or removing pixels using modifier keys

Using modifier keys, you can add or delete pixels from the marquee border. You can also select pixels at the intersection of two overlapping marquee selections.

To add pixels to a marquee selection:

Hold down Shift and select the pixel area you want to add. You can add pixels to the selection that are not adjacent to the original selection.

To deselect pixels inside a marquee to punch out parts of the selection:

Hold down Alt (Windows) or Option (Macintosh) and select the pixel area you want to deselect.

To use a second marquee to select pixels within a marquee:

1 Hold down Alt+Shift (Windows) or Option+Shift (Macintosh) while creating a new marquee selection that overlaps the original marquee border.

2 Release the mouse button. Only the pixels at the intersection of the two marquees are selected.

Rectangular marquee overlapping original marquee

Resulting pixel selection

Expanding and contracting a marquee

Once you have drawn a marquee to select pixels, you can expand or contract its border.

To expand the border of a marquee:

1 After drawing the marquee, choose Modify > Marquee > Expand.

2 Enter the number of pixels by which you want to expand the border of the marquee, and click OK.

To contract the border of a marquee:

1 After drawing the marquee, choose Modify > Marquee > Contract.

2 Enter the number of pixels by which you want to contract the border of the marquee, and click OK.

Selecting an area around an existing marquee

You can create an additional marquee to frame an existing marquee at a specified width. This lets you create special graphics effects, such as feathering the edges of a pixel selection.

Original marquee

After framing with an additional marquee

To select an area around an existing marquee:

1 After drawing a marquee, choose Modify > Marquee > Border.

2 Enter the width of the marquee that you want to place around the existing marquee, and click OK.

Smoothing the border of a marquee

With Fireworks, you can eliminate excess pixels along the edges of a pixel selection. This is useful if excess pixels appear along the border of a pixel selection or marquee after using the Magic Wand tool.

A pixel selection before and after smoothing

To smooth the border of a marquee:

1 Choose Modify > Marquee > Smooth.

2 Enter a sample radius to specify the desired degree of smoothing, and click OK.

Creating a floating selection of pixels

When you draw a marquee and drag it to a new location, the pixels within the marquee selection do not move with the marquee. If you want to move, edit, cut, or copy a selection of pixels, first make the pixels a floating selection.

To create a floating selection of pixels:

After drawing a marquee, drag it with the Pointer tool.

You can move a floating selection anywhere inside the striped border. When you select other pixels or exit bitmap mode, the pixels are permanently placed in the new location.

Painting in bitmap mode

You can create bitmap images by opening or importing them, by drawing and painting in bitmap mode, or by converting vector objects to bitmap objects. For information on importing images, see "Inserting objects into a Fireworks document" on page 69.

In Fireworks, a bitmap image file, such as a JPEG, opens in bitmap mode.

You can convert selected vector objects into a single bitmap object. You can also convert any number of selected bitmap objects into a single bitmap object. A vector-to-bitmap conversion is technically irreversible, except when Edit > Undo or undoing actions in the History panel is still an option. Bitmap images cannot be converted to vector objects.

To create a new bitmap:

Insert an empty bitmap image:

- Drag in an empty area in the document with a marquee or lasso tool.

- Choose Insert > Empty Bitmap.

To convert selected vector objects to a bitmap image:

Choose Modify > Convert to Bitmap.

Using drawing tools in bitmap mode

You can use the basic shape tools, the Line tool, the Pencil tool, and the Brush tool to paint pixels in bitmap mode. When you paint in bitmap mode, you are not drawing vector objects; you are painting pixels. Whatever you draw replaces the pixels in the image.

If a selection marquee is currently in the document, these tools only paint pixels inside the marquee (see "Selecting pixel areas" on page 127).

If you paint lines and strokes that enlarge a bitmap image, its size is automatically trimmed after leaving bitmap mode. It is trimmed to a rectangular shape in the size of the used pixels, removing transparent space around the image.

To paint pixels in bitmap mode:

1 Choose a basic shape tool, the Line tool, the Pencil tool, or the Brush tool.

2 Set stroke options in the Stroke panel. If you are using a basic shape tool, you also can set fill options.

3 Drag to draw.

Changing pixel colors with the Paint Bucket tool

After selecting pixels, you can use the Paint Bucket tool to change them to the color in the fill color box.

Paint Bucket tool

To change selected pixels to the fill color:

1 Choose a color in the fill color box.

2 Double-click the Paint Bucket tool.

3 In the Tool Options panel, choose Fill Selection Only.

4 Click inside the selection marquee. The selected pixels change to the fill color.

Erasing pixels

Use the Eraser tool to remove pixels or color over pixels with a different color.

Eraser tool

By default, the Eraser tool pointer is eraser shaped and represents the size of the current eraser. You can change the size and appearance of the Eraser tool pointer. For information, see "Setting preferences" on page 54.

To erase pixels:

1 Double-click the Eraser tool to open the Tool Options panel.

2 Set the eraser color in the Erase To pop-up menu:

Transparent makes the erased area transparent.

Fill Color selects the color in the fill color box.

Stroke Color selects the color in the stroke color box.

Canvas Color selects the document canvas color.

3 Choose a round or square eraser.

4 Drag the Edge Softness slider to set the softness of the eraser's edge.

5 Drag the Eraser Size slider to set the size of the eraser.

6 Drag the Eraser tool over the pixels you want to erase or paint over with a different color.

Feathering pixel selections

Feathering a selection does not blur the pixels in the image; it blurs the edges of the selection only. This is useful when you want to remove an object from a photo. Feathering helps a copied area blend with the surrounding pixels.

To feather the edges of a pixel selection:

1   Choose Modify > Marquee > Feather to open the Feather Selection dialog box.

2   Type a value to set the feather radius, and click OK.

The radius value determines the number of pixels that are blurred on each side of the selection border.

Cloning an area of pixels

Use the Rubber Stamp tool to duplicate areas of a bitmap image. When you clone an area, two pointers appear. The blue circle indicates the area you want to clone (the *source*), and the rubber stamp pointer indicates where you want to place the cloned area.

Rubber Stamp tool

Cloning is useful when you want to fix a scratched photograph. Simply duplicate an area of the photo and place the cloned area over the scratch.

Rubber Stamp pointers

Cloning is also useful for creating interesting effects, such as duplicating a person's face or particular facial features.

To clone portions of a bitmap image:

1 Double-click the Rubber Stamp tool.

2 In the Tool Options panel, select a Source option:

• Fixed locks the source pointer (the blue circle) to a specific area of the image so you can duplicate the area more than once. The stamp pointer moves independently of the circular source pointer.

• Aligned unlocks the source pointer so that you can duplicate different areas of the image. The two pointers move together.

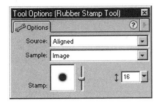

3 Select a Sample option:

• Image lets you clone from the selected image only.

• Document lets you clone any area of the document, including any existing path objects.

4 Drag the Stamp Size pop-up slider to set the size of the Rubber Stamp.

5 In the Edge Softness preview, drag the slider to adjust the softness of the Rubber Stamp tool's edge.

6 Move the pointer to the area you want to clone, and click.

7 Move the Rubber Stamp pointer to the area where you want to place the clone, and click again.

Note: To reposition the source pointer, hold down Alt (Windows) or Option (Macintosh) while clicking with the Rubber Stamp tool.

Cropping a bitmap image

Use Edit > Crop Selected Bitmap to remove portions of a bitmap image. For example, if you have a photograph that was taken at too wide an angle, you can remove elements in the background but retain the subject in the photo.

Crop tool

To crop a bitmap image:

1 Choose Edit > Crop Selected Bitmap. The crop handles appear.

2 Adjust the crop handles until the bounding box surrounds the area of the bitmap image that you want to keep:

• Drag the handles.

• Hold down Shift and use the arrow keys.

3 To crop the bitmap image, double-click inside the bounding box or press Enter. Everything outside the bounding box is removed.

To cancel the crop command, press Esc.

CHAPTER 7
Using Text

Fireworks has many text features typically reserved for sophisticated desktop publishing applications. You can create text in a variety of fonts and sizes and adjust kerning, spacing, color, leading, baseline shift, and more. Combining Fireworks text editing features with the wide range of strokes, fills, effects, and styles makes text a lively element of your graphic designs.

The capability to edit text anytime—even after you apply Live Effects like drop shadows and bevels—means you can easily correct misspellings. You can also copy objects that include text and change the text for each copy. Vertical text, transformed text, text attached to paths, and text converted to paths and images extend the design possibilities.

You can import text while retaining rich text format attributes. Also, when you import a Photoshop document containing text, the text remains editable. Fireworks handles missing fonts upon import by asking you to choose a substitute font.

Entering text

Enter, format, and edit text in your graphics using the Text tool and the Text Editor.

Text tool

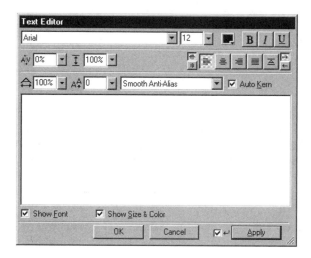

Text Editor

All text in a Fireworks document appears inside a rectangle with handles called a text block.

To enter text:

1 Choose the Text tool.

2 Click in your document where you want the text block to begin.

The Text Editor opens.

3 Choose color, font, size, spacing, and other text characteristics.

4 Type the text. To enter a line break, press Enter (Windows) or Return (Macintosh).

5 Select text in the Text Editor to reformat it after you type it.

6 To see text in the document as you type it in the Text Editor:

• Choose the Auto-Apply option in the Text Editor.

• Click Apply.

7 Click OK.

The text appears as a text block in the Fireworks document.

Note: Fireworks remembers text color separate from fill color and carries this over to your next entry or session.

To open the Text Editor again:

Double-click the text block.

Moving text blocks

You can select a text block and move it anywhere in your document, like any other object. You can even move it while the Text Editor is open.

To move a text block:

Drag it to the new location.

Auto-sizing text blocks

Fireworks has auto-sizing text blocks. As you type a single line, the text block expands. If you remove text, the text block shrinks to fit the remaining text. Multiline text blocks do not auto-size.

To control the width of wrapped text within a text block, resize the text block.

To resize a text block:

Drag a resize handle.

Editing text

Within a text block, you can vary all aspects of text, including size, font, spacing, leading, and baseline shift.

You can change a text block's attributes, using either the Text menu or the Text Editor. The Text menu provides a quick way to change simple attributes. For more detailed editing use the Text Editor.

When you edit text, its stroke, fill, and effect attributes redraw accordingly.

To edit text in the Text Editor:

1 Double-click the text block.

2 In the Text Editor preview area, highlight the text you want to change.

3 Make and apply your changes.

   For information about changing text attributes, see the corresponding sections in this chapter.

4 Click OK.

Choosing a font, type size, and style

When changing the font, size, and style attributes of the text within a text block, you can use either the Text Editor or the Text menu commands.

Note: To use Type 1 fonts on the Macintosh, you need Adobe Type Manager 4 or later.

When you are viewing text in the Text Editor, by default the text appears in the actual font and size. A text block can contain multiple fonts and sizes.

You can also view text in the Text Editor in the system font and size. This is useful if the font or size makes it difficult to read while you are typing.

To view text in the system font:

Deselect Show Font in the Text Editor.

To view text in the default size:

Deselect Show Size & Color in the Text Editor.

To change the font, type size, and style using the Text Editor:

1   In the Text Editor, highlight the characters you want to change.

2   To change the font, choose a font from the font pop-up menu.

3   To change the type size, choose a size from the size pop-up menu.

4   To apply a bold, italic, or underline style, click the corresponding style button.

5   Click OK.

To change the font, type size, and style using the Text menu:

1   Select the text block or blocks. You can change the attributes of more than one text block simultaneously by holding down Shift as you select text blocks.

2   To change the font, choose Text > Font and choose a font from the submenu.

3   To change the type size, choose Text > Size and choose a size from the submenu.

4   To change the style, choose Text > Style and choose a style from the submenu.

Setting baseline shift and leading

Baseline shift determines how closely text sits above, below, or on its natural baseline. Use baseline shift to create subscript and superscript characters.

Leading determines the distance between adjacent lines in a paragraph. Specifically, leading is the percentage of the point size that lines are separated baseline to baseline.

Use the Text Editor to set the leading and baseline shift.

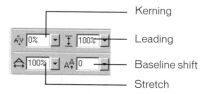

— Kerning

— Leading

— Baseline shift

— Stretch

Leading (top) and Baseline Shift (bottom) pop-up menus

To set leading and baseline shift:

1   In the Text Editor, select the characters you want to change.

2   From the Baseline Shift pop-up menu, choose an amount to subscript or superscript the text.

3   From the Leading pop-up menu, choose a leading value. The default is 100%.

4   Click OK.

Setting kerning

Kerning increases or decreases the spacing between certain pairs of letters to improve their appearance. Most fonts include information that automatically reduces the amount of space between certain letter pairs, such as "TA" or "Va." By default, Fireworks uses a font's kerning information when displaying text, but you may want to turn it off at smaller point sizes, or when the text has no anti-aliasing.

Range kerning increases or decreases the spacing between more than two characters.

Use the Text Editor to set kerning.

To disable automatic kerning:

In the Text Editor, deselect Auto Kern.

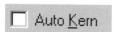

To set kerning:

1 Select characters in the Text Editor:

• To kern two characters, click between them.

• For range kerning, highlight the characters you want to change.

2 Enter a kerning value.

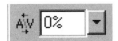

Zero represents normal kerning. Positive values move letters farther apart. Negative values move letters closer together.

Setting direction and orientation

Text direction, or text flow, determines whether text flows right to left or left to right. By default, text flows left to right.

Fireworks

skroweriF

Text flowing left to right and right to left

Text orientation determines whether the text block is oriented horizontally or vertically. By default, text is oriented horizontally.

Fireworks

F
i
r
e
w
o
r
k
s

Horizontal and vertical orientation

Use the Text Editor to set text orientation and text direction. These settings apply to entire text blocks only.

Text orientation, alignment, and direction buttons in the Text Editor

To set orientation using the Text Editor:

Click the Horizontal Text or Vertical Text button.

To set the orientation of selected text using the Text menu:

Choose a command from the Text > Align submenu.

To set direction using the Text Editor:

Click the Left to Right or Right to Left direction button.

Setting alignment

Alignment determines the position of each line of text in a paragraph relative to the left and right edges of the text block. You can align text to the left or right edges of the text block, center it within the text block, or align it to both the left and right edges (full justification). By default, text is left aligned.

To achieve a stretched effect, or to fit text into a specific space, you can set the alignment to stretch the text horizontally (for horizontally oriented text) or vertically (for vertically oriented text).

Fireworks
Fireworks

Horizontal text stretched to fill a text block

Use the Text menu or Text Editor to set text alignment. You can set alignment for individual paragraphs within a text block.

To set alignment with the Text Editor:

1 Select the text within the text block.

2 Click the Left, Center, Right, Justified, or Stretched alignment button.

Applying text color

By default, text is black and has no stroke. If you change the text color, Fireworks continues using that color for text entry until you change it again. The text color you choose is saved between different documents and Fireworks sessions.

You can apply color to the entire text block or to individual characters within the text block.

To set text color:

• Choose a color from the color box pop-up window in the Text Editor.

• Select a text block and choose a color from the color box pop-up window in the Fill panel.

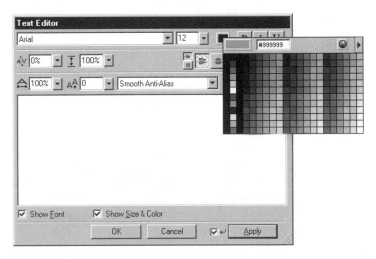

Color box pop-up window

Smoothing text edges

To smooth out a text edge, anti-alias it. This makes the edges of the text blend into the background so that the text is cleaner and more readable when it is large.

Use the Text Editor to set anti-aliasing. Anti-aliasing applies to all characters in a given text block.

To apply an anti-aliased edge to selected text:

1 Open the Text Editor.

2 From the Anti-Alias pop-up menu in the Text Editor, choose an option: Crisp, Strong, or Smooth.

3 Click OK.

Note: When you open vector files, such as FreeHand files, in Fireworks, text is anti-aliased. You can edit this attribute using the Text Editor. For more information on opening vector files, see "Opening FreeHand, Illustrator, or CorelDRAW files" on page 66.

Applying strokes, fills, effects, and styles to text

You can apply strokes, fills, effects, and styles to text, like any other object. You can apply any or all to the same text block. You can apply any style in the Styles panel to the text, even if it is not a text style. Also, you can save text attributes as a style.

Text remains editable. Strokes, fills, effects, and styles update automatically in response to editing.

Text with stroke, fill, effect, and style applied

For more information about strokes and fills, see "Applying Colors, Strokes, and Fills" on page 157. For more about using styles, see "About styles" on page 224. For information about Live Effects, see "Applying a Live Effect" on page 194.

Saving text attributes

Attributes such as stroke, fill, and effects that you apply to text can be saved for reuse as styles in the Styles panel. Saving text attributes as a style does not save the text itself, only the effects.

To save text attributes as a style:

1 Create a text object and apply the effects you want.

2 Select the text object and choose New Style from the Styles panel Options pop-up menu.

3 Choose the properties for the new style and name it.

4 Click OK.

Attaching text to a path

To free text from the restrictions of rectangular text blocks, you can draw a path and attach text to it. The text flows along the shape of the path and remains editable. For more information on drawing different types of paths, see "Drawing rectangles with rounded corners" on page 101 and "Drawing polygons" on page 102.

A path to which you attach text temporarily loses its stroke, fill, and effect attributes. Any stroke, fill, and effect attributes you apply subsequently are applied to the text, not the path. If you then detach the text from the path, the path regains its stroke, fill, and effect attributes.

To place text on a path:

1 Holding down the Shift key, select a text block and a path.

2 Choose Text > Attach to Path.

To detach the text from a selected path:

Choose Text > Detach from Path.

To edit text attached to a path:

• Double-click the text-on-a-path object to open the Text Editor.

• Choose the Text tool and select the text to edit.

To edit the shape of the path:

1 Choose Text > Detach from Path.

2 Edit the path.

3 After editing the path, place the text back on the path.

If text attached to an open path exceeds the length of the path, the remaining text returns and repeats the shape of the path.

Text on a path returns and repeats the path shape.

The order in which you draw a path establishes the direction of the text attached to it. For example, if you draw a path from right to left, the attached text appears backwards and upside down.

Text attached to a path drawn right to left

You can reverse the direction or change the orientation of the text attached to a path. You can also change the starting point of text on a path.

To change the text's orientation on a selected path:

Choose Text > Orientation and select an orientation.

To reverse the text's direction on a selected path:

Choose Text > Reverse Direction.

Text rotated around path

Text vertical around path

Text skewed vertically around path

Text skewed horizontally around path

To move the starting point of text attached to a path:

1 Select the text-on-a-path object.

2 In the Object panel, enter a value in the Text Offset text box.

Transforming text

You can transform text blocks in the same ways you can transform other objects. You can scale, rotate, skew, and flip text to create unique text effects.

You can still edit the transformed text, although severe transformations may make it difficult to read. Transforming text does not change the point size of the text. For more information, see "Transforming and distorting objects" on page 90.

Converting text to paths

You can convert text to paths and then edit the letters' shapes as you would any vector object. All vector editing tools are available to edit text once you have converted it to paths. However, you can no longer edit it as text.

One reason to convert text to paths is when you need to open a document that contains text in a font your computer does not have.

Note: Converting text to paths is not necessary for viewing a particular font in a Web browser, because the text is exported to a bitmap format such as GIF.

To convert selected text to paths:

Choose Text > Convert to Paths.

Text converted to paths retains all of its visual attributes, but you can edit it only as paths.

Importing text

You can use text from other documents by dragging and dropping or copying and pasting from the source document into the current Fireworks document.

You can also open or import an entire text file in Fireworks.

Fireworks can import these text formats:

- RTF (rich text format)
- ASCII (plain text)

To open or import text from a file:

1 Use a File command:

- Choose File > Open.

- Choose File > Import.

2 Navigate to the folder containing the file.

3 Choose the file and click OK.

Importing text from Photoshop

You can open or import an entire Photoshop file, and you can copy and paste or drag and drop text from a Photoshop file into the current Fireworks document.

If you want to use only certain words or characters from another file and don't mind losing the ability to edit the text, use drag and drop or copy and paste. The text comes in as pixels and is not editable as text.

If you want the text to be editable as text, open or import the whole file.

Note: The text layer retains its name.

Importing RTF files

When importing RTF text, Fireworks maintains these attributes:

- Font, size, and style (bold, italic, underline)

- Alignment (left, right, center, justified)

- Leading

- Baseline shift

- Range kerning

- Horizontal scale

- First character's color

All other RTF information is ignored.

Fireworks cannot import RTF text using copy and paste or drag and drop.

Importing ASCII text

You can import ASCII text using any of the import methods. Imported ASCII text is set to the current default font, 12 pixels high, and uses the current fill color.

Handling missing fonts

If you open a document in Fireworks that contains fonts not installed on your computer, the Missing Fonts dialog box opens.

You can choose fonts to replace the missing fonts. If you don't choose replacement fonts, the text appears in the default system font. You can edit and save the text.

When the file is reopened on a computer that contains the original fonts, Fireworks remembers the original font.

To select a replacement font:

1 Choose a missing font from the Change Missing Font list.

2 Choose a replacement font from the To list, and click OK.

   The next time you open a document with the same missing fonts, the Missing Fonts dialog box includes the fonts you chose.

To leave the missing font as is:

Click No Change.

CHAPTER 8
Applying Colors, Strokes, and Fills

Fireworks gives you a broad range of options when it comes to choosing colors for a graphic. You can use color swatches to help you maintain the appearance of your graphic on various Web browsers and computer platforms as you work. In addition to the default color swatches, you can use the Windows or Macintosh system color swatches, or even create your own colors and groups of swatches.

You can mix your own colors using any of several color models—Hexadecimal, RGB, CMY, HSB, or Grayscale. You can also view any color in your document expressed in each of these color models.

Stroke options for Fireworks graphic objects range from pencil-thin lines to wide swaths resembling spray paint; fill options range from solid color to multicolor gradients to bitmap patterns. After applying a gradient or pattern fill, you can edit it in the workspace. In addition to Fireworks patterns, you can use most any image as the basis for a fill pattern. You can also add texture to strokes and fills. Additionally, you can save the stroke and fill attributes of an object as a style, then apply the style to other objects (see "Using Libraries, Styles, and URLs" on page 223).

Choosing colors

You can use the Swatches panel to choose a new color as you create graphics. The colors in the Swatches panel also appear in the color box pop-up windows in the Stroke and Fill panels, the Color Mixer, and the Tools panel.

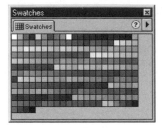

Swatches panel

To open the Swatches panel:

Choose Window > Swatches.

Color boxes in the Tools panel

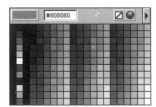

Color box pop-up window

To open a color box pop-up window:

Click the color box or the arrow next to the color box.

Applying colors

You can use the Swatches panel or a color box pop-up window to apply colors to the stroke or fill of path objects.

To apply a color to a selected object:

1 Click the stroke or fill color box to select it.

2 Choose a color:

• In the Swatches panel, click a swatch to apply the color to the stroke or fill of the selected object. This color is then assigned to the active color box.

• Open the color box pop-up window and click a swatch or type a color's hexadecimal value in the value text box.

Sampling colors

You can take a color from anywhere on your screen, including other open Fireworks documents, and apply it to selected objects. This process is called *sampling;* it lets you identify and use the exact colors you need to edit and integrate graphics. You can also identify the hexadecimal value of any color either before or after applying it to selected objects.

Note: You must be using 24- or 32-bit color mode.

To apply a color from anywhere on the screen to a selected object:

1 Select the stroke or fill color box on the Tools panel and the color box's pop-up window displays. The pointer changes to an eyedropper.

2 Click anywhere onscreen to choose a color. The color is applied to the selected object.

Note: Shift-click to choose a Websafe color.

To identify a color's hexadecimal value:

1 Open a stroke, fill, or effect color box pop-up window. The pointer changes to an eyedropper.

2 Move your pointer over a color. The color's hexadecimal value appears in the color box pop-up window.

Note: Click the hexadecimal field to enter a specific hexadecimal color value.

To change color sets:

Choose a color set from the color box panel's Options pop-up menu. The setting used by Swatches panel is the default setting.

Customizing the Swatches panel

You can add, delete, replace, and sort color swatches in the Swatches panel. These changes automatically update in the color box pop-up windows.

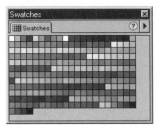

You can also add and delete entire swatch groups. For information, see "Changing swatch groups" on page 162.

Note: Choosing Edit > Undo does not undo swatch additions or deletions.

To add a color from a Fireworks document to the Swatches panel:

 1 Choose the Eyedropper tool from the Tools panel.

2 Click the color you want to add.

3 In the Swatches panel, move the pointer to the open space after the last swatch. The pointer becomes the paint bucket pointer.

4 Click to add the swatch.

To add a color from anywhere onscreen to the Swatches panel:

 1 Open a color box pop-up window. The pointer changes to the eyedropper.

2 Click anywhere onscreen, including in another Fireworks document, to choose a color.

3 In the Swatches panel, move the pointer to the open space after the last swatch. The pointer becomes the paint bucket pointer.

4 Click to add the swatch.

Note: When Snap to Websafe is selected in the Options pop-up menu of the color box pop-up window, any nonWebsafe color picked up by the eyedropper pointer is changed to the nearest Websafe color.

To save a selection of sampled colors:

1 Add sampled colors to the Swatches panel.

2 In the Swatches panel Options pop-up menu, click Save Swatches.

3 The Export Swatches dialog box opens. Choose a file name and directory and click Save.

To replace a swatch with another color:

1 Select the Eyedropper tool from the Tools panel.

2 Click a color.

The color is applied to any selected object and becomes the active stroke or fill color.

3 Hold down Shift and point to a swatch in the Swatches panel.

The pointer becomes the paint bucket pointer.

4 Click the swatch to replace it with the new color.

To delete a swatch from the Swatches panel:

1 Hold down Control (Windows) or Command (Macintosh) and point to a swatch. The pointer becomes the scissors pointer.

2 Click the swatch to delete it from the Swatches panel.

To clear the entire Swatches panel:

Choose Clear Swatches from the Swatches panel Options pop-up menu.

To return to the default color swatches:

Choose Windows System or Macintosh System palette from the Swatches panel Options pop-up menu.

To sort the swatches by color:

Choose Sort by Color from the Swatches panel Options pop-up menu.

Changing swatch groups

You can easily switch to another swatch group or create your own. Fireworks lets you choose from these swatch groups: Color Cubes, Continuous Tone colors, Macintosh System colors, Windows System colors, Grayscale, and custom swatch groups you import from ACT or GIF files.

Use the Swatches panel to choose a swatch group.

Swatches panel Options pop-up menu

To choose a swatch group:

Choose a swatch group from the Swatches panel Options pop-up menu.

To choose a custom swatch group:

1 Choose Replace Swatches from the Swatches panel Options pop-up menu.

2 Navigate to the folder and choose a file.

3 Click Open.

   The color swatches in the custom swatch group replace the previous swatches.

Note: For information on creating a custom swatch group, see "Optimizing color palettes" on page 320.

To append a swatch group to the current swatches in the Swatches panel:

1 Choose Add Swatches from the Swatches panel Options pop-up menu.

2 Navigate to the folder, choose a swatch group file, and click OK.

   Fireworks adds swatches from Photoshop ACT or GIF files. The new swatches are appended to the end of the current swatches.

To save a custom color swatch group:

1 Choose Save Swatches from the Swatches panel Options pop-up menu.

2 Name the new swatch group, and click Save.

Creating colors

Create your own colors and apply them to objects, add them to the Swatches panel, or use them to make a new swatch group. You can create colors using the Color Mixer or use the system color picker to select colors.

Creating colors in the Color Mixer

Use the Color Mixer to view the values of the active color and create new colors.

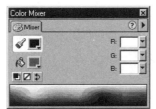

You can create your own colors using any of these color models: RGB, Hexadecimal, HSB, CMY, and Grayscale.

By default, the Color Mixer identifies RGB colors as Hexadecimal, displaying hexadecimal color values for red (R), green (G), and blue (B) color components. Hexadecimal RGB values are calculated based on a range of values from 00 to FF.

Choose	To express color components as
RGB	Values of Red, Green, and Blue, where each component has a value of from 0 to 255. 0-0-0 is black and 255-255-255 is white.
Hexadecimal	RGB values of Red, Green, and Blue, where each component has a hexadecimal value of from 00 to FF. 00-00-00 is black and FF-FF-FF is white.
HSB	Values of Hue, Saturation, and Brightness, where Hue has a value of from 0 to 360 degrees, and Saturation and Brightness have a value of from 0 to 100%.
CMY	Values of Cyan, Magenta, and Yellow, where each component has a value of from 0 to 255. 0-0-0 is white and 255-255-255 is black.
Grayscale	A percentage of black. The single Black (K) component has a value of from 0 to 100%, where 0 is white and 100 is black, and in between are shades of gray.

You can choose alternative color models from the Color Mixer Options pop-up menu. The current color's component values change with each new color model.

To display the Color Mixer:

Choose Window > Color Mixer.

To cycle the color bar through the color models:

Shift-click the color bar at the bottom of the Color Mixer.

The options in the Color Mixer do not change.

To apply a color from the color bar to a selected object:

1 In the Color Mixer, click the stroke or fill color box to make it the active well.

2 Move the pointer over the color bar. The pointer becomes the eyedropper pointer.

3 Click to pick a color.

   The color is applied to the selected object and becomes the active stroke or fill color.

To create a color in the Color Mixer:

1 Deselect all objects before mixing a color to prevent unwanted object editing as you mix colors.

2 Click either the stroke or fill color box to make it the destination for the new color.

3 Choose a color model from the Color Mixer Options pop-up menu.

4 Specify color component values:

• Enter values in the color component text boxes.

• Use the pop-up sliders.

• Pick a color from the color bar.

You can add the color to the Swatches panel for reuse. For information, see "Customizing the Swatches panel" on page 160.

Creating colors using system color pickers

You can create colors using the Windows Color dialog box (Windows) or the Apple Color Picker (Macintosh) instead of using the Color Mixer and Swatches panel.

To display the system color picker:

- Double-click any color box.

 • Click the system color picker button from the color box pop-up window.

Viewing color values

To identify specific color values, use the Info panel, a color box pop-up window, or the Color Mixer. You can view the color value of almost any visible object in any open application, including the desktop, in the color box pop-up window. You can view the color value of the active stroke and fill color in the Color Mixer or the color box pop-up window.

To display the Info panel:

Choose Window > Info.

To display the Color Mixer:

Do one of the following:

- Choose Window > Color Mixer.

- Click the Mixer tab in the Colors panel.

To view the color value of any part of your document using the Info panel:

Move the pointer over the object containing the color you want to view.

To view the color value of the active stroke or fill color:

Do one of the following:

- For the RGB or other color system values, look in the Color Mixer.

- For the hexadecimal value, look in any color box pop-up window.

By default, the color's RGB values appear in the Info panel and the Color Mixer and its hexadecimal value appears in the color box pop-up window. However, you can change the value system displayed in the Color Mixer or the Info panel at any time.

To display color information for an alternate color model:

Choose another color model from the Info panel or the Color Mixer Options pop-up menu.

Applying strokes

You can change the stroke attributes of the Pen, Pencil, and Brush tools so that the next vector object you draw has the new stroke attributes, or you can apply stroke attributes to an object after you draw it. You can apply strokes only to vector or text objects.

The current stroke color appears in the stroke color box in the Tools panel. Use the Tools panel to change a drawing tool's stroke color.

The paintbrush icon indicates the stroke color box in the Tools panel.

You can also change the stroke color, as well as other stroke attributes, in the Stroke panel. You can choose from a variety of brush tips and tip sizes (see "Changing strokes" on page 167).

To change the stroke color of the drawing tools:

1 From the stroke color box in the Tools panel, click the color box or the triangle next to the color box to open the pop-up window.

2 Choose a color for the stroke from the set of swatches.

3 Choose a drawing tool.

4 Drag to draw the object.

To change the stroke color of a selected object:

Choose a color swatch from the stroke or fill color box pop-up window in the Tools panel.

To swap fill and stroke colors:

 Click the Swap Colors button in the Color Mixer or in the Tools panel.

To reset colors to the default:

 Click the Default Colors button.

To remove all stroke attributes from a selected object:

Click the No Stroke or Fill button. The current stroke or fill is set to None.

To use a color from the system color picker:

1 Choose the system color picker from the color box pop-up menu.

The Color dialog box (Windows) or the Apple color picker (Macintosh) opens.

2 Choose a color from the system color picker and click OK.

The color becomes the new stroke color. For information on adding a color to the Swatches panel from the color picker, see "Customizing the Swatches panel" on page 160.

Changing strokes

You can change strokes to create paths with a range of pen or brush characteristics, from thin, pencil-like paths to wide swaths resembling spray paint or splattered oil. Stroke textures add to the range of creative possibilities.

Using the Stroke panel and the Edit Stroke dialog box, you have full control of every brush nuance, including ink amount, tip size and shape, texture, edge effect, and aspect. Additionally, sensitivity settings control how a pressure-sensitive pen affects strokes. You can save the resulting brush for future use.

A newly created stroke assumes the color currently displayed in the stroke color box.

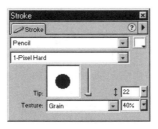

Use the Stroke panel to change the stroke applied to an object.

To view the Stroke panel:

Choose Window > Stroke.

To change the stroke attributes of a selected object:

1 In the Stroke panel, choose a stroke category, such as Pencil, Oil, or Watercolor from the Stroke Category pop-up menu.

2 Choose a stroke from the Stroke Name pop-up menu.

3 To change the stroke color, choose a swatch from the color box pop-up window.

4 Alter the edge softness using the Edge Softness slider next to the Tip preview.

5 Choose a texture from the Texture pop-up menu, and enter a value for its intensity. For more information, see "Adding texture to strokes and fills" on page 175.

Note: Some stroke categories have a texture applied to them by default.

Saving strokes

You can change specific stroke characteristics such as ink amount, tip shape, and tip sensitivity, and save the custom stroke as a style for reuse across many documents. For information about saving styles, see "Using Libraries, Styles, and URLs" on page 223.

To save custom strokes only in the current document, use the Options pop-up menu in the Stroke panel to edit brush stroke attributes. You can edit stroke attributes or create and save your own custom strokes.

Placing the stroke on the path

By default, an object's brush stroke is centered on the path. You can change options for placing the brush stroke completely inside or outside the path. This lets you control the overall size of stroked objects, and lets you create effects such as using strokes on the edges of beveled buttons.

Centered stroke, stroke inside, and stroke outside

 Use the Stroke placement buttons in the Object panel to reorient brush strokes.

To move a brush stroke inside or outside the selected path:

1 Choose a Stroke Placement button in the Object panel: Inside, Centered, or Outside.

2 Optionally, choose Fill over Stroke.

   Normally, the stroke overlaps the fill. Selecting Fill over Stroke draws the fill over the stroke. If you select this option for an object with an opaque fill, any part of the stroke that falls inside the path is obscured. A fill with a degree of transparency may tint or blend with a brush stroke inside a path.

Applying fills

You can change the fill attributes of the Rectangle, Rounded Rectangle, Ellipse, and Polygon drawing tools for the next object of these types that you draw. You can draw objects with solid, gradient, or pattern fills.

The current fill color appears in the fill color box in the Tools panel. Use the Tools panel to change a drawing tool's fill.

The paint bucket icon indicates the fill color box in the Tools panel.

You can also change the fill color for a drawing tool in the Fill panel. You can choose from a variety of gradient and pattern fills. Further, you can change the fill characteristics of an object after you draw it.

Each object you draw using the Brush, Pencil, or Pen tool appears with no fill. You must add the fill after you draw the object.

To change the fill color of the basic shape tools:

1 From the fill color box in the Tools panel, click the down arrow next to the color box to open the color box pop-up window.

2 Choose a color for the fill from the set of swatches.

3 Choose the Rectangle, Ellipse, or Polygon tool.

4 Drag to draw the object.

Changing fills

You can change fills to create paths with a variety of solid, dithered, pattern, or gradient characteristics, ranging from solid colors to gradients resembling satin, ripples, or folds. Additionally, you can change various attributes of a fill, such as color, edge, texture, and transparency.

You can save a custom gradient fill for use within the current document or among several documents. To save the gradient fill for use across multiple documents, save it as a style. For information about styles, see "Using Libraries, Styles, and URLs" on page 223.

A newly created fill assumes the current color displayed in the fill color box in the Tools panel.

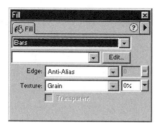

Use the Fill panel to edit fill attributes.

Changing a solid fill

A solid fill is a solid color that fills the interior of an object. You can change an object's fill color in the Tools panel, Fill panel, or Color Mixer.

To edit a selected object's solid fill:

1 In the Fill panel, choose Solid from the Fill Category pop-up menu.

2 From the color box pop-up window, choose a color.

   The fill appears in the selected object and becomes the active fill color.

Applying a gradient fill

Fill categories other than None, Solid, Pattern, and Web Dither are *gradient* fills. Gradient fills blend colors to create various effects.

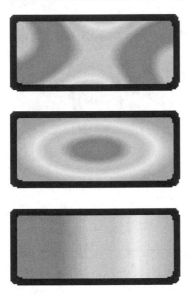

Objects with Satin, Radial, and Linear gradient fills

To apply a gradient fill to a selected object:

1 From the Fill panel, choose a gradient from the Fill Category pop-up menu.

2 From the Fill Name pop-up menu, choose a fill color combination, such as Red, Green, Blue, or Pastels.

The fill appears in the selected object and becomes the active fill.

Changing a gradient fill

You can edit, save, rename, or delete a gradient fill using the Edit Gradient pop-up window.

Edit Gradient pop-up window

To open the Edit Gradient pop-up window:

1 Select an object that has a gradient fill or choose a gradient fill from the Fill Category pop-up menu.

2 Do one of the following:

• Click the Edit button on the Fill panel.

• Choose Edit Gradient from the Fill panel Options pop-up menu.

 The Edit Gradient pop-up window opens with the current gradient in the color ramp and preview.

To adjust the transition between colors in the fill:

Drag color swatches left or right.

To add a new color swatch to the gradient:

Click the area between the color ramp and the preview.

To remove a color swatch from the gradient:

Drag the swatch away from the Edit Gradient pop-up window.

To change the color of a color swatch:

1 Click the color swatch.

2 Choose a color from the pop-up window.

When you have finished editing the gradient, press Enter or click outside the Edit Gradient pop-up window. The gradient fill appears in any selected objects and becomes the active fill.

Saving fills as styles

You can save any change to gradient fill settings as a style for use across many documents (see "Using Libraries, Styles, and URLs" on page 223). You can also save a gradient fill for use within the current document only.

Applying a pattern fill

In addition to solid and gradient fills, you can fill a path object with a bitmap graphic, known as a *pattern* fill. Fireworks ships with more than a dozen pattern fills, including Berber Rug, Photinia Leaves, and Bricks.

You can also use a bitmap file as a pattern fill. You can use files with these formats as patterns: PNG, GIF, JPEG, BMP, TIFF, and PICT (Macintosh only). When a pattern file is a 32-bit transparent image, the transparency affects the fill when used in Fireworks. If an image is not 32-bit, it becomes opaque.

To include an external pattern in the Fill Name pop-up menu for use in all documents, copy the pattern file to the Fireworks 4\Configuration\Patterns folder.

To apply a pattern fill to a selected object:

1 In the Fill panel, choose Pattern from the Fill Category pop-up menu.

2 Choose a pattern:

• Choose the pattern from the pattern name pop-up menu.

• To use an external pattern, choose Other from the pattern name pop-up menu and navigate to a pattern file.

The pattern fill appears in the selected object and becomes the active fill color.

Note: Although the pattern fill is active and is applied to subsequent objects that you draw, it does not appear in the fill color box in the Tools panel, Fill panel, or Color Mixer.

Transforming and distorting gradient and pattern fills

You can move, rotate, skew, and change the width of an object's pattern or gradient fill. When you select an object with a pattern or gradient fill, using the Pointer or Paint Bucket tools, a set of handles appears on or near the object. Drag these handles to adjust the object's fill.

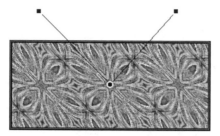

Use the fill handles to interactively adjust a pattern or gradient fill.

To move the fill within an object:

Drag the round handle, or click in a new location within the fill using the Paint Bucket tool.

To rotate the fill:

Drag the lines connecting the handles.

To adjust the fill width and skew:

Drag a square handle.

Setting hard-edged, anti-aliased, or feathered fill edges

In Fireworks, you can set the edge of a fill to be a regular hard line or soften the edge by anti-aliasing it or feathering it. By default, edges are anti-aliased. Anti-aliasing smooths jagged edges that may occur on rounded objects, such as ellipses and circles, by subtly blending the edge into the background.

Feathering, however, makes a noticeable blend on either side of the edge. This gives the edge a softened effect—almost a glow.

To change the fill edge of a selected object:

1   In the Fill panel, choose an option from the Edge pop-up menu: Hard Edge, Anti-Alias, or Feather.

2   For a feathered edge, also choose the number of pixels on each side of the edge that are to be feathered. The default is 10. You can choose from 0 to 100. The higher the level, the more feathering occurs.

Adding texture to strokes and fills

You can create dimensional effects for both strokes and fills by adding texture. Fireworks provides textures, or you can use existing textures. For more information on using external textures, see "Using external files as patterns and textures" on page 177.

Adding texture to a stroke

Textures modify the brightness of the stroke, but not the hue, and give strokes a less mechanical, more organic look, as if you were laying paint on a textured surface. Textures are more effective when used with wide strokes. You can add a texture to any stroke. Fireworks ships with several textures to choose from, such as Chiffon, Oilslick, and Sandpaper.

Use the Stroke panel to add a texture to a brush stroke.

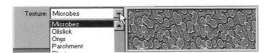

The Texture pop-up menu previews the highlighted texture.

To add texture to the stroke of a selected object:

1 In the Stroke panel, choose a stroke category from the Stroke Category pop-up menu and a specific stroke from the Stroke Name pop-up menu.

2 Choose a texture:

• Choose the texture from the Texture pop-up menu.

• To use an external texture, choose Other from the Texture pop-up menu. Navigate to a texture file. You can use files with these formats as textures: PNG, GIF, JPEG, BMP, TIFF, and PICT (Macintosh only).

3 Enter a percentage from 0 to 100 to control the depth of the texture. Increasing the percentage increases the texture intensity.

Adding texture to a fill

Textures modify the brightness of a fill, but not the hue, and give fills a less mechanical, more organic look. You can add a texture to any fill. Fireworks ships with several textures from which to choose, such as Chiffon, Oilslick, and Sandpaper. You can also use bitmap files as textures. This allows you to create almost any type of custom texture.

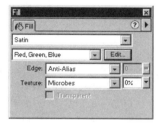

Use the Fill panel to add a texture to a fill.

The Texture pop-up menu displays a preview of the highlighted texture.

To add texture to the fill of a selected object:

1 In the Fill panel, choose a fill type from the Fill Category pop-up menu.

2 Choose a texture:

• Choose the texture from the Texture pop-up menu.

• To use an external texture, choose Other from the Texture pop-up menu and navigate to a texture file.

3 Enter a percentage from 0 to 100 to control the depth of the texture. Increasing the percentage increases the texture intensity.

4 Choose Transparent to introduce a level of transparency to the fill. The Texture percentage also controls the degree of transparency.

Using external files as patterns and textures

You can also use bitmap files from other applications as a texture. You can use files with these formats as textures: PNG, GIF, JPEG, BMP, TIFF, and PICT (Macintosh only). To add an external texture to the Texture pop-up menu for use in all documents, copy the texture file to the Fireworks 4\Configuration\Textures folder.

To use an external texture:

1 In the Fill panel, choose a fill type from the Fill Category pop-up menu.

2 If you didn't add the texture to the Text pop-up menu, choose Other from the Texture pop-up menu and navigate to a texture file. Otherwise, select the texture from the Texture pop-up menu.

3 Enter a percentage from 0 to 100 to control the depth of the texture. Increasing the percentage increases the texture intensity.

4 To make the lighter areas of the texture transparent, choose Transparent. The Texture percentage also controls the degree of transparency.

Dithering with Websafe colors

Sometimes you may need to use a color that is not a Websafe color. For example, your company logo may use a color that is not Web safe. To approximate a Websafe color that neither shifts nor dithers when exported with a Websafe palette, use a Web dither fill.

Web dither is a method whereby two colors in the palette are combined to closely replicate a color that is not in the palette. Note that Web dither can increase the expected file size.

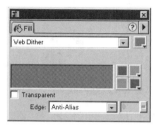

Two Websafe colors create a Web dither fill.

To use the Web dither fill:

1 Select an object containing a non-Websafe color.

2 In the Fill panel, choose Web Dither as the fill category.

The object's non-Websafe fill appears in the fill color box next to the fill type. The two Websafe dither colors appear in the checkerboard color boxes beneath. The Web Dither appears on the object and becomes the active fill color.

Note: Setting the edge of a Web Dither fill to Anti-Alias or Feather results in colors that are not Websafe.

To create the illusion of a true transparent fill in a Web browser:

1 In the Fill panel, apply a Web dither fill to a selected object.

2 Select Transparent.

3 Export the object as a GIF or PNG with Index Transparency or Alpha Channel Transparency set.

When you view the graphic in a Web browser, the Web page background shows through every other pixel of the transparent Web dither fill, creating the appearance of transparency. Note that not all browsers support PNG files.

CHAPTER 9
Adjusting Color and Tone

Filters on the Xtras menu and in the Live Effects panel help improve and enhance the colors in your bitmap images. Fireworks includes many new color adjustment filters. You can adjust the contrast and brightness, the hue and color saturation, and the tonal range.

In addition, you can blur or sharpen an image and give an image a unique look by colorizing it or inverting the colors. But you are not limited to these filters. You can also add Photoshop plug-ins to the Xtras menu and Live Effects panel.

These filters are used primarily for bitmap images, such as a digital photograph. However, you can also apply filters to vector objects. Applying a filter to a vector object using the Xtras menu converts the vector object to a bitmap.

Effects created by filters and plug-ins are reversible using the Undo command or History panel. Additionally, filters and plug-ins applied using the Live Effects panel are reversible and editable using that panel.

Using filters and plug-ins as Live Effects

In Fireworks, you can apply Photoshop plug-ins and built-in filters on the Xtras menu to an image using the Effect panel, making them Live Effects (see "Using Photoshop plug-ins as Live Effects" on page 195 and "Using Fireworks Xtras as Live Effects" on page 194).

Using Levels to adjust tonal range

You can use the Levels filter to correct bitmaps with a high concentration of pixels in the highlights, midtones, or shadows. A bitmap with a full tonal range should have an even number of pixels in all areas: the highlights, the midtones, and the shadows. A bitmap with a high concentration of light pixels (the highlights) looks washed out, while one with too many pixels in the midtones looks bland. A bitmap with too many dark pixels (the shadows) hides many of the details.

The Levels filter sets the darkest pixels and the lightest pixels as black and white, and then redistributes the midtones proportionally. This produces an image with the sharpest detail in all of its pixels.

Original with pixels concentrated in the highlights

After adjusting image with Levels

Use the Histogram in the Levels dialog box to view the pixel distribution of a bitmap. The Histogram is a graphical illustration of the distribution of pixels in the highlights, midtones, and shadows of a bitmap.

Histogram

Use the Histogram to determine the best method of correcting an image's tonal range. A high concentration of pixels in the shadows or highlights indicates that you could improve the image by applying the Levels or Curves feature.

The horizontal axis illustrates the color values from darkest (0) to brightest (255). Read the horizontal axis from left to right: the left depicts the darker pixels, the right depicts the brighter pixels, and the center depicts the midtone pixels. The vertical axis depicts the number of pixels at each brightness level. Typically, you should adjust the highlights and shadows first. Adjusting the midtones second lets you improve their brightness value without affecting the highlights and shadows.

To adjust highlights, midtones, and shadows:

1 Select the image in either vector mode or bitmap mode.

2 Open the Levels dialog box:

• Choose Xtras > Adjust Color > Levels.

• Choose Adjust Color > Levels from the Effect panel's Effect pop-up menu.

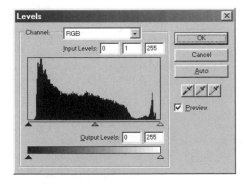

3 To view your changes in the workspace, select Preview. As you make changes, the image updates automatically.

4 From the Channel pop-up menu, choose whether you want to apply changes to individual color channels (red, blue, or green) or to all color channels (RGB).

5 Drag the Input Levels sliders under the Histogram to adjust the highlights, midtones, and shadows.

The slider on the right adjusts the highlights using values from 255 to 0; the slider in the center adjusts the midtones using values from 10 to 0.19; the slider on the far left adjusts the shadows using values from 0 to 255. As you move the sliders, the values are automatically entered in the Input Levels boxes.

Note: The shadow value cannot be higher than the highlight value, and vice versa.

6 Drag the Output Levels sliders to adjust the contrast values in the image.

Drag the right slider to adjust the highlights using values from 255 to 0 and drag the left slider to adjust the shadows from 0 to 255. As you move the sliders, the values are automatically entered in the Output Levels boxes.

For information on using the eye dropper buttons to adjust the tonal range, see "Adjusting the tonal range with the eyedroppers" on page 184.

Adjusting the tonal range automatically

Using the Auto Levels filter, you can automatically define the lightest and darkest pixels in an image. The Auto Levels filter is exactly the same as the Levels filter except that Fireworks makes the adjustments for you.

To adjust highlights, midtones, and shadows automatically:

1 Select the image in either vector mode or bitmap mode.

2 Choose Auto Levels:

• Choose Xtras > Adjust Color > Auto Levels.

• Choose Adjust Colors > Auto Levels from the Effect panel's Effect pop-up menu.

Note: You can also adjust the highlights, midtones, and shadows automatically by clicking the Auto button in the Levels or Curves dialog box.

Adjusting the tonal range using Curves

The Curves feature is similar to Levels, but provides more precise control over the tonal range. Whereas Levels uses the highlights, shadows, and midtones to correct the tonal range, Curves lets you adjust any color along the tonal range instead of only three variables, without affecting other colors. For example, you can use Curves to correct for a color cast caused by lighting conditions.

The grid in the Curves dialog box depicts these brightness values:

• The horizontal axis depicts the original brightness of the pixels (shown in the Input box).

• The vertical axis represents the new brightness values (shown in the Output box).

When you first open the Curves dialog box, the diagonal line indicates that no changes have been made, so the input and output values are the same for all pixels.

To adjust a specific point in the tonal range:

1 Select the image in either vector mode or bitmap mode.

2 Open the Curves dialog box:

- Choose Xtras > Adjust Color > Curves.

- Choose Adjust Color > Curves from the Effect panel's Effect pop-up menu.

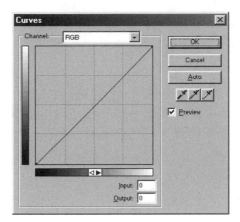

3 Select Preview to view your changes in the workspace. As you make changes, the image updates automatically.

4 From the Channel pop-up menu, choose whether you want to apply changes to individual color channels or to all colors.

5 To adjust the curve, click a point on the grid's diagonal line and drag it to a new position.

- Each point on the curve has its own Input and Output values. When you drag a point, the Input and Output values update automatically.

- The curve displays brightness values of 0 to 255, with 0 representing the shadows.

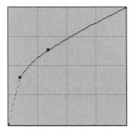

Curve after dragging a point to adjust

Note: Clicking the Auto button yields the same result as clicking the Auto button in the Levels dialog box.

To delete a point along the curve:

Drag the point off the grid.

Note: You cannot delete the endpoints of the curve.

Adjusting the tonal range with the eyedroppers

You can adjust the highlights, shadows, and midtones using the shadow, highlight, or midtone eyedropper button in the Levels or Curves dialog box.

For example, you might have an image that contains a lot of white and is therefore washed out in appearance. Click the highlight eyedropper, and then click a pixel in the image that is not as white. The highlight in the image is remapped to the new color, giving the picture more contrast.

To adjust the tonal range using an eyedropper:

1 Open the Levels or Curves dialog box, and choose a color channel from the Channel pop-up menu.

2 Choose the appropriate eyedropper:

• Highlight eyedropper (eyedropper with white ink) resets the highlight value.

• Shadow eyedropper (eyedropper with black ink) resets the shadow value.

• Midtone eyedropper (eyedropper with gray ink) resets the midtone value.

3 Click a pixel in the image and click OK.

Adjusting brightness and contrast

The Brightness/Contrast filter modifies the contrast or the brightness of all pixels in an image. Using this command affects the highlights, shadows, and midtones of an image.

You can use the Brightness/Contrast filter when correcting images that do not need substantial correction. For more advanced tonal correction procedures, see "Inverting an image's color values" on page 188, and "Adjusting the tonal range using Curves" on page 182.

Original

After adjusting the brightness

To adjust the brightness or contrast:

1 Select the image in either vector mode or bitmap mode.

2 Choose Xtras > Adjust Color > Brightness/Contrast. The Brightness/Contrast dialog box opens.

3 Select Preview to view your changes in the workspace. As you apply changes, the image updates automatically.

4 Drag the Brightness and Contrast sliders to adjust the settings. Values range from −100 to 100.

5 Click OK.

Applying color fills

You can use the Color Fill effect to quickly change the color of objects, either by replacing the pixels entirely with a given color or by blending a color into an existing object. When you blend colors, the color is added on top of the object. Blending a color into an existing object works similarly to the Hue/Saturation filter; however, it allows you to quickly apply a specific color from a color swatch panel.

To add a Color Fill effect to a selected object or area of pixels:

1 From the Effect panel's Effect pop-up menu, choose Adjust Color > Color Fill.

2 Choose a blending mode. The default is Normal.

For information about each blending mode, see "About blending modes" on page 217.

3 Choose a fill color from the color box pop-up menu.

4 Choose a percentage of opacity for the fill color and press Enter.

Adjusting hue and saturation

You can use Hue/Saturation to adjust the color, the purity of the color (known as its *saturation*), and the lightness of the color in an image.

To adjust the hue or saturation:

1 Select the image in either vector mode or bitmap mode.

2 Open the Hue/Saturation dialog box:

• Choose Adjust Color > Hue/Saturation from the Effect panel's Effect pop-up menu.

• Choose Xtras > Adjust Color > Hue/Saturation.

3 Select Preview to view your changes in the workspace. As you apply changes, the image updates automatically.

4 Choose Colorize to change an RGB image to a two-tone image or to add color to a grayscale image.

When you choose Colorize, the value range of the Hue and Saturation sliders changes. Hue changes to 0 to 360. Saturation changes to 0 to 100.

5 Drag the Saturation slider to adjust the purity of the colors. Values range from −100 to 100.

6 Drag the Hue slider to adjust the color of the image. Values range from − 180 to 180.

7 Drag the Lightness slider to adjust the lightness of the colors. Values range from −100 to 100.

8 Click OK.

Inverting an image's color values

You can use the Invert filter to change each color in an object or image to its inverse on the color wheel. For example, applying Invert to a red image object (R=255, G=0, B=0) changes the color to light blue (R=0, G=255, B=255).

Original

After inverting

To invert colors:

1 Select a vector or bitmap object.

2 Choose Xtras > Adjust Color > Invert.

Blurring an image

You can use the Blur commands to blur the pixels in bitmap images. Blur options include Blur, Blur More, and Gaussian Blur. Blur More blurs about three times as much as Blur. Gaussian Blur applies a weighted average of blur to each pixel to produce a hazy effect.

Before using Gaussian Blur

After using Gaussian Blur

To blur an image:

1   Select an image in either vector mode or bitmap mode.

2   Choose a blur option:

•   Choose Xtras > Blur > Blur or Blur More.

•   Choose Blur > Blur or Blur More from the Effects panel's Effect pop-up menu.

To blur an image using Gaussian Blur:

1 Select the image in either vector mode or bitmap mode.

2 Open the Gaussian Blur dialog box:

• Choose Xtras > Blur > Gaussian Blur.

• Choose Blur > Gaussian Blur from the Effect panel's Effect pop-up menu.

3 Select Preview to view your changes in the workspace. As you make changes, the image updates automatically.

4 Drag the Blur Radius slider to set the strength of the blur effect. Values range from 0.1 to 250. An increase in radius results in a stronger blur effect.

5 Click OK.

Changing color transitions to lines

You can use Find Edges to identify the parts of an image that are color transitions. Find Edges changes the color transitions to lines. In bitmap images, Find Edges creates the look of a sketch.

Original

After applying Find Edges

To change color transitions to lines in a selected object:

Choose the Find Edges option:

- Choose Other > Find Edges on the Effect panel's Effect pop-up menu.

- Choose Xtras > Other > Find Edges.

Converting an image

You can use the Convert to Alpha filter to convert an object or text into a gradient transparency based upon the transparency of the image.

To convert a selected image to alpha:

Choose the Convert to Alpha option:

- Choose Other > Convert to Alpha on the Effect panel's Effect pop-up menu.

- Choose Xtras > Other > Convert to Alpha.

Sharpening an image

You can use the Sharpen filter to correct images that are blurry. The Sharpen command includes three options: Sharpen, Sharpen More, and Unsharp Mask. Sharpen adjusts the focus of a blurred image by increasing the contrast of adjacent pixels. Sharpen More increases the contrast of adjacent pixels about three times as much as Sharpen. Unsharp Mask sharpens an image by adjusting the contrast of the image edges. Unsharp Mask offers the most control, so it is usually the best option for sharpening an image.

Original

After sharpening

To sharpen an image:

1 Select the image in either vector mode or bitmap mode.

2 Choose a sharpen option:

• Choose Xtras > Sharpen > Sharpen or Sharpen More.

• Choose Sharpen > Sharpen or Sharpen More from the Effect panel's Effect pop-up menu.

Note: If you sharpen too much, you may degrade the image.

To sharpen an image using Unsharp Mask:

1 Select the image in either vector mode or bitmap mode.

2 Open the Unsharp Mask dialog box:

• Choose Sharpen > Unsharp Mask from the Effect panel's Effect pop-up menu.

• Choose Xtras > Sharpen > Unsharp Mask.

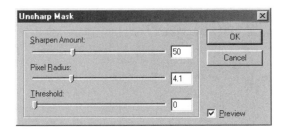

3 Select Preview to view how your changes affect the image.

4 Drag the Sharpen Amount slider to select the amount of sharpening effect from 1 to 500 percent.

5 Drag the Pixel Radius slider to select a radius from 0.1 to 250.

An increase in radius results in a greater area of sharp contrast surrounding each pixel edge.

6 Drag the Threshold slider to select a threshold of 0 to 255. Values between 2 and 25 are most commonly used.

An increase in threshold sharpens only those pixels of a higher contrast in the image. A decrease in threshold includes pixels of lower contrast.

A threshold of 0 sharpens all pixels in the image.

7 Click OK.

CHAPTER 10
Applying Live Effects

Fireworks effects are live, which means that when you edit an object the effects are reapplied so you can see the results right away. These effects can be easily turned on and off, which simplifies comparing different versions of a graphic.

With the wide selection of Fireworks strokes and fills, you can create all kinds of compelling graphics for your Web site. But what about wrapping a bevel edge around your buttons for a raised look? Or making a soft glow emanate from a picture? Or adding a subtle drop shadow to lend depth to text?

These and many other effects are easy to apply in Fireworks. Plus, you can apply effects to an object with only one visit to the Effect panel. You can edit or remove Live Effects as easily as you apply them.

In Fireworks 4 you can use Xtras filters, such as Gaussian Blur and Sharpen, as Live Effects. Many Photoshop plug-ins also now have all the flexibility of Live Effects.

Applying a Live Effect

Use the Effect panel to apply Live Effects. You can apply multiple effects to an object. Each time you add a new effect to the object, it is added to the list in the Effect panel. A check box appears next to each effect in the list. That way, you can turn it on or off.

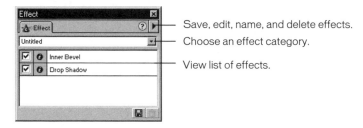

— Save, edit, name, and delete effects.

— Choose an effect category.

— View list of effects.

Effect panel

To apply a Live Effect to a selected object:

1 Choose an effect from the Effect pop-up menu.

The effect is added to the Effect list.

2 If a pop-up edit window or dialog box opens, enter the settings for the effect.

Click OK to close a dialog box. Press Enter or click anywhere in the workspace to close a pop-up window.

Note: The Effect panel is not available in bitmap mode.

3 Repeat steps 1 and 2 to apply multiple Live Effects.

Using Fireworks Xtras as Live Effects

In Fireworks, you can apply all the built-in filters in the Xtras menu as Live Effects using the Effect panel. This ensures that you can edit or remove the filter from an object at any time. You can also edit objects to which you applied the filters.

Use the Xtras menu to apply filters only when you are certain that you will not need to remove or edit the filter. For more information on using the Xtras menu, see "Adjusting the tonal range with the eyedroppers" on page 184.

Note: If you apply an Xtra filter from the Xtras menu, the filter is editable only if Undo is available. When you close and reopen the image, the filter is not removable because the History panel is cleared.

Using Photoshop plug-ins as Live Effects

When you install a Photoshop plug-in in Fireworks, it is added to the Xtras menu and to the Effect panel. Use the Xtras menu to apply Photoshop plug-ins only when you are certain that you will not want to edit or remove the effect from an object.

Use the Effect panel to apply Photoshop plug-ins as Live Effects. Some Photoshop plug-ins cannot be used as Live Effects.

Note: When you share a Fireworks file in which a Photoshop plug-in is applied as a Live Effect, the recipient must have the plug-in installed to view the effect. Built-in Fireworks effects, however, are saved with the Fireworks file. The recipient does not need to install additional software to view the effect.

To install Photoshop plug-ins:

1 In the Effect panel Options pop-up menu, choose Locate Plugins.

2 Navigate to the folder where the Photoshop plug-ins are installed, and click OK.

3 Restart Fireworks to load the plug-ins.

   Note: If you move the plug-ins to a different folder, repeat the above steps, or choose File > Preferences and click the Folders tab to change the path to the plug-ins. Then restart Fireworks.

To apply a Photoshop plug-in to a selected object as a Live Effect:

Choose the plug-in from the Effect pop-up menu in the Effect panel.

Applying traditional effects

With Fireworks, you can create Web effects, such as bevels, drop shadows, glows, and embossing. You can customize each effect to get exactly the look you want. Effect settings can be changed anytime.

When you choose the Bevel, Emboss, Shadow, or Glow effect, a pop-up edit window appears in the Effect panel so you can adjust the effect settings. The options on the pop-up edit window change depending upon the effect you choose.

Experiment with the settings until you get the look you want. If you want to change the effect settings later, see "Changing Live Effects" on page 198.

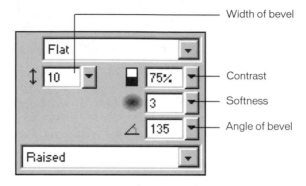

— Width of bevel

— Contrast

— Softness

— Angle of bevel

Inner Bevel pop-up edit window

Applying beveled edges

Applying a beveled edge to a button gives it a raised look. You can create an inner bevel or an outer bevel.

Inner Bevel and Outer Bevel

To apply a beveled edge to a selected object:

1 In the Effect panel, choose a Bevel option:

• Bevel and Emboss > Inner Bevel

• Bevel and Emboss > Outer Bevel

2 Edit the effect settings in the pop-up edit window.

3 Click outside the edit window or press Enter to close it.

Applying emboss effects

Use the Emboss effect to make an image appear raised or inset from its background. Emboss makes buttons appear to press into or raise out from their surroundings. You can apply an inset emboss effect or a raised emboss effect.

Inset Emboss and Raised Emboss on blue canvas

To apply an emboss effect:

1 Open the Effect pop-up menu to view a list of available effects.

2 Choose an Emboss effect:

• Bevel and Emboss > Inset Emboss

• Bevel and Emboss > Raised Emboss

3 Edit the effect settings in the pop-up edit window.

If you want the original object to appear, check Show Object.

4 When you have finished, click outside the edit window or press Enter to close it.

Note: For backward compatibility, emboss effects on objects in older documents open with the Show Object check box deselected.

Applying shadows and glows

Fireworks makes it easy to apply drop shadows, inner shadows, and glows to objects. You can specify the angle of the shadow to simulate the angle of the light shining on the object.

Drop Shadow, Inner Shadow, and Glow effects

To apply a shadow or inner shadow:

1 Open the Effect pop-up menu to view a list of available effects.

2 Choose a shadow option:

• Shadow and Glow > Drop Shadow

• Shadow and Glow > Inner Shadow

3 Edit the effect settings in the pop-up edit window:

• Drag the distance slider to set the distance of the shadow from the object.

• Drag the Opacity slider to set the percentage of transparency in the shadow.

• Select Knock Out to hide the object and display the shadow only.

4 When you have finished, click outside the edit window or press Enter to close it.

To apply a glow:

1 Open the Effect pop-up menu to view a list of available effects.

2 Choose Shadow and Glow > Glow.

3 Edit the effect settings in the pop-up edit window:

• Drag the Offset slider to specify the distance of the glow from the object.

• Drag the Opacity slider to set the transparency of the glow.

• Select the color box pop-up menu to set the glow color.

4 When you have finished, click outside the edit window or press Enter to close it.

For more information on effects, see "Adjusting the tonal range with the eyedroppers" on page 184.

Changing Live Effects

Use the associated Info button in the Effect panel to change an effect applied to an object.

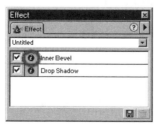

To edit a Live Effect:

1 In the Effect panel, click the Info button next to the effect you want to edit. Either a pop-up edit window or a dialog box opens.

   Note: If an effect is not editable, the Info button is dimmed. For example, you cannot edit Auto Levels.

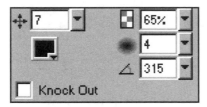

The Drop Shadow pop-up edit window

2 Adjust the effect settings.

3 When you have finished, click outside the pop-up edit window or press Enter to close it.

Reordering Live Effects

You can reorder the effects applied to an object. Reordering effects changes the sequence in which the effects are applied. This can alter the object's appearance.

In general, effects that change the interior of an object, such as the Inner Bevel effect, should be applied before effects that change the object's exterior. For example, apply the Inner Bevel effect before you apply the Outer Bevel, Glow, or Shadow effects.

To reorder effects applied to a selected object:

In the Effect panel, drag the effect that you want to move to the desired position in the list.

Effects at the top of the list are applied before the effects at the bottom.

Removing Live Effects

You can also easily remove effects from an object. If several effects are applied to an object, you can remove a single effect or remove all of them.

For information on temporarily disabling an effect, see "Handling Live Effects redraw" on page 202.

To remove a single effect applied to a selected object:

1 In the Effect panel, select the effect you want to remove from the list.

2 Click the Delete button at the bottom of the Effect panel, or drag the effect to the Delete button.

To remove all effects from a selected object:

In the Effect panel, choose None from the Effect pop-up menu.

Creating custom Live Effects

Use the Effect panel Options pop-up menu to save a custom effect setting, rename an effect, or delete an effect. In Fireworks 4, saved effects are stored with the application. If you name and save the effect settings for an object, the effect is available to all documents you open subsequently.

If you name and save multiple effects that are applied to an object, all of the effects can be applied to other objects at once.

Note: When you open documents from previous versions of Fireworks that contain saved effects, the effects are titled Unnamed. However, all effect settings are retained. Rename the effects using the Effect panel.

To save an effect setting:

1 Choose Save Effect As from the Effect panel Options pop-up menu.

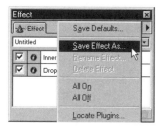

Options pop-up menu in the Effect panel

2 Type a name for the effect and click OK. The effect is added to the Effect pop-up menu.

To rename a custom effect setting:

1 Select the custom effect you want to rename from the Effect panel.

2 Choose Rename Effect from the Effect panel Options pop-up menu.

3 Enter a new name and click OK.

   You cannot rename or delete a standard Fireworks effect.

To delete a named custom effect:

1 Select the object that contains the custom effect you want to delete, or choose the custom effect from the Effect pop-up menu.

2 Choose Delete Effect in the Effect panel Options pop-up menu.

Saving Live Effects as styles

You can save and reuse an effect by creating a style based on it. Live Effects are among the attributes that you can save as a style or as part of a style. For more information, see "About styles" on page 224.

Using the default Live Effects settings

If you frequently use particular settings for a Live Effect, you can make those settings the default. For example, if you are using a particular drop shadow and glow combination for buttons, save this combination of settings as the default and apply it to buttons throughout your document. The default is remembered between documents and sessions.

To save a combination of effect settings as the default:

1 Select the object that contains the effect settings you want to use as the default.

2 Choose Save Defaults from the Effect panel Options pop-up menu.

To apply the default effects to an object:

Choose Use Defaults from the Effect panel pop-up menu.

Handling Live Effects redraw

It may take slightly longer to open a file in which numerous Live Effects are used. In addition, when you resize or edit an object with numerous effects, it may take Fireworks longer to redraw the object on the screen.

You can temporarily disable an effect to speed the redraw.

To temporarily enable or disable an effect applied to an object:

Select or deselect the check box next to the effect in the Effect panel.

To temporarily enable or disable all effects applied to an object:

Choose All On or All Off in the Effect panel Options pop-up menu.

For information on permanently removing effects, see "Removing Live Effects" on page 199.

Applying effects to grouped objects

When you apply an effect to a group, the effect is applied to all objects in the group. If the objects are ungrouped, each object reverts to any effect settings applied to the object individually.

You can apply an effect to an object within a group by selecting only that object, using the Subselection tool. For information on selecting a group or objects within a group, see "Selecting objects within groups" on page 95.

CHAPTER 11
Layers and Masking

Layers divide a Fireworks document into discrete planes, as though the components of the illustration were drawn on separate tracing paper overlays. A document can be made up of many layers and each layer can contain many objects. In Fireworks, the Layers panel contains a list of layers and the objects contained in each layer. Fireworks layers are equivalent to layer sets in Photoshop 6. Photoshop layers are equivalent to individual Fireworks objects.

Masking and blending techniques give you another level of creative control. You can create unique effects by blending the colors in overlapping objects. Fireworks has several blending modes to help you achieve just the look you want.

Another way to create a unique effect is to use a mask. With masking, you can use a vector object or a bitmap object to block out part of the underlying image. For example, you can create an elliptical vector object to use as a mask on top of a photograph. Use Paste as Mask to paste the vector object as a mask on top of the photograph. All areas outside the ellipse are effectively cropped, showing only the part of the picture inside the ellipse.

About Layers

Each object in a document resides on a layer. You can either create all layers before you draw or add layers as needed. The canvas is below all layers and is not itself a layer. For information on working with the canvas, see "Changing the canvas" on page 75.

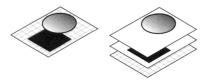

You can view the order of objects in the Layers panel. This is the order in which they appear in the document. Within a document, Fireworks stacks layers based on the order in which you created them, placing the most recently created layer on the top of the stack. The stacking order of layers determines how objects on one layer overlap objects on another. You can rearrange the order of layers as well as the order of objects within a single layer.

The Layers panel displays the current state of all layers in the current frame of a document. The name of the active layer is highlighted. You can expand a layer to view a list of all the objects on it. The objects are displayed in thumbnails.

Masks are also shown in the Layers panel. You can create new masks using the Layers panel. Selecting the mask thumbnail lets you edit it. For more information, see "Editing masks" on page 214.

Opacity and blend mode controls are also found on the Layers panel. For more information, see "Adjusting opacity and applying blends" on page 220.

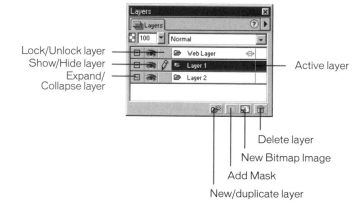

When you want to protect objects on all but the active layer from unwanted selection or changes, choose Single Layer Editing from the Layers panel Options pop-up menu. A check mark (Windows) or bullet (Macintosh) shows Single Layer Editing is enabled. When Single Layer Editing is enabled, only objects on the current layer can be selected and edited.

The Web Layer

The Web Layer is a special layer that appears as the top layer in each document. The Web Layer contains Web objects, such as slices and hotspots, used for assigning interactivity to exported Fireworks documents. For more information on Web objects, see "Using Hotspots and Slices" on page 249.

You cannot unshare, delete, duplicate, move, or rename the Web Layer. It is always shared across all frames, and Web objects are visible on every frame.

To rename a slice or hotspot in the Web Layer:

1   Double-click on the slice or hotspot in the Layers panel.

2   Enter a name and click outside the window or press Enter.

Note: When you rename a slice, that name is used when exporting the slice.

Working with layers

When you create a new layer, a blank layer is inserted before the currently selected layer. The new layer becomes the active layer and is highlighted in the Layers panel. Creating a duplicate layer adds a new layer that contains the same objects as the currently selected one. Duplicated objects retain the opacity and blending mode of the objects from which they were copied. Changes can be made to the duplicated objects without affecting the originals.

Each layer can be edited independently. This means that you can make changes to the objects on one layer without affecting objects on any other.

To add a layer:

Do one of the following:

*   Choose New Layer from the Layers panel Options pop-up menu. Select Share across Frames to share the objects on that layer across all frames. Click OK.

*   Click the New/Duplicate Layer button with no layer selected.

*   Choose Insert > Layer.

To activate a layer:

Do one of the following:

- Click the layer name in the Layers panel.

- Select an object on that layer.

  Objects you draw or paste reside initially on the active layer.

To expand or collapse the objects on a layer:

Click the plus sign (Windows) or the triangle (Macintosh) to the left of the layer name in the Layers panel.

To name a layer:

1 Double-click a layer name in the Layers panel.

   The Layer Name window opens.

2 In the Layer Name text box, type a new name for the layer. Close by clicking outside the window or pressing Enter.

   Note: Objects on layers can be renamed. Double-click on the selected object and enter a new name.

To delete a layer:

Select a layer and click the Delete button, or drag the layer to the Delete button.

To show or hide a layer or objects on a layer:

Click the square in the middle column to the left of a layer or object name.

The eye icon indicates that a layer is visible.

To show or hide multiple layers or objects:

Drag the pointer along the eye column in the Layers panel.

To show or hide all layers and objects:

Choose Show All or Hide All from the Layers panel Options pop-up menu.

Note: Hidden layers and objects are not exported.

To lock a layer:

Click the square in the column immediately to the left of a layer name.

A padlock indicates that the layer is locked.

To lock multiple layers:

Drag the pointer along the padlock column in the Layers panel.

To lock or unlock all layers:

Choose Lock All or Unlock All in the Layers panel Options pop-up menu.

Note: Objects on a locked layer are not editable.

To share a selected layer across frames:

 Choose Share This Layer in the Layers panel Options pop-up menu.

Note: If a layer is shared across all frames, when you update any object on that layer, the object updates in all frames. This is useful when you want objects such as background elements to appear on all frames of an animation.

To turn on or off Single Layer Editing:

In the Layers panel Options pop-up menu, choose Single Layer Editing. A check mark indicates that Single Layer Editing is active.

Moving objects on the Layers panel

Objects can be moved within a layer or between layers. Moving objects in the Layers panel changes the ordering of the objects in the document. Moving objects in a document using the Modify > Arrange commands changes the ordering of the objects in the Layers panel. Objects at the top of a layer appear in front of other objects on that layer.

Objects are shown as thumbnails in the Layers panel. When you select an object in a document, it is highlighted in the Layers panel.

To view the list of individual objects on a layer, click the plus sign (Windows) or the triangle (Macintosh) to the left of the layer name on the Layers panel. To expand or collapse all the layers, Alt-click on the plus or minus sign (Windows) or Option-click on the triangle (Macintosh).

To move an object to another layer:

Drag the object to the desired layer.

Note: Drag objects within a layer to change their stacking order in that layer.

To copy selected objects to another layer:

Hold down Alt (Windows) or Option (Macintosh) and drag the object to the desired layer.

To rename an object:

1 Double-click an object's name in the Layers panel.

2 Type a new name for the object. Close by clicking outside the text box or press Enter.

Duplicating layers

You can add duplicate layers and choose where to position them in the Layers panel. A duplicate layer contains the same objects as the currently selected layer. Duplicated layers have the same name as the original layer but with a number appended.

To duplicate a layer:

1 Do one of the following:

• Drag a layer to the New/Duplicate Layer button.

• Select a layer and choose Duplicate Layer from the Layers panel Options pop-up menu.

2 If you did the latter, choose the number of duplicate layers to insert and where to place them in the stacking order.

Note: The Web Layer is always the top layer, so choosing At the top places the duplicate layer below the Web Layer.

Arranging layers

Moving layers in the Layers panel changes the order in which objects appear in a document. The topmost layer appears in front of other layers. Objects on the topmost layer appear in front of objects on lower layers.

To move a layer:

Select and drag a layer name up or down in the Layers panel.

Masking images

Masks are added to an object to create a cut-out effect on that object. An empty mask or another object can be used to mask an existing object. Masks are fully editable.

You can use either a vector or a bitmap object as the mask object.

A mask has two primary uses:

• The path of a vector mask can outline another object or image. It masks the underlying object or image to its path.

• A mask object's pixels can affect the visibility of another object. In Photoshop this is called a *layer mask*. Masks are commonly used to define gradient transparency for other objects.

By editing the stroke and fill attributes of the mask object, you can create many unique effects.

Image and masking object

Vector mask

Bitmap mask

Creating bitmap and vector masks

You can create a mask for an object using the Layers panel or the Modify menu. A vector object or a bitmap object can be used as a mask. A mask can be made up of more than one object.

To create a bitmap mask from scratch:

1 Select the object you want to mask.

 2 Click the Add Mask button at the bottom of the Layers panel.

3 Draw the mask using a bitmap tool from the Tools panel.

Note: Bitmap tools such as the Brush, Pencil, Rectangle, and Ellipse tools can be used to draw masks.

To create a vector mask from scratch:

1 Create the path or text object or objects you want to use as a mask.

2 Cut or Copy the object or objects.

Shift-click to select multiple objects.

3 Select the object you want to mask.

4 Paste the mask:

• Choose Edit > Paste as Mask.

• Choose Modify > Mask > Paste as Mask.

Creating a mask using an existing object

Any object can be used as a mask. To do this, use the Paste as Mask command to add the Clipboard contents as a mask. You can also create a mask using multiple objects.

To use the Clipboard contents as a mask:

1 Create the object or objects you want to use as a mask.

Shift-click to select multiple objects.

2 Place the object or objects on the Clipboard:

• Choose Edit > Cut.

• Choose Edit > Copy.

3 Select the object you want to mask.

4 Choose Edit > Paste as Mask or Modify > Mask > Paste as Mask.

If a mask already exists, you can choose to Replace it or Add to it. Choosing Add creates a mask made up of more than one object.

To add a mask to the Clipboard contents:

1 Select the object to be masked.

2 Choose Edit > Cut.

3 Select the object you want to use as a mask.

4 Choose Edit > Paste Inside.

Grouping objects to form a mask

You can select two or more existing objects and group them to form a masked object. The top object becomes the mask object. Check in the Layers panel to see which object is at the top. Objects from different layers can be grouped as a mask object. The top object on the topmost layer becomes the mask object.

You can group objects as either bitmap or vector masks. Group as Mask results in a bitmap mask. The command for Group as Vector Mask is found in the Keyboard Shortcuts under the Miscellaneous category. This is the same as using Group as Mask and choosing Path Outline in the Object panel. For more information, see "Using the Object panel in masking" on page 216.

To group objects into a masked object:

1 Shift-click two or more objects.

2 Choose Modify > Mask > Group as Mask.

Using text as a mask

Text is commonly used as a mask to create interesting effects. Select Show Fill and Stroke in the Object panel to display any extra effects you apply to the text mask using the Fill and Stroke panels. You can also choose to apply the mask using its Path Outline or Grayscale Appearance. For more information, see "Using the Object panel in masking" on page 216.

To create a mask using text:

1 Create the text using the Text Editor.

See "Entering text" on page 142.

2 Copy or Cut the text object to the Clipboard.

3 Select the object to be masked and choose Edit > Paste as Mask.

A vector mask is added to the object.

Creating an empty mask

You can add an empty mask to an object. This is either a white mask, which shows the whole object, or a black mask, which obscures the whole object. The empty mask is fully editable.

Using Reveal/Hide All commands

The Reveal All command adds an empty white mask to an object. The Hide All command adds a black mask to an object.

To use Reveal All and Hide All commands to create a mask:

1 Select the object you want to mask.

2 Create the mask:

• Choose Modify > Mask > Reveal All to show the object.

• Choose Modify > Mask > Hide All to hide the object.

3 Select the mask thumbnail in the Layers panel.

4 Select a drawing tool from the Tools panel to edit the mask.

Using Reveal/Hide Selection commands

The Reveal Selection and Hide Selection commands can be used on bitmap objects. The Reveal Selection command adds a white pixel mask that represents the current pixel selection. The other pixels in the object are hidden. The Hide Selection command adds a black pixel mask that represents the current pixel selection. The other pixels in the object are shown.

To use Reveal Selection and Hide Selection commands to create a mask:

1 Choose the Marquee or Lasso Tool from the Tools panel.

2 Select pixels in the bitmap:

• Choose Modify > Mask > Reveal Selection to show the area defined by the pixel selection.

• Choose Modify > Mask > Hide Selection to hide the areas defined by the pixel selection.

Editing masks

Masks remain fully editable after you create them. Masks can be edited, deleted, and disabled. Disabling a mask temporarily removes it. A disabled mask can be enabled to show its effect on an object.

  Masks and objects can be easily identified and edited using the thumbnails in the Layers panel. When you select a mask for editing, the mask icon appears beside it in the Layers panel. When you select an object for editing, the pencil icon appears.

The size of the thumbnails in the Layers panel can be changed to show details of objects and masks more clearly. Choose Thumbnail Options in the Layers panel Options pop-up menu. Turn off thumbnails to save memory.

To edit a mask:

1 Select the mask:

• Click on the mask thumbnail in the Layers panel.

• Choose Edit Mask from the Layers panel Options pop-up menu.

• Double-click the Move Handle on the masked object.

2 Make changes to the mask:

• Choose a tool from the Tools panel and draw the changes.

• Drag the Move Handle on the mask.

• Apply effects to the mask.

Although the mask itself is not visible, the effects of editing are immediately visible while editing.

To edit an object without affecting the mask:

1 Click on the object thumbnail in the Layers panel.

2 Make changes to the object.

> **Note:** When you select a masked object, the effects applied to the object are shown in the Fill and Stroke panels.

To move an object without affecting the mask:

1   Click the link icon on the mask thumbnail in the Layers panel.

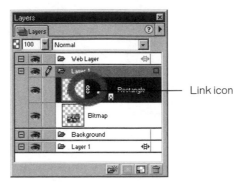

Link icon

This unlinks the object from its mask so the object moves independently.

2   Drag the object.

To convert a vector mask to a bitmap mask:

1   In the Layers panel, select the mask thumbnail.

2   Choose Modify > Convert to Bitmap.

Note: You cannot convert a bitmap mask to a vector mask.

To disable or enable a mask:

1   Select the masked object.

2   Enable or disable the mask:

•   Choose Disable or Enable Mask from the Layers panel Options pop-up menu.

•   Choose Modify > Mask > Disable or Enable Mask.

A red X appears on the mask thumbnail when it is disabled. Clicking on the X enables the mask.

To delete a mask:

1 Select the mask.

2 Delete the mask:

• Choose Delete Mask from the Layers panel Options pop-up menu.

• Choose Modify > Mask > Delete Mask.

3 Choose whether to apply the mask to the image before the deletion occurs:

• Apply keeps the changes you have made to the mask, but the mask is no longer editable.

• Discard gets rid of the changes you have made and restores the object to its original form.

Using the Object panel in masking

Use the Object panel to ensure that you are editing a mask and to identify the type of mask you are working on. When a mask is selected, the Object panel lets you change the way the mask is applied.

Vector masks can be applied using their Path Outline. This uses the outline of the path or text as the mask. Select Show Fill and Stroke to show the mask's fill and stroke on the masked object. The area outside the mask is cut out. This is the same as Paste Inside in FreeHand.

You can apply bitmap masks using their Alpha Channel, rather than the brightness of the pixels, to mask the object.

Both vector and bitmap masks can be applied using their Grayscale Appearance. When a mask is applied using grayscale appearance, the lightness of its pixels determines how much of the masked object is displayed. Light pixels display the masked object. Darker pixels in the mask knock out the image and show the background.

Blending the fill colors of overlapping objects

Compositing is the process of using blending modes to vary the transparency or color interaction of two or more overlapping objects. Blending modes manipulate the color values of overlapping objects. They also add a dimension of control to the opacity effect.

About blending modes

Choosing a blending mode applies it to the entire appearance of selected objects. Objects within a single document or a single layer can have blending modes that differ from other objects within the document or layer.

When objects with different blending modes are grouped, the group's blending mode overrides individual blending modes. Ungrouping the objects restores each object's individual blending mode.

A blending mode contains these elements:

*   Blend color is the color to which the blending mode is applied.
*   Opacity is the degree of transparency to which the blending mode is applied.
*   Base color is the color of pixels underneath the blend color.
*   Result color is the result of the blending mode's effect on the base color.

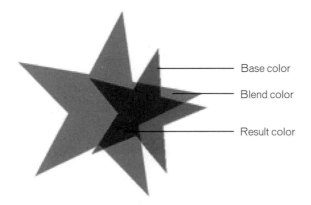

These are the blend modes in Fireworks:

Normal applies no blending mode.

Multiply multiplies the base color by the blend color, resulting in darker colors.

Screen multiplies the inverse of the blend color by the base color, resulting in a bleaching effect.

Darken selects the darker of the blend color and base color to use as the result color. This replaces only pixels that are lighter than the blend color.

Lighten selects the lighter of the blend color and base color to use as the result color. This replaces only pixels that are darker than the blend color.

Difference subtracts the blend color from the base color or the base color from the blend color. The color with less brightness is subtracted from the color with more brightness.

Hue combines the hue value of the blend color with the luminance and saturation of the base color to create the result color.

Saturation combines the saturation of the blend color with the luminance and hue of the base color to create the result color.

Color combines the hue and saturation of the blend color with the luminance of the base color to create the result color, preserving the gray levels for coloring monochrome images and tinting color images.

Luminosity combines the luminance of the blend color with the hue and saturation of the base color.

Invert inverts the base color.

Tint adds gray to the base color.

Erase removes all base color pixels, including those in the background image.

Blending mode examples

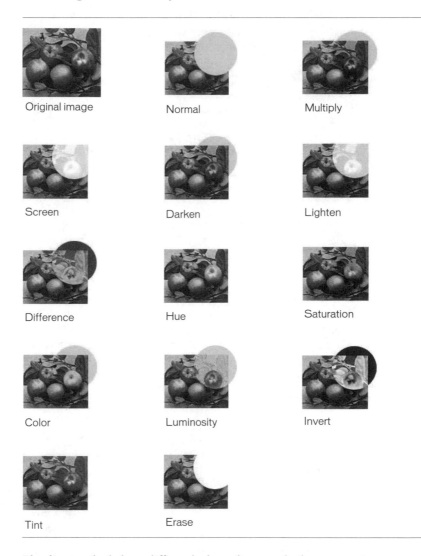

Original image

Normal

Multiply

Screen

Darken

Lighten

Difference

Hue

Saturation

Color

Luminosity

Invert

Tint

Erase

Blending modes behave differently depending on whether you are in vector mode or bitmap mode.

- In vector mode, a blending mode affects the selected object.

- In bitmap mode, a blending mode affects a floating selection of pixels.

- In bitmap mode without a floating selection, a blending mode affects the brushes and fills of subsequently drawn objects.

Adjusting opacity and applying blends

Use the Layers panel to adjust the opacity of selected objects and to apply blending modes. A setting of 100 renders an object completely opaque. A setting of 0 (zero) renders an object completely transparent.

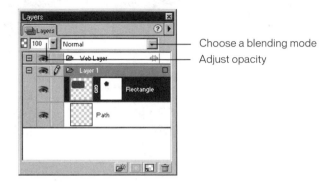

Set opacity and choose a blending mode in the Layers panel.

To set a blending mode for existing objects:

1 With two objects overlapping, select the top object.

2 In the Layers panel Blending Mode pop-up menu, choose a blending option.

To set a default blending mode to be applied to objects as you draw them:

1 Choose Edit > Deselect to avoid inadvertently applying a blending mode.

2 In the Layers panel, choose a blending mode as the default.

Applying the Fill Color Live Effect

Fill Color is a Live Effect that lets you adjust the color of an object by altering the object's opacity and blend mode. This gives the same effect you would get by overlapping the object with one that had a different opacity and blend mode.

The Fill Color Live Effect is completely compatible with Photoshop's Color Fill Layer Effect. You can import a Photoshop graphic containing the effect into Fireworks and export it to Photoshop again when you are ready.

To apply a Color Fill Live Effect to an object:

1 Select the object to apply the color to.

2 In the Effect panel pop-up menu, choose Color Fill from the Adjust Color submenu.

3 Select a color, blend mode, and opacity.

Working with Photoshop

Masked objects can be exported to Photoshop. They are converted into Photoshop layer masks. The masks, including text, remain editable. For total editability, choose Maintain Editability over Appearance when exporting to Photoshop.

Importing Photoshop layer masks

In Photoshop, you can mask images using layer masks or grouped layers. Fireworks lets you successfully import images that employ layer masks without losing the ability to edit them. Layer masks are imported as bitmap masks.

For more information on Photoshop layer masks, see "Masks" on page 393.

Importing Photoshop grouped layers

Photoshop files that contain layers are imported with each layer placed as a separate object on a single Fireworks layer. Grouped layers are imported as individual layers, as if the layers were ungrouped in Photoshop before importing into Fireworks. The clipping effect on Photoshop grouped layers is lost on import.

For more information on clipping groups in Photoshop, see "Groups" on page 393.

CHAPTER 12
Using Libraries, Styles, and URLs

This chapter covers three panels where you can store and reuse symbols, styles, and URLs. Symbols are stored in the Library panel. Similarly, styles are stored in the Styles panel, and URLs are stored in the URL panel.

The Styles panel contains a set of predefined Fireworks styles to choose from. However, if you like the way you have used strokes, fills, and other attributes to make an object unique, you can save the attributes as a style. Rather than rebuilding attributes each time, simply save them in the Styles panel and then apply that combination of attributes to other objects.

Symbols are stored in the Library panel. There are three different types of symbols: buttons, graphics, and animations. You can create new symbols and duplicate symbols, import existing ones, and edit symbols.

URLs, or Uniform Resource Locators, are stored in the URL panel. A URL is an address of a specific page or file on the Internet. If you are using the same URL many times, you can add it to the URL panel. You can organize and group your URLs in URL libraries.

About styles

You can save and reapply a set of predefined fill, stroke, effect, and text attributes by creating a style. Styles in Fireworks are more like paint mixes on an artist's palette than styles in a word processor. When you apply a style to an object, that object takes on the style's characteristics.

Fireworks has many predefined styles. You can add, change, and remove styles. The Fireworks CD-ROM and the Macromedia Web site have many more predefined styles that you can import into Fireworks. You can also export styles and share them with other Fireworks users or import styles from other Fireworks documents.

Using styles

Use the Styles panel to store and apply styles to objects or text. Choose Window > Styles to open the Styles panel.

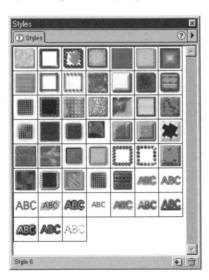

Styles panel

When you apply a style to an object, you can later update the style without affecting the original object. Fireworks does not keep track of which style you applied to an object. If you delete a style you cannot recover it. If you delete a style supplied in Fireworks, you can recover it and all other deleted styles using the Reset Styles command in the Styles panel Options pop-up menu. However, resetting styles also deletes your custom styles.

To apply a style to a selected object or text block:

Click a style in the Styles panel.

To create a new style:

1 Create an object or text with the stroke, fill, effect, or text settings you want.

 2 Click the New Style button at the bottom of the Styles panel.

3 Choose the properties you want to be part of the style, name it if you wish, and click OK.

An icon depicting the style appears in the Styles panel.

To edit a style:

1 Choose Edit > Deselect.

2 Double-click a style in the Styles panel.

3 In the Edit Style dialog box, select or deselect components of the style you wish to apply, and click OK.

To base a new style on an existing style:

1 Apply the existing style to a selected object.

2 Edit the attributes of the object.

3 Save the attributes as a new style.

To delete a style:

1 Select a style from the Styles panel.

To select multiple styles for deleting, hold down the Shift key while clicking.

 2 Click the Delete Styles button in the Styles panel.

To export styles:

1 Select one or more styles from the Styles panel.

 To select multiple styles, hold down the Shift key while clicking.

2 Choose Export Styles from the Styles panel Options pop-up menu.

3 Enter a name and location for the saved-styles document.

4 Click Save.

To import styles:

1 Choose Import Styles from the Styles panel Options pop-up menu.

2 Choose a styles document to import.

 All styles in the styles document are imported and placed directly after the selected style in the Styles panel.

To reset the Styles panel to the default styles:

Choose Reset Styles from the Options pop-up menu.

Note: Resetting styles to the default overwrites any custom styles you may have saved.

To change the size of the style preview icons:

Choose Large Icons from the Styles panel Options pop-up menu to switch between large and small preview sizes.

About symbols and instances

A symbol represents an object, text block, or group and is either a graphic, an animation, or a button. Instances are representations of an original Fireworks object. The object is designated as the symbol. When the symbol object (the original) is edited, the instances (copies) automatically change to reflect the modifications to the symbol.

Symbols are useful whenever you want to reuse a graphic element. They can be used across documents. Symbols are also necessary for creating buttons and animating objects across multiple frames. For more on creating animated objects, see "Creating animation symbols" on page 291.

Use symbols and instances to easily modify copies of the same object, to share components across rollover states, and to do animations.

Using the symbol library

Create and save symbols in the Library panel. The Library panel stores graphic, button, and animation symbols. You can create a symbol from any object, text block, or group. Symbols can include other symbols.

To create a new symbol:

1 Do one of the following:

- To create a new symbol from scratch, choose Insert > New Symbol, or choose New Symbol in the Library panel Options pop-up menu.

- To create a symbol from an existing object, select the object and choose Insert > Convert to Symbol.

2 In the Name text box of the Symbol Properties dialog box, type a name for the symbol.

3 Choose a symbol type, either Graphic, Animation, or Button, and click OK.

4 If you are creating a symbol from scratch, the Symbol Editor or Button Editor opens. Create the object to be used as a symbol and close the editor.

The symbol appears in the library and in the document.

For more information on creating button symbols, see "Inserting buttons from the library" on page 243. For more on creating animated symbols, see "Creating animation symbols" on page 291.

Placing instances

You can add one or more instances of a symbol to the current document.

To place an instance, drag a symbol from the Library panel to the current document.

Arrow icon representing an instance

Changing symbols

You can modify a symbol in the Symbol Editor and automatically modify all associated instances.

Note: Modifying an instance affects the symbol and all other instances. To modify an instance only, see "Breaking the link between an instance and its symbol" on page 229.

To change a symbol:

1 Open the Symbol Editor:

• Double-click an instance.

• Double-click the symbol object in the Library panel.

2 Make changes to the symbol and close the window.

The symbol and all instances reflect your modifications.

To rename a symbol:

1 Double-click the symbol name in the Library panel.

2 Change the name in the Symbol Properties dialog box and click OK.

To duplicate a symbol:

1 In the Library panel, select the symbol.

2 From the Options pop-up menu, choose Duplicate.

To delete a symbol:

1 In the Library panel, select the symbol.

2 Choose Delete from the Options pop-up menu.

3 If the symbol is in use, click Delete. The symbol and all of its instances are deleted.

To select all symbols in the library that have not yet been used in the current document:

From the Library panel Options pop-up menu, choose Select Unused Items.

Breaking the link between an instance and its symbol

When you modify an instance, the change affects the symbol and all other instances. However, you can modify an instance without affecting the symbol or other instances by first breaking the link between it and the symbol.

To release an instance from a symbol:

1 Select the instance.

2 Choose Modify > Symbol > Break Apart.

The instance reverts to a group. The symbol in the Library panel is no longer associated with that group. Button symbols stop functioning as buttons and animation symbols stop functioning as animations.

Note: To edit the released instance as an object, select the instance and choose Modify > Ungroup.

Using symbols from other libraries

You can export symbols for use in other Fireworks documents and import symbols from other documents.

If you change a symbol in the original document, you can update those changes in any document into which the symbol was imported.

For example, suppose you have created a symbol for your company logo in a master file. Then you import the logo symbol into other documents. If the logo changes, you can modify it in the master file and update all the files into which you imported it.

You can automatically break the link between the imported symbol and the original document by editing the symbol in the current document. Breaking the link lets you edit the imported symbol independently from the original symbol.

To export symbols:

1 From the Library panel Options pop-up menu, choose Export Symbols.

2 Select the symbols to export and click Export.

3 Navigate to a folder, type a name for the symbol file, and click Save.

Fireworks saves the symbols in a single PNG file.

To import symbols using drag and drop or copy and paste:

• Drag a symbol into the current document.

• Paste a symbol into the current document.

To import symbols using the Library panel:

1 From the Library panel Options pop-up menu, choose Import Symbols.

2 Navigate to the folder containing the file, choose the file, and click Open.

3 Select the symbols to import and click Import.

The imported symbols appear in the Library panel with "(imported)" next to the file type.

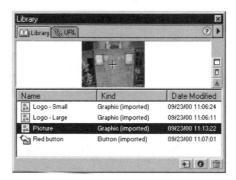

To update a symbol imported from another document:

1 In the original document, modify the symbol and save the file.

2 In the document to which the symbol was imported, select the symbol from the Library panel.

3 Choose Update from the Library panel Options pop-up menu.

Note: To update all imported symbols, select all the symbols in the Library panel and choose Update.

About the URL panel

Assigning a URL to a Web object creates a link to a file. This file can be a Web page. You can assign URLs to hotspots, buttons, and slice objects. When you intend to use the same URLs several times, create a URL library in the URL panel, and store the URLs in the library. Use the URL panel to add, edit, and organize your URLs.

For example, if your Web site contains several navigation buttons to return to your home page, add the URL for your home page to the URL panel. Then assign this URL to each navigation button by selecting it in the URL library. Use Find and Replace to change a URL across multiple documents (see "Finding and replacing" on page 365).

URL libraries are available for all Fireworks documents and are saved between sessions.

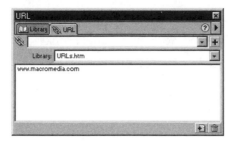

URL panel

Working with URLs

You can group URLs together in libraries. This keeps related URLs together, making them easier to access. You can save URLs in the default URL library, URLs.htm, or in new URL libraries that you create. URLs are stored in an HTML bookmark file in the Fireworks 4\Settings\URL Libraries folder. These file names appear in the URL panel.

To create a new URL library:

1 Choose New URL Library from the URL panel Options pop-up menu.

2 Enter the library name in the text box and click OK.

The new library name appears in the Library pop-up menu in the URL panel.

To add a new URL to a URL library:

1 Choose a library from the Library pop-up menu.

2 Enter a URL in the Link text box.

3 Click the plus (+) sign.

The plus sign adds current URLs to the library.

You can further organize your URLs by adding only those that are in use in your document.

To add used URLs to a URL library:

1 Choose a library from the Library pop-up menu.

2 Choose Add Used URLs to Library from the URL panel Options pop-up menu.

To assign a URL to a Web object:

1 Select the object.

2 Enter the URL:

• From the URL panel Options pop-up menu, choose Add URL. Enter an absolute or relative URL and click OK.

• Enter a URL in the Link text box. Click the plus (+) sign.

The URL appears in the URL preview pane.

See "Attaching a URL to the button" on page 240, "Assigning URLs to hotspots" on page 251, and "Assigning URL links to rollovers" on page 282.

To edit a URL:

1 Select the URL to be edited from the URL preview pane.

2 From the URL panel Options pop-up menu, choose Edit URL.

3 Edit the URL. Select Change All Occurrences in Document if you want to update this link throughout the entire document.

4 Click OK.

To delete a selected URL from the URL preview panel:

Click the Delete URL from library button at the bottom of the URL panel.

To delete all unused URLs from the library:

From the URL panel Options pop-up menu, choose Clear Unused URLs.

To import a URL:

1 From the URL panel Options pop-up menu, choose Import URLs.

2 Select an HTML file and click Open.

All URLs contained within this file are imported.

To export a URL:

1 From the URL panel, select the URL to be exported.

2 From the Options pop-up menu, choose Export URLs.

3 Enter a file name and click Save.

A Fireworks bookmark file is created. This file contains the URLs you have exported.

Entering absolute or relative URLs

When you enter a URL in the URL panel, you can enter an absolute or relative URL:

• If you are linking to a Web page that is beyond your own Web site, you must use an absolute URL.

• If you are linking to a Web page within your Web site, you can use an absolute URL or a relative URL.

Absolute URLs are complete URLs that include the server protocol, which is usually http:// for Web pages. For example, http://www.macromedia.com/support/fireworks is the absolute URL for the Macromedia Fireworks Support Web page. Absolute URLs remain accurate regardless of the location of the source document, but they do not link correctly if the target document is moved.

Relative URLs are relative to the folder containing the source document. These examples show the navigation syntax of relative URLs:

• file.htm links to a file located in the same folder as the source document.

• ../../file.htm links to a file located in the folder two steps above the folder containing the source document. Each ../ represents one step.

• htmldocs/file.htm links to a file located in a folder named htmldocs, which is below the folder containing the source document.

Relative URLs are usually the simplest ones to use for links to files that will always remain in the same folder as the current document.

CHAPTER 13
Creating Buttons and Navigation Bars

In Fireworks, you can create a variety of JavaScript buttons even if you know nothing about JavaScript. The Fireworks Button Editor leads you through the button creation process, automating many button-making tasks. The result is a convenient button symbol that you can position and transform as a single object. You can quickly replicate a button to create a navigation bar and easily update text across the button's frames.

A button is controlled by JavaScript that runs in the background. When you export a button, Fireworks automatically generates the JavaScript necessary to display it in a Web browser. In Macromedia Dreamweaver you can easily insert JavaScript and HTML code from Fireworks into your Web pages. Also, you can cut and paste the code into any HTML file.

A navigation bar is a group of buttons that typically remains, or seems to remain, on a Web page as other parts of the page change.

About buttons

In Fireworks a button is a type of rollover that encapsulates up to four different states. Each state represents a button's appearance in response to a pointer action:

- The Up state is the default or at-rest appearance of the button.

- The Over state is the way the button appears in a Web browser when the pointer is moved over it.

- The Down state is the appearance of the button after it has been clicked, typically as displayed on the destination Web page.

- The Over While Down state is the appearance of the Down-state button when the pointer is moved over it.

You can create a new button from scratch or convert an existing object into a button. The Button Editor lets you edit all the different states, including the active area for triggering the button—a slice that the Button Editor automatically creates.

Many buttons on the Web have only two states—Up and Over. The Over state is useful because it alerts the user that clicking the mouse is likely to result in an action. The Up and Down states communicate dormancy, while the Over While Down state can alert the user that clicking will likely have no further effect.

A button created in the Button Editor is more than just a JavaScript rollover:

- A button is a special type of symbol. You can drag instances of it from the library into your document. For more information on symbols, see "About symbols and instances" on page 226.

- A button is encapsulated. Dragging the button in the document moves all of the components and states associated with it. No more messy multiframe editing.

- A button is easy to edit. Double-click it, and then change it in the Button Editor.

- A selected button has a convenient text box in the Object panel where you can update text on all states simultaneously.

- Like other symbols, buttons have a registration point. The registration point is a center point that helps you align text and the different button states.

Creating buttons

The easiest way to create a JavaScript button or navigation bar is to use the Button Editor. The tips on each panel in the Button Editor help you make design decisions. The Button Editor lets you draw all four button states and set the button's URL settings.

Buttons can be created on any foreground layer of Frame 1. When designing odd-shaped buttons, note that Fireworks uses only the Frame 1 background, regardless of any background set up in another frame.

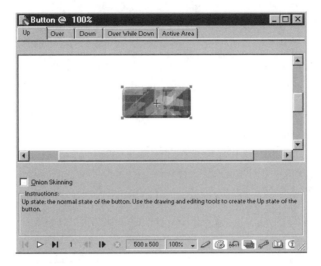

The Button Editor

Creating a button

You can create a button in the Button Editor. If your button is part of a navigation bar, you may need to use all four button states. However, if your button resides on just one Web page, you probably need just the Up state and Over state.

Note: When you create or insert a button, Fireworks places it automatically on Frame 1. Buttons work correctly only on Frame 1. If a button is moved to another frame, it will not work correctly.

To create a button:

1 Choose Insert > New Button to open the Button Editor.

The Button Editor opens to the Up state tab.

2 In the work area of the Button Editor, place the graphic that will appear as the button's Up state:

• Use the drawing and editing tools to create a graphic.

• Import or drag and drop a graphic into the Button Editor.

3 If you want the button to display text, use the Text tool.

Note: It is a good idea to center-align text so that if you need to edit it later, the text maintains its central position on the button.

4 Click the Over tab.

5 Check the Onion Skinning box so you can visually align each button state graphic.

6 Place a graphic for the button's Over state:

• Click Copy Up Graphic to paste a copy of the Up state graphic into the Over window, and then edit it to change its appearance.

• Create a unique Over state graphic.

• Import a graphic into the Over window.

If you want the button to display text, use the Text tool.

Adding a Down state

In a Web browser, the Down state appears when a clicked button remains visible on the Web page. The Down state is often used in navigation bars. Many buttons exist only on one Web page, so your button might not need a Down state or Over While Down state.

To add a Down state to a button:

1 Click the Down tab in the Button Editor.

2 Place a graphic in the Button Editor:

• Click Copy Up Graphic to paste a copy of the Up state graphic into the Over window, and then edit it to change its appearance.

• Create a unique Over state graphic.

• Import a graphic into the Over window.

  If you want the button to display text, use the Text tool.

3 Optionally, if you want the Down state to appear immediately when the Web page loads, check the Show Down State Upon Load box.

Note: When you insert an image in the work area of the Down state, Include Nav Bar Down State is automatically checked.

Adding an Over While Down state

The Over While Down state appears when the pointer moves over the button in the Down state. Like the Down state, the Over While Down state is often used for navigation bars.

To add an Over While Down state to a button:

1 Click the Over While Down tab in the Button Editor.

2 Place a graphic in the Button Editor:

• Click Copy Up Graphic to paste a copy of the Up state graphic into the Over While Down window, and then edit it to change its appearance.

• Create a unique Over While Down state graphic.

• Import a graphic into the Over While Down window.

  If you want the button to display text, use the Text tool.

  Note: When you insert an image in the work area, the Include Nav Bar Over While Down State is automatically checked.

Attaching a URL to the button

Attach a URL to a button to link it to another Web page or Web site, or to an anchor on the same Web page. Use the Link Wizard to enter the button's URL. You can also enter alternative text that displays when the pointer passes over the button, and a status bar message. The Link Wizard also lets you control the button's export settings and naming convention. For more information on naming conventions, see "Auto-naming slices" on page 264.

To attach a URL to a button using the Link Wizard:

1 Click the Active Area tab in the Button Editor.

The Active Area appears, containing a single slice.

Note: By default, the Button Editor automatically creates the slice. When Set Active Area Automatically is checked. the size of the slice expands to cover all the images used to build the button.

2 Click the Link Wizard button to attach a URL to the rollover.

3 Click on the Link tab and enter the URL address in the first field. For information on static versus relative URLs, see "Entering absolute or relative URLs" on page 233.

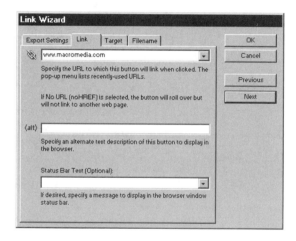

4 If required, enter alternate text and a status bar message in the remaining fields.

5 If you want the URL to point to a target frame or window, click the Target tab and select a target from the list, or enter a target.

6 Click OK.

When you close the Button Editor, the button appears in the Library and an instance of the button appears in the document. When you move or resize the button as a unit, all the states and the active area are moved or resized.

To place additional copies of a button in the document:

Drag the button from the library to the document.

Alternatively, you can drag an instance while holding down Alt (Windows) or Option (Macintosh) to create a new instance.

Changing a button

You can edit a button symbol after you have created it. When you edit a button symbol, all instances reflect the edits.

If you have imported the button from a library or another Fireworks document, editing the button in the current document breaks the link to the previous document. In other words, the changes you make do not affect the original.

For more information on importing and updating buttons, see "Inserting a button from an external source" on page 230.

To edit an existing button symbol:

1 Double-click a button to open the Button Editor.

2 Click the tab for any state.

3 Select the object and edit it as you would any object in the document.

Drawing and editing in the active area

The active area of a button is what triggers the rollover when the pointer is moved over it in a Web browser.

With Set Active Area Automatically selected, Fireworks automatically creates a slice large enough to enclose all the states encapsulated in the button. If you need the active area to be a different size or shape, you can edit the slice accordingly. If you resize the slice or draw another one, Set Active Area Automatically turns off.

Web objects in a button's Active Area tab appear on the Web Layer when the Button Editor is open.

To draw a slice or hotspot Web object:

1 Double-click a button.

2 Click the Active Area tab of the Button Editor.

3 Deselect Set Active Area Automatically.

4 Select a Slice or Hotspot tool and draw in the Button Editor.

To edit a button's active area:

1 Double-click a button.

2 Click the Active Area tab.

3 Use the Pointer tool, Slice tool, or Polygon Slice tool to move, reshape, or redraw the current active area.

Editing button text

In Fireworks, it is easy to change the text on a rollover button without editing each rollover frame.

To simultaneously change the text on all states of a button:

1 Select the button in the document.

2 In the Object panel, type the new text in Button Text, and press Enter.

The text updates on all states of the button.

To simultaneously change text on all states of a button in the Button Editor:

1 Change text in the top text block on any state of the button.

A message appears asking if you want to update the text in the other button states.

2 Click Yes.

Using bevel effects to draw button states

You can use any object to create a rollover state. However, because buttons are a common type of JavaScript rollover, Fireworks includes Live Effects presets to simplify the creation of common button appearances. Apply an Inner Bevel or Outer Bevel effect to an object, and then choose Raised, Highlighted, Inset, or Inverted from the Button Presets pop-up menu in the Effect panel.

Button Presets effect	Description
Raised	The bevel appears raised from the underlying objects.
Highlighted	The button's colors lighten.
Inset	The bevel appears sunken into the underlying objects.
Inverted	The bevel appears sunken into the underlying objects and the colors lighten.

For example, if you are creating a four-state button, you could apply Raised to the Up state graphic, Highlighted to the Down state graphic, and so on.

For more information about Live Effects, see "Applying a Live Effect" on page 194.

Inserting buttons from the library

The library helps you streamline the creation of consistent buttons for your Web site. You can create an original button symbol and use it as the source for all of your site's buttons.

To use the button symbol in the current document, import it into the library. Then drag the symbol onto the canvas to create new instances.

Note: Editing an instance breaks the link between it and the original.

If at some point you need to change the buttons on your Web site, you can just edit the original symbol and then use the Library panel's Update command to implement the changes in each of your documents. For more information about using the Library panel, see "About symbols and instances" on page 226.

Importing a copy of a button symbol into the current document

To import a copy of a button symbol into the current document:

1 Select Window > Library to open the Library panel.

2 Choose Import Symbols from the Options pop-up menu.

3 Locate the button symbol file or Fireworks document you created earlier, and click Open.

4 Click Import to bring the copy into the library.

Inserting a button from the library

To insert a button from the library:

1 Open the Library panel.

2 Drag the button symbol onto the document.

Importing a preinstalled button symbol

Fireworks comes with several button styles.

To import a preinstalled button into the current document:

1 Choose Insert > Libraries > Buttons.

2 Select the button you want to use from the symbols list.

3 Click Import.

Creating a navigation bar with buttons

A navigation bar, also called a *nav bar*, is a group of buttons that typically remain, or seem to remain, on a Web page as other parts of the page change. Use navigation bars to create a consistent navigation aid throughout your Web site. An easy way to create a navigation bar is to duplicate a button several times and change the text and the URL link on each one. The nav bar thus looks the same from Web page to Web page, but the links are specific to the function of each page.

Although nav bar buttons generally look identical, each should be able to display unique text. The problem is to create a button symbol that allows unique text but can still be used to update the appearance of all the buttons on your Web site. You can resolve the problem by nesting button symbols. Build one button symbol containing only the graphic elements and no text. Then build a second button that takes its graphic information from the first and has its text on an unshared layer. Duplicate this button to create your navigation bar.

To create a navigation bar using nested symbols:

1 Create a button with only the graphic elements and no text.

The button appears automatically in the library.

2 Select Insert > New Button.

3 The Button Editor displays the Up state work area.

4 Drag the original button from the library into the new button's Up state work area.

5 In the Layers panel, select a layer that is not a shared layer and is above the layer the original button is placed on.

6 Add text to the new button for each button state.

7 In the Down and Over While Down tabs, select the Include options as appropriate.

8 Close the Button Editor.

9 In the document, duplicate the button.

10 For each duplicate button, change the text using the Object panel.

Note: You can nest a series of buttons in a symbol to make a portable navigation bar.

To update the graphics for all the buttons in a simple navigation bar:

Use the Button Editor to edit the original button (the button without text).

Fireworks updates the other buttons to reflect the new appearance. Because the text is unique to the newer button symbols, it is not affected when the graphic is updated.

You can also create a more complex navigation bar using the Down and Over While Down states.

Converting Fireworks rollovers into buttons

You can create buttons from rollovers that you have previously created (see "Creating Rollovers" on page 271). You can convert these rollovers, including ones from previous versions of Fireworks, into buttons to take advantage of button symbol conveniences.

The components of the rollover convert to a button, and the new button is placed in the library. The button automatically creates its own slice, so the rollover's hotspot or slice is no longer needed.

To convert a Fireworks rollover into a button:

1 In the Frames panel, choose Show All Frames from the Onion Skinning pop-up menu.

2 Select all components of the rollover.

3 Choose Insert > Convert to Symbol.

4 Enter a name, choose Type: Button, and click OK.

Inserting a button from an external source

You can choose a button from a Fireworks library or from another Fireworks document. When you import a button from an external source, Fireworks remembers the source. Then, if the source file changes, you can update the imported button to reflect the changed original.

To insert a ready-made button from a library into the document:

1 Choose Insert > Libraries > Other and choose the library or Fireworks document from which you want to insert a button.

2 Choose a symbol from the library and click Import.

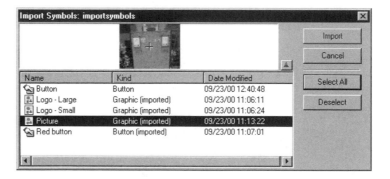

To update an imported button:

1 In the Library panel, select the button symbol to update.

2 Choose Update from the Options pop-up menu.

Fireworks updates the imported button to match the appearance of the original button.

CHAPTER 14
Using Hotspots and Slices

Hotspots and slices are the primary tools you use to create interactive objects like rollovers and image maps.

Hotspots and slices are called Web objects; that is, they exist not as images, but ultimately as HTML code that assigns interactivity to your document. You can view, select, and rename them through the Web Layer in the Layers panel.

This chapter describes the basic concepts you need to understand to create hotspots and slices.

Creating hotspots and image maps

Web designers use hotspots and image maps extensively, to make navigating Web sites much easier. A *hotspot* is an area of a Web graphic that links to a URL. An image map is nothing more than a graphic upon which several hotspots have been placed. Fireworks lets you generate hotspots in virtually any shape you need, and allows you to export the HTML code to reproduce your image map on the Web.

Note: Because an image map is just a collection of hotspots over a graphic, this section deals only with creating hotspots. See "Exporting image maps" on page 254 for special considerations on exporting.

After you identify areas on a source graphic that would make good navigation points, you create the hotspots and then assign URL links to them. There are two ways to create hotspots:

- You can draw the hotspot around a target area in the graphic using the Rectangle, Circle, or Polygon (odd-shaped) Hotspot tools.

- You can select an object and insert the hotspot over it.

To create a rectangular or circular hotspot:

1   Choose the Rectangle Hotspot or Circle Hotspot tool.

2   Drag the Hotspot tool to draw a hotspot over an area of the graphic. Hold down Alt (Windows) or Option (Macintosh) to draw from a center point.

A hotspot need not always be a rectangle or a circle. You can also create polygon hotspots composed of many points. This can be a good approach when working with intricate images.

To create an odd-shaped hotspot:

 1   Choose the Polygon Hotspot tool.

2   Click to place vector points, much as you would draw straight segments with the Pen tool. Whether the path is open or closed, the fill defines the hotspot area.

To create a hotspot by tracing one or more selected objects:

1   Choose Insert > Hotspot.

If you selected more than one object, a dialog box asks whether you want to create a single rectangular hotspot covering all objects or multiple hotspots, one for each object.

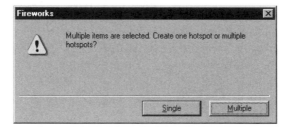

2   Click Single or Multiple. The Web Layer displays the new hotspot or hotspots.

Another way to create a polygon hotspot is to convert a circle hotspot into a polygon hotspot, and then drag the points. For more information, see "Changing hotspots" on page 252.

Assigning URLs to hotspots

A URL, or Uniform Resource Locator, is the address of a specific page or file on the Internet. When you assign a URL to a hotspot, the user can navigate to that address by clicking on the hotspot in their Web browser. Use the Object panel to assign a URL to a hotspot.

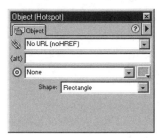

To assign a URL to a selected hotspot:

1 Choose Window > Object to open the Object panel.

2 Enter a URL in the Link text box.

3 Optionally, enter alternate text, which appears in a Web browser as the Web page downloads.

4 Enter an HTML frame name or choose a reserved target from the Target pop-up menu. A target is an alternate Web page frame or Web browser window in which the linked file opens (see "Choosing a Target option" on page 252).

5 If you wish, choose an alternative hotspot color from the Overlay Color pop-up window. This can be helpful in organizing Web objects.

Organizing URLs with the URL panel

If you intend to use the same URLs several times, you can create a URL library in the URL panel and then store your URLs in the library. For more information, see "Using Libraries, Styles, and URLs" on page 223.

Specifying alt text

Alt (alternate) text appears on the image placeholder while the image is downloading from the Web or in place of a graphic if it fails to download. In some newer versions of browsers, the text also appears next to the pointer as a tooltip.

To specify alt text:

In the Object panel, type the text in the alt text box.

Choosing a Target option

A target is an alternate Web page frame or Web browser window in which the linked document opens. You can specify a target for a selected hotspot or slice in the Object panel Target text box.

To specify a target:

• Type the name of the HTML frame in which to open the linked document.

• Choose a reserved target from the Target pop-up menu.

These are the reserved target options:

• **_blank** loads the linked documents in a new, unnamed browser window.

• **_parent** loads the linked document in the parent frameset or window of the frame that contains the link. If the frame containing the link is not nested, then the linked document loads into the full browser window.

• **_self** loads the linked document in the same frame or window as the link. This target is implied, so you usually need not specify it.

• **_top** loads the linked document in the full browser window, thereby removing all frames.

Changing hotspots

Web objects have points and paths like vector objects. Use the Pointer, Subselection, and Transform tools to reshape or resize a hotspot. Other editing tools, such as the Freeform tool, do not edit hotspots. For information on using the Transform and Skew tools, see "Working with Objects" on page 85.

To edit a selected hotspot using points:

1   Choose the Pointer tool or Subselection tool.

2   Drag the points:

• A rectangle hotspot changes position and dimensions but remains rectangular.

• A circle hotspot changes position and diameter but remains circular.

• A polygon hotspot changes shape according to the location of the moved point.

To convert a selected hotspot into a rectangle, circle, or polygon hotspot:

1   Choose Window > Object to open the Object panel.

2   Choose Rectangle, Circle, or Polygon from the Shape pop-up menu.

Applying drag-and-drop behaviors to hotspots

You can use drag-and-drop behaviors to configure a hotspot to trigger a disjoint rollover effect. Drag-and-drop behaviors are applied to hotspots the same way as they are to slices. For more information, see "Creating Rollovers" on page 271.

Note: A hotspot can only trigger a disjoint rollover. It cannot be the target of a drag-and-drop behavior coming from another hotspot or slice.

Once you have attached a drag-and-drop behavior to a hotspot, the connecting blue line remains visible only while the hotspot is selected.

Exporting image maps

After you build an image map of hotspots, you must export the image map before it actually functions in a Web browser.

Fireworks produces only client-side image maps when exporting. Exporting a client-side image map generates the graphic file and the HTML file containing map information for hotspots and corresponding URL links.

Exporting a sliced image map typically generates many graphic files. For more information about slicing, see "Creating slices" on page 256.

To export an image map:

1 Optimize the graphic to prepare it for export.

   For more information, see "Optimizing Graphics" on page 307.

2 Choose File > Export.

3 Navigate to the folder where you want to place the HTML file, and name the file.

   If you have already built a local file structure for your Web site, you can save the graphic in the appropriate folder for the site from here.

4 For Save as type, choose HTML and Images.

5 For HTML, choose Export HTML File.

6 For Slices, choose None.

7 If necessary, check the Put Images in Subfolder box and browse to the appropriate folder.

8 Click Save to export the image map.

You can select Copy to Clipboard from the HTML list and paste the image map into Dreamweaver or another HTML editor.

When you are exporting files, Fireworks can use HTML comments to clearly label the beginning and end of code for image maps and other Web features created in Fireworks. By default, HTML comments are not included in the code. To include them, select Include HTML Comments in the HTML Setup dialog.

After you have exported HTML, the Update HTML feature delivers Fireworks-generated HTML to the right location within HTML files in your Web site. For information on placing image maps into Dreamweaver or another HTML editor, see "Using Dreamweaver and Fireworks Together" on page 349.

About slicing

Slicing cuts up a Fireworks document into different segments and exports each segment to a separate file for downloading. There are three reasons why it is useful to take this step: to optimize an image's file size, to create interactivity, and to swap out parts of an image. You can also use slicing to replace part of an image with HTML text.

Optimizing an image

One challenge of Web graphic design is ensuring that images are small enough to download quickly. Slicing provides a powerful tool to meet this challenge by letting you cut up your graphic into smaller chunks, which a user's computer can handle more efficiently. Fireworks enables you to convert each individual slice into the most appropriate file format and then export it in a variety of HTML styles (Dreamweaver and Microsoft Frontpage, for example).

See "Optimizing Graphics" on page 307 and "Exporting" on page 329 for more information on optimizing and exporting respectively.

Assigning interactivity to areas of your document

You can assign interactivity to slices, creating areas that respond when the user's pointer passes over or clicks them. For example, an image may change when the pointer passes over it, giving a rollover effect, or the pointer may change to an open hand, indicating a hyperlink to another Web page.

You can use slices to create many interactive effects, such as buttons, navigation bars, and rollovers.

You can also use slices to insert HTML-based text into a graphic so that the text remains editable.

Swapping out part of an image

Another reason for slicing is to swap out parts of an image that change frequently without having to download the entire image. For example, your Web site may include a page that recognizes the employee of the month. Each month you can update the slice containing the employee picture without updating the other graphics on the page.

Creating slices

You can create slices in either of two basic ways, depending on your purpose. You can automatically insert a rectangular slice over the object or you can draw a slice. If you want to make an entire object interactive, then you can simply select the object and insert a slice on top of it. This step encloses the entire object in a rectangular slice, regardless of the object's shape.

If a hotspot is selected, you can convert it to a slice by selecting Insert > Slice.

If you want to convert a smaller part of the object into an interactive area, cut the object into a number of slices, or convert several objects, then you can use the Slice tool or Polygon Slice tool to draw slices. When you draw a slice onto all or part of an image, that area becomes a slice object.

The red lines extending from the slice object are slice guides, which determine the boundaries of the separate image files into which the object is split on export.

Note: You can copy and paste slice objects into other Fireworks documents.

To insert a rectangular slice based on an object:

1   Select the object.

    You can select more than one object by holding down Shift while selecting.

2   Choose Insert > Slice. The slice is a rectangle whose area includes the outermost pixels of the selected object.

3 If you have selected more than one object, choose an option in the dialog box:

• Single creates a single slice object that covers all selected objects.

• Multiple creates a slice object for each selected object.

To draw a rectangular slice object:

  1 Choose the Slice tool.

2 Drag to draw the slice object. The slice object and slice guides appear on the Web Layer.

Overlapping slices

Occasionally, slices meant to be drawn close to each other end up overlapping. Instead of creating extra slices in the overlapping areas, Fireworks 4 considers only the frontmost of the slices as the active slice in the overlapping region. Therefore fewer extraneous sliced graphics are exported. The problem of overlapping slices is normally due to simple oversight. It is recommended that you redraw or edit such slices to eliminate any overlap.

Assigning URLs to slices

You can assign a URL to a slice using the Object panel.

1 Choose Window > Object to open the Object panel.

2 Enter a URL in the Link text box.

3 Optionally, enter alt text.

4 Enter an HTML frameset name or choose a reserved target from the Target pop-up menu. A target is an alternate Web page frame or Web browser window in which the linked file opens (see "Choosing a Target option" on page 252).

Creating text slices

A text slice designates an area of a sliced image where ordinary HTML text appears in the browser. A text slice does not export any pixel image data; it exports HTML text that appears in the table cell defined by the slice.

Text slices are useful if you want to quickly update messages that appear on your Web site without having to create new graphics.

To create a text slice:

1 Draw a slice object.

2 In the Object panel, choose Text from the Type pop-up menu.

3 Type your text in the large text box at the bottom of the Object panel.

4 To format text in a text slice:

• Use HTML text formatting tags in the text box of the Object panel.

• Use HTML text formatting tags in the HTML file that you plan to transfer to your Web site after exporting the image containing the text slice.

The text in a text slice does not appear in your Fireworks PNG file, but it appears in a Web browser when previewing in a browser and after exporting HTML.

Note: Text created in this way may vary in appearance when viewed in different browsers and on different operating systems.

Creating nonrectangular slices

Rectangular slices may not be sufficient for building some rollovers. If a rollover contains slice objects that overlap or have irregular shapes, then a rectangular slice may swap unwanted background information along with the swap image. Fireworks solves this problem by allowing you to draw slices in any shape. These slices are called *polygon slices*. They are usually required only when rollover images would otherwise overlap.

You can also convert vector paths to slices to create irregular slice shapes.

To create a polygon slice automatically:

1 Select the object.

2 Choose Insert > Hotspot.

3 Choose Insert > Slice.

The hotspot converts to a polygon slice.

To manually draw a polygon slice object:

1 Choose the Polygon Slice tool.

2 Click to place the vector points of the polygon. The Polygon Slice tool draws only straight line segments.

3 When drawing a polygon slice object around objects with soft edges, be sure to include the entire object to avoid creating unwanted hard edges in the slice graphic.

4 To quit the Polygon Slice tool, choose an alternative tool from the Tools panel. You do not have to click the first point again to close the polygon.

Note: Be careful not to overuse polygon slices, as they require more JavaScript code than similar rectangular slices. A high number of polygon slices could adversely affect Web browser processing time.

To convert a vector path into a slice:

1 Select a vector path.

2 Choose Insert > Hotspot.

3 Choose Insert > Slice.

A slice is generated that conforms to the shape of the vector path.

Displaying slices and slice guides

If an object is covered by a slice, you may need to hide the slice in order to edit the object. Hiding a slice renders the slice invisible. You can turn off all the Web objects in the document or only specific ones.

Slice guides appear automatically when you draw a slice object. The slice guides show how Fireworks will cut the image when the slices are exported. You cannot edit slice guides like normal guides, but they redraw when you add, move, or edit slice objects. For information on normal guides, see "Using rulers, guides, and the grid" on page 80.

Slices and slice guides are visible in Preview, although slices show as a white overlay.

You can organize slices by assigning a unique color to each slice object. You can also change the color of slice guides.

To hide particular slices and hotspots:

Click the eye icon next to the individual Web objects in the Layers panel.

Note: Click in the same (now blank) square to turn visibility back on. The eye icon reappears when Web objects are visible again.

To hide or show all hotspots, slices, and guides:

• Click the Hide Hotspots and Slices or Show Hotspots and Slices button in the Tools panel.

• Click the eye icon next to the Web Layer in the Layers panel.

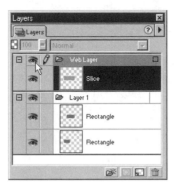

To hide or show slice guides in any document view:

Choose View > Slice Guides.

To change the color of a selected slice object:

In the Object panel, choose a new color from the Slice color box pop-up window.

To change the color of slice guides:

1 Choose View > Guides > Edit Guides.

2 Choose a new color from the Slice Color pop-up menu.

Using the slice overlay

Use the slice overlay to differentiate the area of the document currently being optimized from the rest of the document. For more information, see "Optimizing Graphics" on page 307.

Viewing and naming slices in the Layers panel

Managing slices and other Web objects in your document is easy using the Web Layer in the Layers panel. The Web Layer displays all the Web objects in the document so that you can select, view, and name each one.

To view and select a slice using the Layers panel:

1 Choose Windows > Layers to open the Layers panel.

2 Expand the Web Layer by clicking on the plus sign (Windows) or triangle (Macintosh).

The full list of Web objects currently in your document is displayed beneath the Web Layer.

3 Click to select a slice.

The slice becomes highlighted in the Web Layer and on the document canvas.

Slicing cuts an image into pieces. Each piece exports as a separate file, so each file must have a name. If an image has more than one frame, each piece in each frame is a separate, uniquely named file.

An image can be cut into multiple slices.

Fireworks automatically names each slice file upon export. You can accept the default naming convention, change the convention, or enter custom names for each slice:

- Click the name of the slice in the Web Layer and enter a new name.

- Choose Auto-Name Slices in the Object panel to name the files using the current naming convention. See "Custom-naming slice files" on page 267 for more information on naming conventions.

- Deselect Auto-Name Slices and enter a name for each slice in the Slice Name text box.

Naming slices through the Web Layer

The easiest way to name an individual slice is through the Web Layer in the Layers panel.

To name a layer through the Web Layer:

1 Choose Window > Layers to open the Layers panel.

2 Expand the Web Layer by clicking on the plus sign (Windows) or triangle (Macintosh).

   The full list of Web objects currently in your document is displayed beneath the Web Layer.

3 Double-click the default name of the Web object (either Slice or Hotspot).

4 Type the new name.

Auto-naming slices

If you do not want to enter custom names for each slice, you can let Fireworks assign a unique name to each slice file automatically, based on the default naming convention.

Fireworks lets you build your own naming convention using a wide range of naming options. You can create a naming convention that comprises up to six elements. An element can consist of any of the following auto-naming options.

Option	Description
None	No name is applied to the element.
doc.name	The element takes the name of the document.
"slice"	You can insert the word "slice" into the slice's naming convention.
Slice # **(1,2,3...)** Slice # **(01,02,03...)** Slice # **(A,B,C...)** Slice # **(a,b,c...)**	The element is labeled numerically or alphabetically, according to the particular style you choose.
row/column (r3_c2, r4_c7...)	**Row (r##)** and **Col (c##)** designate the rows and columns of the table that Web browsers use to reconstruct a sliced image. You can use this information in the naming convention.
Underscore Period Space Hyphen	The element uses any of these characters typically as separators between other elements.

For example, if the document name is mydoc, the naming convention doc.name + "slice" + Slice # (A,B,C...) results in a slice called mydocsliceA. Chances are that you will never require a naming convention that uses all six elements.

To automatically name slice files:

1 Select one or more slices.

2 In the Object panel, choose Auto-Name Slices.

3 When you export your sliced image, enter a name in the File Name (Windows) or Name (Macintosh) text box in the Export dialog box. Do not add a file extension. Fireworks automatically adds file extensions to slice files upon export.

You can change the naming convention in the HTML Setup dialog box.

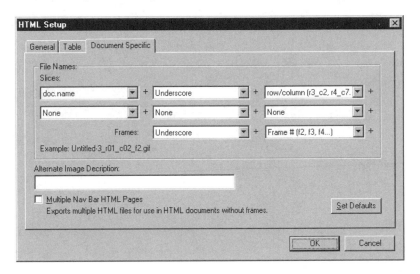

HTML Setup dialog box

To change the default auto-naming convention:

1   Choose File > HTML Setup to open the HTML Setup dialog box.

2   Click the Document Specific tab.

3   In the File Names section, build your new naming convention by selecting from the desired lists.

For example, the naming convention doc.name + "slice" + Slice # (A,B,C...) would appear as follows:

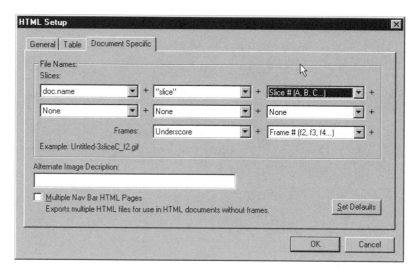

Note: To save all information in the HTML Setup dialog box as the default settings for new Fireworks documents, click Set Defaults.

Custom-naming slice files

You may want to use specific names for slices, so you can easily identify slice files in your Web site file structure. For example, if you have a button on a navigation bar that returns to the Home page, you could name the slice "home."

To enter a custom name for a selected slice:

1 In the Object panel, deselect Auto-Name Slices.

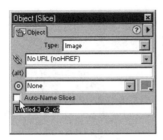

2 Enter a name in the Slice Name text box. If you do not enter a name, Fireworks reverts to auto-naming. Do not add a file extension to the base name. Fireworks automatically adds file extensions to slice files upon export.

If a slice has more than one frame, by default Fireworks adds a number to each frame's file. For example, if you enter the custom slice file name "home" for a three-state rollover, then Fireworks names the Up state graphic home.gif, the Over state graphic home_f2.gif, and the Down state graphic home_f3.gif. You can create your own naming convention for multiframe slices using the HTML Setup dialog box.

To change the default auto-naming convention of a multiframe slice file:

1 Choose File > HTML Setup to open the HTML Setup dialog box.

2 Click the Document Specific tab.

3 In the File Names section, beside Frames, build the appropriate naming convention from the two lists.

For example, the naming convention Underscore + Rollover (over, down, overdown) adds "_over" to the name of an Over state slice file. The name of the Over state for mydocsliceA would be mydocsliceA_over.

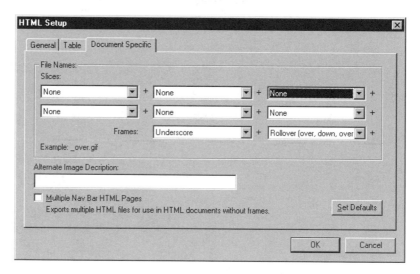

Note: To save a naming convention to use for new documents, click Set Defaults in the Document Specific tab.

Using nested tables and spacers

In the HTML Setup dialog box, under the Table tab, you can choose how the table in your Web page will be constructed. You can also determine how browsers reassemble tables using spacers or nested tables when slicing (see "Using nested tables and spacers" on page 268).

Updating a slice within an HTML document

You can update the image under a single slice of an existing sliced image without having to export and upload the entire sliced image. It is recommended that you use custom slice naming so that you can easily locate the replacement slice.

To update a single slice of an image:

1 Hide the slice and edit the area underneath.

2 Show the slice again and select it.

3 Choose File > Export.

4 Check Selected Slices Only.

5 Export the slice into the same folder as the original slice using the same base name.

If you retain the original file name for the updated slice and upload the slice to the same place on your Web site where the original came from, the new slice replaces the original slice in the image.

15

CHAPTER 15
Creating Rollovers

The Button Editor lets you create buttons using a single slice to convey visual effects. But you may need more complex rollover behavior than you can create in the Button Editor. For example, you may want to create a disjoint rollover that displays an image away from the pointer, or a customizable pop-up menu that appears as the pointer passes over a graphic.

This chapter describes how to build simple and disjoint rollovers using slices and frames. It also describes how to create pop-up menus.

The basic building blocks for creating rollovers in Fireworks are slice objects, hotspot objects, and drag-and-drop behaviors. Drag-and-drop behaviors let you create rollover and swap image effects that link slices and hotspots to target slices. For more information on hotspots and slices, see "Using Hotspots and Slices" on page 249.

About rollovers

JavaScript rollovers are graphics that change appearance in a Web browser when you move the pointer over them or click them. They include buttons and swap images.

In whatever form, rollovers all work the same way: one graphic triggers the display of another when the pointer rolls over or clicks it. Rollover images can be placed on two or more frames. The trigger is always a Web object, that is, a slice or hotspot. Web objects can have one or more behaviors attached to them.

The simplest rollover swaps an image on Frame 1 with an image directly below it on Frame 2. You can build more complicated rollovers: swap image rollovers can swap an image from any frame; disjoint rollovers display an image away from the pointer.

Creating simple rollovers using the Behaviors panel

A simple rollover is one in which an image appears beneath the pointer when the pointer rolls over or clicks a trigger image. This is the easiest rollover to build because it requires only one slice, since the trigger and target areas of the canvas are the same.

A simple rollover always takes the image from Frame 2.

Setting up the slice, images, and frames

You create a simple rollover in two stages. The first stage involves setting up the slice, the two images that create the effect, and the frames they reside on. The two images that comprise the rollover are located in the same space on the canvas, but are on different frames.

To set up the slice, images, and frames for a simple rollover:

1 Select the image you want to trigger the rollover effect.

2 Choose Insert > Slice to attach a slice to the image.

3 Create a new frame using the Frames panel:

Choose Window > Frames, and click the New/Duplicate Frame button.

Note: If you already have a second frame, then you may not need to create another one.

4 Select the new frame in the Frames panel, if it is not already highlighted.

5 Place the second image in the space on the canvas occupied by the slice:

• Use the drawing and editing tools to create a graphic.

• Import or drag a graphic onto the slice.

Applying the simple rollover behavior to the slice

When you have set up the images and frames, apply the simple rollover behavior to the slice.

To apply the simple rollover behavior:

1 Select the slice.

   Note: Slices are shared between frames. If you have turned on Show Hotspots and Slices, slices remain visible no matter what frame you are working on.

2 Choose Window > Behaviors to open the Behaviors panel.

3 Select Simple Rollover from the Add Action (+) pop-up menu.

Using the Behaviors panel

You can use the Behaviors panel to create, edit, and delete behaviors attached to a selected slice or hotspot.

The Behaviors panel lets you create other types of effects and lets you specify the type of event (such as clicking) that triggers the effects. The Behaviors panel also gives you more flexibility in editing existing behaviors.

To attach a behavior to a selected slice or hotspot using the Behaviors panel:

1 Click the Add Action (+) button in the Behaviors panel.

Add a behavior.

Remove a selected behavior

2 Select the behavior from the Add Action (+) pop-up menu.

These behaviors are available:

- **Simple Rollover** creates a rollover using Frame 1 as the Up state and Frame 2 as the Over state. Once you select this behavior, you have to create an image in a second frame, using the same slice, to create the Over state. The Simple Rollover option is actually a behavior group containing Swap Image and Swap Image Restore.

- **Swap Image** replaces the image under the specified slice with the contents of another frame under the slice or the contents of an external file.

- **Swap Image Restore** restores the rollover to its default appearance on Frame 1.

- **Set Nav Bar Image** sets a slice to be a part of a navigation bar. Each slice that is part of the navigation bar must have this behavior. The Set Nav Bar Image option is actually a behavior group containing Nav Bar Over, Nav Bar Down, and Nav Bar Restore. For more information, see "Creating Buttons and Navigation Bars" on page 235.

- **Nav Bar Over** specifies the Over state for the currently selected slice when it is part of a navigation bar and optionally specifies the Over While Down state.

- **Nav Bar Down** specifies a Down state for the currently selected slice when it is part of a navigation bar.

- **Nav Bar Restore** restores all the other slices in the navigation bar to their Up state.

- **Set Pop-Up Menu** attaches a pop-up menu to a slice or hotspot.

- **Set Text of Status Bar** lets you define text for display in the status bar at the bottom of most browser windows.

Behaviors in Fireworks 4 are compatible with Dreamweaver 4 behaviors. When you export a Fireworks rollover to Dreamweaver 4, you can edit Fireworks behaviors using the Dreamweaver 4 Behaviors panel.

Note: Pop-up menus work in Dreamweaver 4, but they must be edited in Fireworks.

To change the mouse event that activates the behavior:

1 Select the trigger slice or hotspot containing the behavior you want to modify.

All the behaviors associated with that Web object are displayed in the Behaviors panel.

2 Select the behavior you want to edit.

All selected behaviors, except Simple Rollover, show a list of associated events.

3 Select a new event from the list.

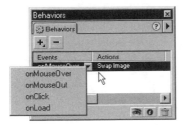

Note: The OnLoad event triggers the behavior as soon as the Web page is loaded. For example, if you change the event that triggers a disjoint rollover to OnLoad, the swap image displays immediately.

Using drag-and-drop behaviors to create swap image effects

Use drag-and-drop behaviors to create swap image rollovers. Drag-and-drop behaviors are a fast and efficient way to specify what happens to a hotspot or slice when the pointer passes over it. Until Fireworks 4, you had to go through the Behaviors panel to set up swap image events. Drag-and-drop behaviors are a faster method that lets you create rollovers by dragging the drag-and-drop behavior handle from a triggering slice or hotspot onto a target slice. The drag-and-drop behavior handle is a circle with cross hairs located in the center of the slice.

When you select a trigger Web object, Fireworks displays all its behavior relationships. By default, a drag-and-drop behavior relationship is represented by a blue line.

Creating a swap image rollover using a single slice

Use a swap image rollover with one slice to create a button or an image that seems to change when the pointer passes over or clicks it.

To create this type of rollover, you drag a drag-and-drop behavior line from the slice's behavior handle to the edge of the slice. You can take the swap image from any frame.

There are two parts to creating a swap image: the first part involves setting up the slice, the rollover image, and the frame on which the rollover image resides.

To set up the slice, rollover image, and frame for a swap image rollover:

1 Select the image you want to trigger the rollover effect.

2 Choose Insert > Slice to attach a slice to the image.

3 Create a new frame using the Frames panel:

Choose Window > Frames, and click the New/Duplicate Frame button.

4 Select the new frame in the Frames panel, if it is not already highlighted.

5 Place the second image in the space on the canvas occupied by the slice:

• Use the drawing and editing tools to create a graphic.

• Import or drag a graphic into the correct position on the slice.

Attaching drag-and-drop behaviors

The second stage is to attach the swap image behavior to the slice.

To finish creating the swap image using drag-and-drop behaviors:

1 Select the slice covering the trigger area.

Note: You can select the slice in any frame.

2 Place the pointer over the drag-and-drop behavior handle in the center of the slice. The pointer changes into a hand.

3 Click and hold down the mouse button so that the pointer changes to a fist.

4 Drag the fist to the edge of the slice.

A blue drag-and-drop behavior line loops from the center to the top left corner of the slice.

The Swap Image dialog displays.

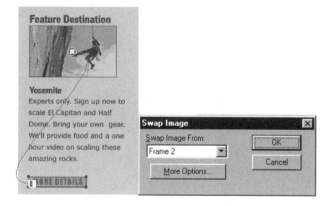

5 From the Swap Image From pop-up menu, select the frame the rollover image resides on.

6 Choose File > Preview in Browser or click the Preview tab to view the rollover as it would appear in a browser.

Creating disjoint rollovers using drag-and-drop behaviors

A disjoint rollover is slightly more complicated than a swap image rollover that uses a single slice. In response to a pointer rolling over or clicking a trigger image, an image appears in a different location on the Web page. Each image resides on its own frame. Disjoint rollovers therefore require two Web objects: a slice or hotspot object to trigger the rollover, and a target slice object covering the area you want to swap out.

You have three options when choosing a Web object for the trigger:

* If the trigger area is not a rollover or does not change appearance itself, then draw a hotspot.

* If you intend for the trigger area to change appearance, draw a slice.

* If you intend to use the Button Editor to build the trigger, place a button symbol. You can attach behaviors to button symbols the same way you attach them to slice and hotspot objects.

As with swap images that use just one slice, creating a disjoint rollover involves two parts. First, you have to set up the trigger and target Web objects and the frame on which the swap image resides. Second, you link the trigger to the target slice with a drag-and-drop behavior line.

Setting up the Web objects, images, and frames

For a disjoint rollover to work, you must locate the two images on separate frames.

To set up the Web objects, target, and frames for a disjoint rollover:

1 Select the image you want to trigger the disjoint rollover effect.

2 Attach a Web object to the image:

* Choose Insert > Slice or Insert > Hotspot to enclose the entire image with a Web object.

* Use the Slice tool or Hotspot tool to draw the Web object over a particular part of the image.

3 Create a new frame using the Frames panel:

Choose Window > Frames, and click the New/Duplicate Frame button.

4 Place the target rollover image.

5 Choose Insert > Slice to attach a slice to the target rollover image.

Using drag-and-drop behaviors to create the disjoint rollover

The second part of creating a disjoint rollover is linking the trigger Web object to the target slice with a drag-and-drop behavior line.

To set up a swap image behavior for a disjoint rollover:

1 Select the Web object covering the trigger area.

2 Place the pointer over the drag-and-drop behavior handle in the center of the Web object.

The pointer changes into a hand.

3 Click and hold down the mouse button so that the pointer changes to a fist.

4 Drag the fist to the slice covering the image you want to swap out.

The line loops from the center of the trigger Web object to the top left corner of the target slice, and the Swap Image From dialog box appears.

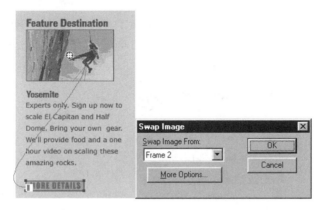

5 From the Swap Image From pop-up menu, select the frame that the rollover image resides on.

Deleting drag-and-drop behaviors

You can delete drag-and-drop behavior relationships (those blue lines) using the Pointer tool.

To delete a drag-and-drop behavior attached to a hotspot or slice:

1 Select the hotspot or slice.

The Web object displays any drag-and-drop behavior relationships (blue lines) associated with it.

2 Click on the blue line you want to delete.

A dialog box appears asking you to confirm that you want to delete the swap image behavior.

3 Click OK to delete the behavior.

Assigning URL links to rollovers

If you want your rollover to link to another Web page, assign a URL link to the rollover's hotspot or slice object.

To assign a URL link to a selected hotspot or slice object:

*   In the Object panel, choose or enter a URL in the URL link pop-up menu.

*   Choose a URL from the URL panel.

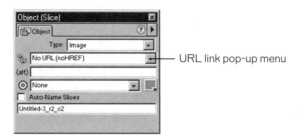

URL link pop-up menu

Creating pop-up menus

Pop-up menus are menus that display as the pointer rolls over or clicks a triggering slice or hotspot. They give your pages a great deal more navigational flexibility without long download times. You can define the appearance of the pop-up menu so that it matches the overall look and feel of your Web site. A pop-up menu is similar to a table: each menu entry is like a table cell. You can customize the menu by choosing from a selection of font types, cell colors, and background image styles.

The Set Pop-up Menu wizard walks you through building the menus from start to finish. Menus are created in two stages. In the first stage you can enter menu text, create submenus, and specify the URL addresses the menu entries point to.

The second stage lets you define the menu's appearance and lets you specify a background image, a font, and the Up and Over states for the menu entries.

Creating pop-up menu entries

The following steps show how to create basic menu entries for a pop-up menu.

To create pop-up menu entries:

1 Place a slice or hotspot onto the object you want to use to trigger the pop-up menu.

2 Choose Insert > Pop-Up Menu.

The Set Pop-Up Menu Wizard displays.

3 Enter a menu item in the Text field.

4 Specify the Web address of the menu item in the Link field.

5 If necessary, set a Web target.

6 Click the Add Menu (+) button to add the entry to the preview list.

7 To create a submenu, select the menu item you want to demote from the preview list, and click the Indent Menu button. To return it to menu-item level, click the Outdent button.

Note: You cannot demote the first item in the list to a submenu.

8 Repeat Steps 3 through 7 until you've added all menu items to the preview list.

9 Click the Next button to continue.

Setting the appearance of a pop-up menu

Once you have entered your menu text, the wizard's next screen lets you define the menu's appearance.

To set the appearance of a pop-up menu:

1   For Cells, choose either HTML or Image:

   HTML sets the Up and Over states for the menu background using HTML formatting.

   Image lets you use images for the menu's Up and Over background.

2   Select the appropriate font, and enter any other font information, such as size, justification, and typeface.

3   In the Up State and Over State boxes, define the appearance of the menu:

•   If you selected HTML in step 1, choose the text and cell colors for each state.

•   If you selected Image in step 1, then select the two background images the menu will use.

4   Click Finish.

When you insert a pop-up menu, a blue outline of the menu appears on or near the slice. The outline looks like a blank table linked to the slice by a drag-and-drop behavior line.

Note: The number of cells in the outline mirrors the number of main menu entries. Submenu entries are not represented by cells in the outline.

Editing a pop-up menu

You can edit the contents of a pop-up menu, rearrange the menu items, and move the pop-up menu outline so it appears anywhere on the canvas. You can edit a pop-up menu by opening the Set Pop-Up Menu wizard and updating the menu's contents. There are two ways to open the Set Pop-Up Menu wizard:

•   Double-click the pop-up menu outline.

•   Double-click the Show Pop-Up Menu behavior for the slice in the Behaviors panel.

To change the text of a menu item:

1   Open the Set Pop-Up Menu wizard.

2   Select the menu item.

   The menu item's details fill the Text, Target, and Link fields.

3   Edit the menu item.

4   Click the Change button.

To rearrange a menu item in the menu:

1 Open the Set Pop-Up Menu wizard.

2 Drag the menu item to a new location in the preview list.

Changing the position of a pop-up menu

You can move a menu outline so that the pop-up menu appears anywhere on the canvas. By default, the menu appears on the slice to which it is attached.

To move a pop-up menu:

1 Select the slice that the pop-up menu is attached to.

2 Drag the outline to the new position.

Exporting a pop-up menu

Fireworks generates all the JavaScript necessary to view the menu on a Web browser. When the document is exported, this JavaScript is exported to the same location as the rest of the files, in a file called menu.js. When you upload your files, menu.js should be uploaded to the same directory location as the Web page containing the pop-up menu. If you want to post the file to a different location, then all the hyperlinks referencing menu.js in the Fireworks HTML code must be updated to reflect the custom location.

If your document contains several pop-up menus, Fireworks does not create extra menu.js files; only a single file is used per document.

When you include submenus, Fireworks generates an image file called Arrow.gif. This image is the tiny arrow that appears next to a main menu entry that tells users a submenu exists. No matter how many submenus your document contains, Fireworks always uses the same Arrow.gif file.

Creating odd-shaped rollovers

Fireworks simplifies the task of creating odd-shaped rollovers. A slice object may be drawn in any shape using polygon slices. For information on creating polygon slices, see "Creating nonrectangular slices" on page 259.

Fireworks lets you use each object as a rollover without writing additional JavaScript code to swap out the appropriate slices.

With regular and more manageable shapes, a single slice is all that's necessary to set up a rollover. However, for more difficult shapes, you need to combine several slices together to cover the target area.

Fireworks exports a number of slices and states to recreate the appearance of the irregular shape. The JavaScript that Fireworks creates during export triggers several slices to display at the same time, each revealing a portion of the irregular shape.

To create odd-shaped rollovers:

1 Draw polygonal slices that match the shape of each object, using the Polygon Slice tool.

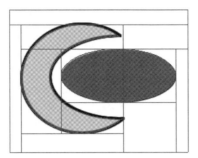

Fireworks creates a number of slices, automatically defining multiple rectangular slice areas for the irregular slice objects.

2 Assign Swap Image behaviors to each slice to set up the rollover.

3 Export the file.

Creating rollovers with overlapping slices

When objects used in a disjoint rollover are irregularly shaped and positioned closely together, the bounding boxes (defined by the slice guides) often overlap. Rectangular slices swap out the entire rectangular block defined by the green slice highlight, including any background area not part of the second image. If the swap image on the second frame and the image on the first interlock very closely, the rollover effect may obscure part of the trigger image. Use the Polygon Slice tool to prevent this.

Note: Although the bounding boxes of the slice overlap, the Polygon Slice tool lets you avoid overlapping the green part of the slice (see "Creating nonrectangular slices" on page 259).

To create a rollover with overlapping slices:

1 Insert a rectangular slice onto the Frame 1 image.

2 Select Frame 2 from the Frames panel.

3 Click on the Onion Skinning button at the bottom of the Frames panel to turn on Onion Skinning, so that an outline of the image on Frame 1 is visible.

4 Using the Polygon Slice tool, draw a slice over the Frame 2 image, being careful to avoid covering the Frame 1 image under the green slice highlight.

5 Set up the Swap Image behavior for the trigger slice.

When previewed, the swap image appears without cutting off any part of the trigger image.

Using external files as rollover images

You can use a GIF, animated GIF, JPEG, or PNG as the source for a rollover. When you choose an external file as the rollover source, that file is swapped with the target slice when the rollover is triggered in a Web browser.

The file must have the same width and height as the slice it is swapping into. If it does not, the browser resizes the file to fit within the slice object. Resizing the file may reduce its quality, especially in the case of an animated GIF.

If you are an advanced user of HTML, it is important to note that precaching can interrupt the display of animated GIFs as rollover states. Uncheck the Preload Images box when setting up the rollover to help avoid this problem.

To select an external file as the source of a rollover:

1 Choose Image File in the Swap Image, Nav Bar Over, or Nav Bar Down dialog box.

2 Navigate to the file you want to use.

3 If necessary, uncheck the Preload Images box (if the external file is an animated GIF).

Using hotspots on top of slices for complex interactivity

Fireworks lets you place hotspots on top of slices. This gives you a lot of flexibility when choosing the location and size of a trigger.

For example, if you want a rollover to appear when the pointer rolls over the center of the swap image, then you could place a smaller hotspot in the center of the slice as a trigger. This prevents the swap image from appearing inadvertently.

When you place a hotspot on top of a slice, no behavior is attached to the slice, only to the hotspot.

To set up a hotspot as a trigger on top of a slice:

1 Insert a slice on top of the image you want to swap out.

2 Draw a hotspot onto the area of the slice object you want to trigger the rollover.

3 Drag and drop a behavior line from the hotspot to the slice.

The Swap Image dialog displays.

4 Choose the frame holding the rollover image from the Swap Image From list.

5 Click OK.

16

CHAPTER 16
Creating Animation
. . . .

Animated graphics add an exciting, sophisticated look to your Web site. In Fireworks, you can create animated graphics with banner ads, logos, and cartoons that move. For example, you can make your company mascot dance across a page while the logo fades in and out.

You make animations in Fireworks by creating symbols and changing their properties over time to create the illusion of motion. A symbol is like an actor whose movements you choreograph. The action of each symbol is stored on a frame. When you play all the frames together in a sequence you get motion.

You can apply different settings to the symbol to gradually change the content of successive frames. You can make a symbol appear to move across the canvas, fade in or out, get bigger or smaller, or rotate.

Because you can have multiple symbols in a single file, you can create a complex animation where different types of action occur all at once.

Your animation won't move until the symbol (or the slice surrounding the symbol) is optimized as an Animated GIF. The Optimize panel lets you set optimization and export settings to control how your file is created. Fireworks can export animations as Animated GIF or Flash SWF files.

About animation

In Fireworks, you create animation by assigning properties to objects called *animation symbols*. The animation of a symbol is broken down into *frames*, which determine how long it takes the symbol to complete its motion. You can have more than one symbol in an animation, and each symbol can have a different action. Different symbols can contain differing numbers of frames. The animation ends when all the action of all the symbols is complete.

Building an animation in Fireworks is a four-step process:

1 Create an animation symbol, either by creating a symbol from scratch or by converting an existing object into a symbol.

2 Use the Symbol Properties dialog box to enter settings for the animation symbol. You can set the degree and direction of movement, scaling, opacity (fading in or out), and angle and direction of rotation.

3 Use the Frame Delay controls on the Frames panel to set the speed of the animated motion.

4 Optimize and export the document as an Animated GIF.

Working with animation symbols

Animation symbols perform the action like actors in a movie. For example, in an animation of three geese flying across the sky, each goose is a cast member.

An animation symbol can be any object you create or import and you can have many symbols in one file. Each symbol has its own properties and animates independently. So you can create symbols that move across the screen while others fade or shrink.

Note: If you convert an existing object into an animation symbol, you must make sure that it is set to be optimized as an Animated GIF in the Optimize panel. Otherwise the symbol's motion will not be exported. For more information, see "Optimizing an animation" on page 302.

You can change animation symbol properties at any time using the Animate dialog box or the Object panel. You can also edit symbol artwork in the Symbol Editor. The Symbol Editor lets you edit your symbol without affecting the rest of the document. You can also change a symbol's motion by moving its motion path.

Since animation symbols are automatically placed in the library, you can reuse them to create other animations.

Creating animation symbols

Once you have created a symbol, you can set properties that determine the number of frames in the animation and the type of action, such as scaling or rotation. By default, the new animation symbol has five frames, each with a delay time of 0.20 seconds.

To create an animation symbol:

1 Choose Insert > New Symbol.

2 In the Symbol Properties dialog, enter a name for the new symbol.

3 Choose Animation and click OK.

4 In the Symbol Editor, use the drawing or text tools to create a new object.

You can draw either vector or bitmap objects.

5 Close the Symbol Editor window.

Fireworks places the symbol in the library and a copy in the center of the document.

6 You can add new frames to the symbol using the Frames slider in the Object panel.

To convert an object to an animation symbol:

1 Select an object.

2 Choose Modify > Animate > Animate selection.

3 Enter the desired setting in the dialog box. For more information on settings, see "Editing symbol properties" on page 292.

Animation controls appear on the object's bounding box and a copy is added to the library.

Editing symbol properties

Changing the symbol's features makes your Web sites come alive. You can change a variety of features, from the animation speed to the opacity and rotation. By manipulating these features, you can make a symbol appear to rotate, speed up, fade in and out, or any combination of the above.

A key property for any animation symbol is its number of frames. This property sets how many steps it takes the symbol to complete its animation. When you set the number of frames for a symbol, Fireworks automatically adds the required number of frames to the document to complete the action. If the symbol requires more frames than currently exist in the animation, Fireworks adds extra frames.

You can change properties using either the Animate dialog box, or the Object panel.

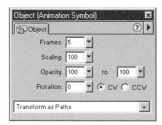

The Object Panel

To change symbol properties:

1 Select a symbol.

2 Choose Modify > Animate > Settings. Or choose Window > Object to display the Object panel.

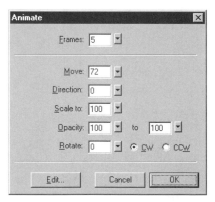

3 Change any of the following properties:

Frames is the number of frames you want to include in the animation. Although the slider only lets you set a maximum of 250, you can use the edit field to type in any number you wish. The default is 5.

Movement is the distance, in pixels, that you want each object to move. Possible values range from 0 to 250 pixels. The default is 72.

Direction is the direction, in degrees, in which you want the object to move. Possible values range from 0 to 360 degrees.

Note: You can also change Movement and Direction values by dragging the object's animation handles (see "Editing symbol motion paths" on page 294).

Scaling is the percent change in size from start to finish. Possible values range from 0 to 250. The default is 100%.

Opacity is the degree of fading in or out from start to finish. Possible values range from 0 to 100. The default is 100%.

Rotation is the amount, in degrees, that the symbol rotates from start to finish. Possible values range from 0 to 360 degrees. You can type in higher values for more than one rotation. The default is 0 degrees.

CW and CCW are the direction in which the object rotates. CW indicates clockwise and CCW indicates counter-clockwise rotation.

To remove a symbol from the Library:

1 In the Library panel, select the animation symbol you want to remove.

2 Drag the symbol to the Trash can icon in the lower right corner.

To remove the animation from a selected animation symbol:

Choose Modify > Animate > Remove animation.

The symbol becomes a graphic symbol and is no longer animated. If you later convert the symbol back into an animation symbol, the previous animation settings return.

Editing symbol graphics

You can change the graphic your symbol is based on as well as its properties. You edit symbol graphics in the Symbol Editor. The Editor lets you use any of the drawing, text, or color tools to edit the graphic. While you're working in the Symbol editor, only the selected symbol is affected.

Since the symbol is a Library item, if you change one of its instances, you change them all.

To change a selected symbol's graphic attributes:

1 Open the Symbol Editor:

• Double-click the symbol object.

• Choose Modify > Symbol > Edit Symbol.

• Click the Edit button on the Animate dialog box.

2 Modify the animation symbol and change any text, strokes, fills, and effects as appropriate.

3 Close the Symbol Editor.

Editing symbol motion paths

When you select an animation symbol, it has a unique bounding box and a motion path attached that indicates the direction in which the symbol moves.

The green dot on the motion path indicates the starting point, while the red dot shows the end point. The blue points on the path represent frames. For example, a symbol with five frames would have five blue points on its path. The position of the object on the path indicates the current frame. So if the object appears at the third dot, Frame 3 is the current frame.

You can change the direction of the motion by changing the angle of the path.

To change movement or direction:

Drag one of the symbol's animation handles to a new location.

• The green point indicates the starting point; the red indicates the ending point.

• To constrain the direction of movement to 45-degree increments, hold down Shift while dragging.

Working with frames

You build animations by creating a number of frames. You can see the contents of each frame using the Frames panel. The Frames panel is where you create and organize frames. You can name the frames, reorganize them, manually set the timing of the animation, and move objects from one frame to another.

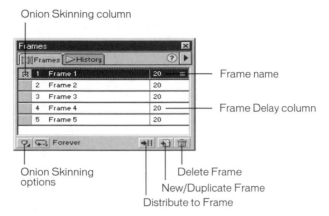

Each frame also has a number of associated properties. By setting the frame delay or hiding a frame you can make your animation look the way you want during the building and editing process.

Setting the frame delay

The frame delay determines how long the current frame is displayed. It is specified in hundredths of a second. For example, a setting of 50 displays the frame for half a second, while a setting of 300 displays it for 3 seconds.

To set the frame delay value:

1 Select one or more frames:

• To select a contiguous range of frames, Shift-click the first and last frame names.

• To select a noncontiguous range of frames, hold down Control (Windows) or Command (Macintosh) and click each frame name.

2 Click the Options pop-up menu and choose Properties, or double-click the frame delay column, to open the Frame Properties dialog box.

3 Enter a value for the frame delay.

4 Press Enter, or click outside the panel to close the dialog box.

Showing and hiding frames for playback

You can show or hide frames for playback. If a frame is hidden, it is not displayed during playback and it is not exported.

To show or hide a frame:

1   Double-click the frame delay column for that frame or click the Options pop-up menu and choose Properties.

    The Frames Property dialog box opens.

2   Deselect Include when Exporting.

    A red X displays in place of the frame delay time.

3   Press Enter or click outside the Frame Properties dialog box to close it.

Naming animation frames

As you set up an animation, Fireworks creates the appropriate number of frames and displays them in the Frames panel. The frames are named with a default of Frame 1, Frame 2, and so on. When you move a frame in the panel, Fireworks renames each one to reflect the new order.

It's a good idea to name your frames for easy reference and to keep track of them. That way you always know which frame contains which part of the animation. When you rename a frame and then move it, its name doesn't change.

To change a frame's name:

1   In the Frames panel, double-click the frame's name.

2   In the pop-up text box, type a new name and press Enter.

Adding, moving, copying, and deleting frames

You can add, copy, delete, and change the order of frames in the Frames panel.

To add a new frame after the current one:

 Click the New/Duplicate Frame button at the bottom of the Frames panel.

To add frames to a specific place in the sequence:

1 Choose Add Frames from the Frames panel Options pop-up menu.

2 Enter the number of frames to add.

3 Choose where to insert them: before the current frame, after it, or at the beginning or end, and click OK.

To make a copy of a frame:

 Drag an existing frame to the New/Duplicate Frame button at the bottom of the Frames panel.

To copy a selected frame and place it in a sequence:

1 Choose Duplicate Frame from the Frames panel Options pop-up menu.

2 Enter the number of duplicates to create for the selected frame, choose where the duplicate frames are to be inserted, and click OK.

Duplicating a frame is useful when you want objects to reappear in another part of the animation.

To reorder frames:

Drag them one by one to a new location in the list.

To delete the selected frame:

• Click the Delete Frame button in the Frames panel.

• Drag the frame to the Delete Frame button.

• Choose Delete Frame from the Frames panel Options pop-up menu.

Moving selected objects in the Frames panel

You can use the Frames panel to move objects to a different frame. Objects that appear on only a single frame appear to vanish as the animation plays. You can move objects to make them appear or disappear at different points in the movie.

To move a selected object to a different frame:

In the Frames panel, drag the blue square to the right of the frame delay time to the new frame.

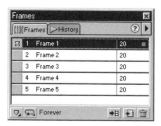

Sharing layers across frames

Layers divide a Fireworks document into discrete planes, like separate tracing paper overlays. With animations, you can use layers to organize objects that are part of the scenery or backdrop for the animation. This gives you the convenience of being able to fix objects so that they don't interfere with the rest of your animation.

If you want objects to appear throughout an animation, you can place them on a layer and then use the Layers panel to share the layer across frames.

You can edit objects on shared layers on any frame; those edits are reflected on all other frames.

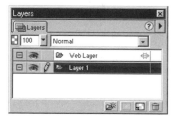

In this example, the Background layer is shared across frames.

To share a layer across frames:

1 Double-click the layer.

2 Select Share Across Frames.

Note: All the contents in a shared layer appear on every frame involved in the sharing.

To disable sharing a particular layer across frames:

1 Double-click the shared layer.

2 Deselect Share Across Frames.

3 Choose how to copy objects to frames:

• Leave the contents of the shared layer in the current frame only.

• Copy the contents of the shared layer to all frames.

Using onion skinning

Use onion skinning to view the contents of frames preceding and following the currently selected frame. Onion skinning helps you smoothly animate frames without having to flip back and forth through them. The term *onion skinning* comes from a traditional animation technique of using thin, translucent tracing paper to view animated sequences.

When onion skinning is turned on, objects in frames before or after the current frame are dimmed so that you can distinguish them from objects in the current frame.

The darker bird in the middle is in the current frame with the Onion Skinning Before and After option active.

By default, you can select and edit dimmed objects in other frames without leaving the current frame.

To adjust the number of frames visible before and after the current frame:

1 In the Frames panel, click the Onion Skinning button.

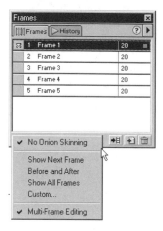

2 Choose a display option:

No Onion Skinning turns off onion skinning and displays only the contents of the current frame.

Show Next Frame displays the contents of the current frame and the next frame.

Before and After displays the contents of the current and adjacent frames.

Show All Frames displays the contents of all frames.

Custom sets a custom number of frames and controls the opacity of onion skinning.

Multi-Frame Editing lets you select and edit all visible objects.

Deselect this option lets you select and edit only objects in the current frame.

Previewing an animation

You can preview an animation while you are working on it to check its progress. You can also preview an animation after optimization to see how the exported Animated GIF will look in a Web browser.

To preview an animation in the workspace:

Use the frame controls that appear at the bottom of the document window.

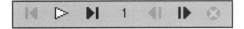

Frame controls

Note these concepts when previewing animations:

- To set how long each frame appears in the document window, enter frame delay settings in the Frames panel.

- Frames excluded from the export do not appear when previewing.

- Previewing the animation in the Original document window displays the full-resolution source graphic, not the optimized 8-bit preview used for the exported Animated GIF.

- The document or slice containing the animation must be set to Animated GIF in the Optimize panel.

To preview an animation in the Preview window:

1 Click the Preview tab at the top of the document window.

2 Use the frame controls.

Note: Previewing animations in 2-Up or 4-Up view is not recommended.

To preview an animation in a Web browser:

Choose File > Preview in Browser, and choose a browser from the submenu.

Exporting your animation

Once you have set up the symbols and frames that make up your animation, you are ready to export the file as an animation. Before you export the files, you first need to enter a few settings to make your animation load more easily and play more smoothly. You can set playback settings like looping and transparency and then use optimization to make your exported file smaller and easier to download.

Note: Your file format must be set to Animated GIF in the Optimize panel to export any type of motion.

Setting the animation repetition

The loop setting on the Export Preview dialog box determines how many times the animation repeats. This feature loops frames over and over so you can minimize the number of frames needed to build the animation.

To set the selected Animated GIF to repeat:

1 Choose Window > Frames to display the Frames panel.

2 Click the looping button at the bottom of the panel.

3 Choose the number of times to repeat after the first time.

If you choose 4, for example, the animation plays five times in all. Forever repeats the animation continuously.

Setting transparency

As part of the optimization process, you can set one or more colors within an Animated GIF to display as transparent in a Web browser. This is useful when you want a Web page background color or image to show through the animation.

To display a color as transparent in a Web browser:

1 From the Transparency pop-up menu in the Optimize panel, choose either Index Transparency or Alpha Transparency.

2 Use the transparency tools in the Optimize panel to select colors for transparency.

Optimizing an animation

Optimization compresses your file into the smallest package for fast loading and exporting, making viewing time much quicker on your Web site.

To optimize an animation:

1 In the Optimize panel, choose Animated GIF from the Export File Format pop-up menu.

Choose Window > Optimize if the panel is not visible.

2 Set the Palette, Dither, or Transparency options. For more information on optimizing options, see "Choosing optimization settings for GIFs and PNGs" on page 316.

3 In the Frames panel, set the frame delay. For more information, see "Setting the frame delay" on page 295.

Exporting as GIF, SWF, or multiple files

After you create and optimize an animation, it is ready to export as an Animated GIF, as multiple files, or as a Flash SWF file. Animated GIFs give the best results for clip art and cartoonlike graphics.

Exporting multiple files is helpful when you have many symbols on different layers for the same object. For example, you can export a banner ad as multiple files if each letter of a company name is animated in a graphic. Each letter is separate from the others.

SWF files import easily into other programs such as Macromedia Flash for further editing. If you export the animation as a Flash SWF file, you can import it into Macromedia Flash for further editing. For more information, see "Exporting to Macromedia Flash" on page 339.

Note: Your file format must be set to Animated GIF in the Optimize panel to export any type of motion.

To export as an Animated GIF:

1 Choose Animated GIF as part of the optimizing process. For more information, see "Choosing optimization settings for GIFs and PNGs" on page 316.

2 Choose File > Export.

3 In the Export dialog box, type a name for the file and choose the destination.

To export as multiple files:

1 Choose File > Export.

2 From the Save as type pop-up menu choose either Layers to Files or Frames to Files.

3 Type a base name for the files and specify the destination.

To export as a Flash SWF file:

1 Choose File > Export.

2 From the Save as type pop-up menu, choose Flash SWF.

3 Click Options to set SWF options. The Options dialog box provides suggestions on picking settings.

4 Click OK to close the dialog box and then click Save.

Working with existing animations

You can use an existing Animated GIF file as part of your Fireworks animation. There are two ways of using the file: you can import the GIF into an existing Fireworks file, or you can open the GIF as a new file.

When you import an Animated GIF, Fireworks converts it to an animation symbol and places it on the currently selected frame. If the animation has more frames than the current movie, you can choose to automatically add more frames.

Imported GIFs lose their original frame delay settings and assume the frame delay of the current document. Since the imported file is an animation symbol, you can apply additional motion to it. For example, you can import an animation of a man walking in place and then apply direction and motion properties to have it walk across the screen.

When you open an Animated GIF in Fireworks, a new file is created and each frame in the GIF is placed on a separate frame. Although the GIF is not an animation symbol, it does retain all the frame delay settings from the original file.

Once the file is imported you need to set its file format to Animated GIF in order to export the motion from Fireworks.

To import an Animated GIF:

1 Choose File > Import.

2 Locate the file and click Yes to add additional frames to your animation.

If you click Cancel, only the first frame of the Animated GIF is displayed. Although the whole document is imported, you must add additional frames to view it.

To open an Animated GIF:

Choose File > Open and locate the GIF file.

Using multiple files as one animation

Fireworks can create an animation based on a group of image files. For example, you can create a banner ad based on several existing graphics by opening each graphic and placing it on a separate frame in the same document.

To open multiple files as an animation:

1 Choose File > Open.

2 Select multiple files by Shift-clicking each one.

3 Select Open as Animation and click OK.

   Fireworks opens the files in a new single document, placing each file on a separate frame in the order in which you selected it.

CHAPTER 17
Optimizing Graphics

The ultimate goal in Web graphic design is to create great-looking images that download as fast as possible. To do that, you must select a format with the best compression for your image while maintaining as much quality as possible. This balancing act is known as optimization—finding the right mix of color, compression, and quality.

In Fireworks, optimization settings apply only to exported images. Therefore, you can work freely through the creative process of design without worrying too much about limiting color usage or applying effects. Then when you are ready to export, choose, customize, and compare optimization settings that are best for your image.

Optimizing images in Fireworks is a three-part task:

- Choose the best file format. Each file format has a different way of compressing color information in the file. Choosing the appropriate format for certain types of graphics can greatly reduce file size.

- Set format-specific options. Each Web file format has a unique set of options for controlling image compression. For example, you can use dithering on a GIF to compensate for fewer colors stored in the image, and you can use smoothing on a JPEG to blur the image slightly, which helps JPEG compression reduce the file size.

- Adjust the colors in the image. Limit colors by confining the image to a specific set of colors called a *color palette*. Then trim unused colors from the color palette. Fewer colors in the palette means fewer colors in the image, which results in smaller file size. Reducing the number of colors can also diminish image quality, so you must try various color palettes to find the best balance of quality and size.

Optimizing in the workspace

Fireworks optimization controls are conveniently located on panels in the workspace:

- The Optimize panel contains the key controls for optimizing.
- The Color Table panel displays the colors in the current export color palette.
- The Preview window shows you a preview of how the exported graphic will look.

Note: In Fireworks, all the optimization controls are in the workspace. However, you can also optimize the image prior to export by choosing File › Export Preview. For more information, see "Optimizing and previewing during export" on page 333.

You can choose from common optimization settings to quickly set a file format and apply several format-specific settings. You can adjust the preset settings.

If you need more precise optimization control than the presets offer, you can also create custom optimization settings using the Optimize panel.

To choose a preset optimization:

Choose a setting from the Optimize panel Settings pop-up menu.

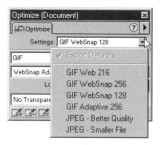

The following preset options are available:

GIF Web 216 forces all colors to Websafe colors. The color palette contains up to 216 colors (see "Setting Websafe colors" on page 324).

GIF WebSnap 256 converts non-Websafe colors to their closest Websafe color. The color palette contains up to a maximum of 256 colors.

GIF WebSnap 128 converts non-Websafe colors to their closest Websafe color. The color palette contains up to 128 colors.

GIF Adaptive 256 is a color palette that contains only the actual colors used in the graphic. The color palette contains up to a maximum of 256 colors.

JPEG - Better Quality sets quality to 80 and smoothing to 0, resulting in a high-quality but larger graphic.

JPEG - Smaller File sets quality to 60 and smoothing to 2, resulting in a graphic less than half the size of a Better Quality JPEG but with reduced quality.

Note: The type of GIF settings you choose for a graphic may depend on the number of colors in the graphic. A palette with 128 colors is suitable for images with few colors and results in a smaller graphic.

For more information, see "Selecting file formats" on page 314.

To specify optimization settings for an image:

1 In the Optimize panel, choose a file format.

2 Set format-specific options, such as color, dither, and quality.

3 Choose other optimization settings from the Optimize panel Options pop-up menu, as necessary.

Specifying optimization settings for slices

You can specify unique optimization settings for each slice in a sliced document. For example, you might want to do this when one part of your graphic contains a photographic image best exported as a JPEG, while another part is a solid area, which would be better compressed as a GIF. By drawing a slice over each part, you can set each part to export differently.

When you select a slice object on the Web Layer, the Optimize panel displays the settings for that slice.

To set optimization settings for a slice:

1 Select a slice object.

  If slice objects are not visible, click the Show Hotspots and Slices button in the Tools panel. These buttons hide and show the Web Layer.

2 Enter optimization settings in the Optimize panel.

The selected slice is now ready to be exported with the specified optimization settings.

For more information about slicing, see "Creating slices" on page 256.

Using the slice overlay

In the Preview, 2-Up, and 4-Up views, the slice overlay differentiates the area currently being optimized from the rest of the document. The slice overlay, which is turned on by default, displays areas not currently being optimized with a dimmed, transparent white tint. This lets you easily identify the areas you are optimizing. The slice overlay is not shown in the Original view.

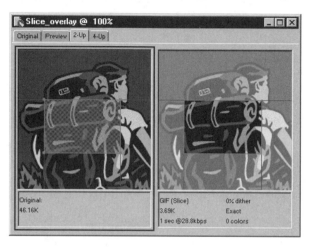

When you are preparing to optimize a selected slice, the portions not being optimized are dimmed.

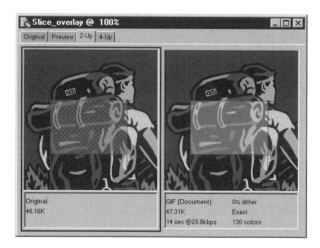

When no slices are selected, sliced areas are dimmed and the rest of the document is optimized.

You can select areas to optimize in the Preview, 2-Up, or 4-Up window. When a slice is selected, its overlay is turned off. You can select multiple slices by holding down Shift and clicking with the Pointer tool.

To select an area to optimize:

1 Click the Preview, 2-Up, or 4-Up tab.

2 Click the area to optimize.

To hide or show the slice overlay:

Choose View > Slice Overlay.

Hiding the Slice Overlay is useful in 2-Up and 4-Up previews when you want to compare an original view with visible slices to an optimized preview with hidden slices.

Saving and reusing optimization settings

You can save custom optimization settings for future use in optimization or batch processing. Saving custom presets store this information:

• Settings in the Optimize panel

• The color palette in the Color Table panel

• Frame delay settings chosen in the Frames panel (for Animated GIFs only)

To save optimization settings as a preset:

1 Click the Save button in the Optimize panel.

2 Type a name for the optimization preset and click OK.

Saved optimization settings appear at the bottom of the Settings pop-up menu in the Optimize panel. They are available in all subsequent documents. The preset file is saved in the Fireworks 4\Configuration\Export Settings folder.

To share saved optimization settings with another Fireworks user:

Copy the saved optimization preset file from the Fireworks 4\Configuration\ Export Settings folder to the same folder on another computer.

To delete a custom preset optimization:

1 In the Optimize panel Settings pop-up menu, choose the optimization setting you want to delete.

2 Click the Delete button at the bottom of the Optimize panel.

You cannot delete a Fireworks preset optimization setting.

Previewing optimization settings and behaviors

The Preview window displays what your exported image would look like based on the current optimization settings. Also, you can test behaviors and rollovers before export using the Preview window.

To preview an image based on the current optimization settings:

Click the Preview tab in the upper left corner of the document window.

To show or hide slice objects and guides in a Preview:

Click the Show (or Hide) Slices and Hotspots button in the Tools panel.

Previewing buttons and rollovers

Move the pointer over the rollover or button in the Preview window to see how the object appears in a Web browser.

Note: You must be viewing Frame 1 to preview buttons or rollovers. To change to Frame 1, click it in the Frames panel.

Estimating file download time

The Preview window displays the image's total size and estimated download time. The estimated download time is the average amount of time it would take to download all the image's slices and rollover states using the current optimization settings and a 28.8 bps modem.

Comparing optimization settings

If you want to compare the same graphic under different optimization settings, you can split the document window into two or four previews using the 2-Up and 4-Up tabs. You can assign unique settings to each preview to compare how each choice of settings affects the image.

When you display the 2-Up or 4-Up preview, the first view is the original view. You can continue editing in that view and compare the original graphic with an optimized version.

The bottom of each preview displays statistics of the current preview settings, including the file format, estimated download time, file size, palette, and number of colors.

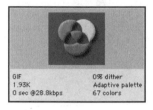

Preview window

To compare two or four different optimization settings:

1 Click the 2-Up or 4-Up tab in the upper left of the document window.

2 Click one of the split-view previews to select it.

3 Enter settings in the Optimize panel and the Color Table panel.

4 Select the other preview and specify different optimization settings to compare with the first one.

When you choose 2-Up or 4-Up preview, the first view displays the original Fireworks PNG document so that you can compare it with optimized versions. You can switch this view with another optimized version.

To switch the original view with an optimized view in the 2-Up or 4-Up preview:

1 Select the view containing the original.

2 In the document window, choose Export Preview from the Preview pop-up menu.

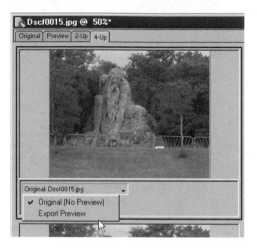

To switch any optimized view with an original view in the 2-Up or 4-Up preview:

1 Select an optimized view.

2 Choose Original (No Preview) from the Preview pop-up menu at the bottom of the document window.

Selecting file formats

GIF and JPEG are graphic file formats that are common in Web development because they are highly compressible. PNG format is not as common because not all Web browsers support it. Compression ensures a faster transfer across the Internet. However, a graphic's appearance can vary from one format to another, depending upon each format's method of compression. Therefore, base your choice of file format upon the design and use of your graphic.

Choosing GIF

Graphics Interchange Format, or GIF, is a popular Web graphic format. GIFs contain a maximum of 256 colors. This format offers good image compression, but if the image contains more than 256 colors quality is significantly reduced. GIFs can also contain a transparent area and multiple frames for animation.

Images compressed with lossless compression normally lose no image quality. A GIF compresses by scanning horizontally across a row of pixels, finding solid areas of color, and then abbreviating identical areas of pixels in the file. GIFs are only lossless if the image contains very few colors, as line or geometric art usually does.

Therefore, images with areas of solid color compress best when exported as GIFs. A GIF is usually ideal for cartoonlike graphics, logos, graphics with transparent areas, and animations. Vector objects are often saved as GIFs.

Note: Dithering or anti-aliasing GIF images produces larger files.

Choosing JPEG

JPEG was developed by the Joint Photographic Experts Group specifically for photographic or high-color images. JPEG supports millions of colors (24-bit), whereas GIF supports only 256 colors. JPEG always produces higher quality for photographic image data.

JPEG is a lossy format, which means that some image data is discarded when it is compressed, reducing the quality of the final file. However, image data can sometimes be discarded with little or no noticeable difference in quality.

When exporting a JPEG, use the Quality slider pop-up menu in the Optimize panel to control how much quality is lost when compressing the file.

- A high percentage setting maintains image quality but compresses less, producing larger files.

- A low percentage setting yields a small file, but produces a lower quality image.

Use the 2-Up and 4-Up previews to test and compare the appearance and estimated file size with different Quality settings for an exported JPEG.

The JPEG format is best for scanned photographs, images using textures, images with gradient color transitions, and any images that require more than 256 colors.

Choosing PNG

Portable Network Graphic, or PNG, is a versatile Web graphic format. However, not all Web browsers can take full advantage of PNG characteristics without using plug-ins. Therefore it is not a common file format for the Web. A PNG can support up to 32-bit color, can contain transparency or an alpha channel, and can be progressive.

PNG compression is lossless, even in high color depths. It compresses across rows and columns of pixels. For high-color images, JPEG produces a superior quality. PNG allows transparency with 32-bit color images, but the image size is large.

The PNG format is best for creating complex live transparency, high-color graphics, and better compressed low-color graphics.

PNG is the native file format for Fireworks. However, Fireworks PNG files contain additional source information that is not saved when you export a PNG for use on the Web.

Choosing optimization settings for GIFs and PNGs

Fireworks optimization settings are similar for GIFs and 8-bit PNGs (PNG8).

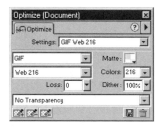

Choosing the color depth

Color depth is the number of colors in the exported graphic. GIF images are always exported in 8-bit color (256 colors) or less. You can export PNG at higher color depths.

Higher color depths create larger exported files, and are typically not ideal for Web graphics. Use PNGs with 24- or 32-bit color depths or JPEGs when exporting photographic images with continuous tones or complex gradient blends of colors.

Choosing a color palette

Exported GIFs and 8-bit PNGs each contain a color palette. A color palette is a list of up to 256 colors available to the file. Only colors defined in the color palette appear in the graphic; however, some color palettes contain colors that are not in the graphic. Adjusting the color palette during optimization affects the colors in the exported image. For more information, see "Optimizing color palettes" on page 320.

Dithering to approximate lost colors

Dithering approximates colors not in the current palette by alternating two available similar colors from pixel to pixel. Dithering is especially helpful when exporting images with complex blends or gradients or when exporting photographic images to an indexed image format such as GIF.

Dithering can greatly increase file size.

To dither an image to be exported:

Enter a percentage value in the Dither text box of the Optimize panel.

Setting loss to reduce file size

To make GIF files compress even smaller than usual, enter a Loss setting in the Optimize panel. Higher loss settings can yield smaller files but lower image quality.

A loss setting between 5 and 15 typically yields the best results.

Defining transparent areas

You can set transparent areas in both GIFs and PNGs so that, in a Web browser, the background of the Web page is visible through those areas. For more information, see "Assigning transparency" on page 325.

Removing all unused colors from the palette

Removing unused colors from an image before exporting makes its file size smaller.

To remove unused colors:

Select Remove Unused Colors in the Optimize panel Options pop-up menu.

Deselect Remove Unused Colors to include all colors in the palette, including colors that are not present in the exported image.

Interlacing: Downloading in segments

When viewed in a Web browser, interlaced images quickly appear at a low resolution and then transition to full resolution as they continue to download.

To make an exported GIF or PNG interlaced:

Choose Interlaced from the Optimize panel Options pop-up menu.

Choosing optimization settings for JPEGs

JPEGs are always saved in 24-bit color. JPEG compression specializes in compressing color transitions and gradients. This format is particularly useful for photographic or high-color images. Selective JPEG compression allows you to compress different parts of an image at different levels.

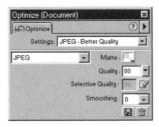

Selective JPEG compression

Selective JPEG compression lets you compress different areas of a JPEG graphic at different levels. Areas of particular interest in an image can be compressed at a high level. Areas of lesser significance, such as backgrounds, can be compressed at a low level, reducing the overall size of the image while retaining the quality of the more interesting areas.

To compress selected areas of a JPEG:

1 Using the Marquee tools, select an area of the graphic for compression.

2 Choose Modify > Selective JPEG > Save Selection as JPEG Mask.

3 Choose a JPEG format from the Optimize panel Settings pop-up menu.

4 Click the Selective Quality button in the Optimize panel. The Selective JPEG Settings dialog box appears.

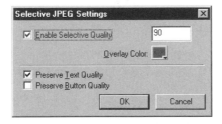

5 Select Enable Selective Quality and enter a compression value in the text box.

Enter a low value to set the Selective JPEG overlay area to compress more than the rest of the image. Enter a high value to set the Selective JPEG overlay area to compress less than the rest of the image.

6 Choose an Overlay Color to highlight the selected area. This does not affect the output.

7 Select Preserve Text Quality. All text items will automatically be exported at a higher level, regardless of the Selective Quality value.

8 Select Preserve Button Quality. All button symbols will automatically be exported at a higher level.

9 Click OK.

Note: You can see the effects of the compression by switching to the Preview tab or choosing File > Preview in Browser.

To modify the selective JPEG compression area:

1 Choose Modify > Selective JPEG > Restore JPEG Mask as Selection.

The selection is highlighted.

2 Use the Marquee tool or another selection tool to make changes to the size of the area.

3 Choose Modify > Selective JPEG > Save Selection as JPEG Mask.

4 Change selective quality settings in the Optimize panel if desired.

Note: To undo a selection, choose Modify > Selective JPEG > Remove JPEG Mask.

Reducing quality to reduce file size

Adjust the Quality setting in the Optimize panel to increase or decrease the quality of the JPEG image. Choosing a lower quality makes the resulting JPEG file smaller.

Blurring edges to increase compression

Set Smoothing in the Optimize panel to help decrease the file size of JPEGs. Smoothing blurs hard edges, which do not compress well in JPEGs. Higher numbers produce more blurring in the exported JPEG, typically creating smaller files.

A smoothing setting of about 3 reduces the size of the image while still maintaining reasonable quality.

Sharpening color edges and fine detail

Choose Sharpen JPEG Edges from the Optimize panel Options pop-up menu to help preserve fine edges between two colors. Use Sharpen JPEG Edges when exporting JPEGs with text or fine detail to preserve the sharpness of these areas.

Choosing Sharpen JPEG Edges increases file size.

Progressive JPEGs

Choose Progressive JPEG from the Optimize panel Options pop-up menu to export a progressive JPEG. Progressive JPEGs, like interlaced GIFs, display at low resolution and then increase in quality as they continue to download.

Some older bitmap editing applications cannot open progressive JPEGs.

Optimizing color palettes

GIFs and PNGs exported in 8-bit color or less use a color palette to store and reference colors used in the exported image file. Optimize and customize color palettes using the Color Table panel.

Choosing the appropriate color palette

Choose a palette from the Optimize panel Palette pop-up menu, and then optimize it.

These palettes are available by default:

Adaptive is a custom palette derived from the actual colors in the document. Adaptive palettes most often produce the highest quality image.

Web Adaptive is an adaptive palette in which colors that are close to Websafe colors are converted to the closest Websafe color.

Web 216 is a palette of the 216 colors common to both Windows and Macintosh computers. This palette is often called a *Websafe* or browser-safe palette because it produces fairly consistent results in various Web browsers on either platform when viewed on 8-bit monitors.

Exact contains the exact colors used in the image. Only images containing 256 or fewer colors may use the Exact palette. If the image contains more than 256 colors, the palette switches to Adaptive.

System (Windows) and **System (Macintosh)** each contain the 256 colors defined by the Windows or Macintosh platform standards, respectively.

Grayscale is a palette of 256 or fewer shades of gray. Choosing this palette converts the exported image to grayscale.

Black and White is a two-color palette consisting only of black and white.

Uniform is a mathematical palette based on RGB pixel values.

Custom is a palette that has been modified or loaded from an external palette or a GIF file.

To import a palette:

1 Load an ACT or GIF palette:

• Choose Load Palette from the Color Table panel Options pop-up menu.

• Choose Custom from the Optimize panel Palette pop-up menu.

2 Navigate to an ACT or GIF file and click Open.

The colors from the ACT or GIF file are added to the Color Table panel.

Setting the number of colors in the palette

Enter or select a number in the Colors pop-up menu of the Optimize panel to set the maximum number of colors allowed in the color palette of the exported image. Fireworks often optimizes an image using the actual colors in the image. This can be lower than the maximum number you specify. The number on the bottom left of the Color Table panel indicates the actual number of colors visible in the image. Create smaller files by reducing the number of colors.

Setting a lower number of colors than the number actually used discards some colors, beginning with those used least. Pixels containing discarded colors convert to the closest color remaining in the palette.This reduces the size and quality of the image.

Viewing colors in a palette

The Color Table panel displays colors in the current preview when working in 8-bit color or less and lets you modify an image's palette. The Color Table updates automatically when you are in Preview mode. It appears empty if you are optimizing more than one slice at a time or if you are not optimizing in an 8-bit format such as GIF.

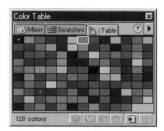

A variety of tiny symbols appears on some color swatches, indicating certain characteristics of individual colors, as follows:

This symbol	Indicates
	The color has been edited, affecting only the exported document. This does not change the color in the document.
	The color is locked.
	The color is transparent.
	The color is Websafe.
	The color has multiple attributes. In this case, the color is Websafe, locked, and has been edited.

If you edit the document, the Color Table panel may no longer show all the colors in the document. In this case, the panel title changes to Colors (Rebuild), indicating that you must rebuild the color palette.

To update the colors in the Color Table panel to reflect edits in the document:

Choose Rebuild Color Table from the Color Table panel Options pop-up menu.

To select a color:

Click the color in the Color Table panel.

To select multiple colors:

Hold down Control (Windows) or Command (Macintosh) as you click colors.

To select a range of colors:

1 Click a color.

2 Hold Shift and click a second color.

To preview all the pixels in the document that contain a specific color:

1 Click the Preview tab of the document window.

2 Click and hold on a swatch in the Color Table panel.

The pixels that contain the selected swatch temporarily change to another highlight color until you release the mouse button.

Note: When previewing pixels in the document using the 2-Up or 4-Up view, select a view other than the Original view.

Locking colors in a palette

You can lock individual colors so that you cannot remove or change them when changing palettes or reducing the number of colors in a palette. If you switch to another palette after colors have been locked, locked colors are added to the new palette.

To lock a selected color:

 Click the Lock button at the bottom of the Color Table panel, or choose Lock Color from the Options pop-up menu.

To unlock a color:

1 Select a color in the Color Table panel.

2 Click the Lock button in the Color Table panel or deselect Lock Color from the Options pop-up menu.

To unlock all colors:

Choose Unlock All Colors from the Color Table panel Options pop-up menu.

Editing colors in a palette

You can change a color in the palette by editing it in the Color Table panel. Editing a color replaces all instances of that color in the image to be exported. Editing does not replace the color in the original image.

To edit a color:

1 Open the system color picker by doing one of the following:

- Select a color and click the Edit Color button at the bottom of the Color Table panel.

- Double-click a color in the Color Table panel.

2 Change the color using the system color picker.

The new color replaces every instance of the replaced color in the preview area.

Note: Right-click (Windows) or Control-click (Macintosh) a color in the palette to display a shortcut menu of edit options for the color.

Setting Websafe colors

Websafe colors are colors that are common to both Macintosh and Windows platforms. These colors are not dithered when viewed in a Web browser on a computer display set to 256 colors.

Fireworks has several methods of applying and using Websafe colors.

To force all colors to Websafe colors:

Choose the Web 216 palette.

To create an adaptive palette that favors Websafe colors:

Choose the Web Adaptive palette. Non-Websafe colors that are close to Websafe colors are converted to the closest Websafe color.

To force a color to its closest Websafe equivalent:

1 Select a color in the Color Table panel.

2 Click the Snap to Websafe button.

Changing colors to Websafe in the Color Table panel affects only the exported version of the image, not the actual image.

Saving palettes

You can save custom palettes as external palette files. Use saved palettes with other Fireworks documents or in other applications that support external palette files, such as Adobe Photoshop, Macromedia FreeHand, and Flash 5.

To save a custom color palette:

1 Choose Save Palette from the Color Table panel Options pop-up menu.

2 Type a name for the palette and choose a destination folder.

3 Click Save.

You can load the saved palette file into the Swatches panel or use it when exporting other documents.

Assigning transparency

You can make the canvas color and other colors in your file appear transparent when exported as a PNG or GIF. When this is done, a Web page's background image or color can be seen through a portion of the graphic. This can make the graphic appear to be a part of the Web page, rather than resting on top.

In Fireworks, a gray-and-white checkerboard denotes transparent areas in both the Original and Preview windows.

You can also set the canvas color to be transparent (see "Changing the canvas" on page 75). If the canvas color is set to transparent, you can set your optimization transparency by choosing Alpha Transparency from the Transparency pop-up menu.

Use the Transparency eyedropper buttons in the Optimize panel to make a color appear transparent when viewed in a Web browser.

Note: Setting optimized colors to transparent does not affect the actual image, only the exported version of the image. You can see what the exported image will look like in the Preview window. For information on exporting, see "Optimizing and previewing during export" on page 333.

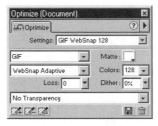

To select a color for transparency:

1 Click Preview, 2-Up, or 4-Up. In 2-Up or 4-Up, click a view other than the original.

2 In the Optimize panel, choose Index Transparency from the Transparency pop-up menu at the bottom of the panel.

The canvas color is made transparent in the preview.

 3 To choose a different color, click the Set Transparency button.

The pointer changes to an eyedropper.

4 Choose the color to make transparent:

• Click a color swatch in the Color Table panel.

• Click a color in the document.

For more information on Preview windows, the Optimize panel, and Color Table panel, see "Optimizing in the workspace" on page 308.

To add colors to or remove colors from the transparency:

1 Click Preview, 2-Up, or 4-Up. In 2-Up or 4-Up, click a view other than the original.

2 In the Optimize panel, click the Add to Transparency or Remove from Transparency button.

Add to Transparency button

Remove from Transparency button

3 Choose another color to make transparent or remove transparency:

• Click a color swatch in the Color Table panel.

• Click a color in the preview.

Anti-aliasing to match the target background color

Anti-aliasing makes an object appear smoother by blending the color of the object into the canvas color. For example, if the object is black and the canvas is white, anti-aliasing adds several shades of gray to the pixels surrounding the object's border to make a smooth transition between the black and white.

To prevent halos, make your canvas color match the background of the target Web page, anti-alias the object to the canvas, and then make the canvas transparent.

If you want to anti-alias a graphic for multiple exports with different-colored backgrounds, use the Matte pop-up menu in the Optimize panel. This is useful if the graphic will appear on Web pages with different-colored backgrounds.

To change the anti-alias colors to match the target background color:

In the Optimize panel, select a color from the Matte pop-up menu. Match it as closely as possible to the color in the target Web page's background color.

Note: This works on soft-edged objects that are directly on top of the canvas.

Removing halos from Web graphics

When viewing an anti-aliased graphic with a transparent canvas color in a Web browser, sometimes an off-colored ring, or halo, of pixels appears around the borders of the graphic.

When you make the canvas color transparent, the pixels from the anti-aliasing remain. When you place the graphic on a Web page that has a background color other than the color to which it was anti-aliased, the perimeter pixels of the anti-aliased object may be apparent on the Web page's background. These form the halo, which is especially noticeable on a dark background.

For native Fireworks files or imported Photoshop files, you can prevent halos by making the canvas color match the Web page's background color.

You must remove the halo for GIF files missing the source file and for imported image files that are anti-aliased to an index color (usually a transparent canvas color). To remove the halo, make the lighter anti-alias colors in the halo transparent using the Optimize panel.

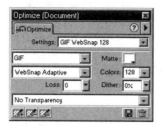

Use Index Transparency and manually trim the halo colors using the Eyedropper buttons in the Optimize panel.

To remove the halo from a graphic:

1 Click Preview, 2-Up, or 4-Up. In 2-Up or 4-Up, click a view other than the original.

   The Optimize panel displays Index Transparency in the transparency pop-up menu.

 2 Choose the Zoom tool and zoom in until you can distinguish the pixels surrounding the borders of the objects in the graphic.

3 In the Optimize panel, click the Add to Transparency button.

   The pointer changes to an eyedropper.

4 Click the off-color pixels that form the halo to make them transparent.

CHAPTER 18
Exporting

After you create graphics in Fireworks, you can easily optimize them and export them in common Web formats, as well as vector application formats. Export and optimization settings do not change the original Fireworks document.

Before you export for the Web, you can optimize the file to be exported. For more information, see "Optimizing in the workspace" on page 308.

If you want to optimize as part of the export process, the Export Preview dialog box offers all optimization options except selective JPEG compression. Export Preview displays any changes you make so you can see how the changes affect image quality and file size.

If you are new to optimizing and exporting Web graphics, use the Export Wizard. This wizard guides you through the export process and suggests settings.

You can export graphics for other vector applications such as Macromedia FreeHand and Flash and Adobe Illustrator and Photoshop. You can also copy and paste Fireworks paths into vector applications.

Exporting an image

Use File > Export if you have finished optimizing your graphic in the workspace. This bypasses Export Preview and opens the Export dialog box.

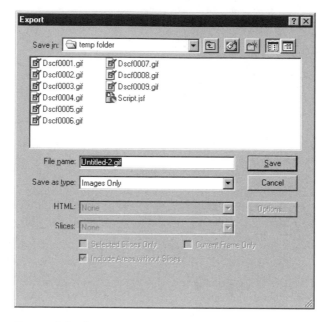

Export dialog box

To export an image:

1 Choose File > Export.

2 Choose a location to store the HTML file in.

   Typically, the best location is a folder within your local site.

3 Enter a file name.

4 Choose HTML and Images from the Save as type pop-up menu.

   Note: Images Only exports just the image and not the HTML.

5 If your image contains slices, choose slicing options. For more information, see "Exporting a slice" on page 336.

6 Select Put Images in Subfolder to choose a separate folder for saving images. If you do not select a folder, your images are placed in a folder called Images, which is automatically created.

Note: Fireworks automatically generates links between the HTML file and the image.

7 Click Save.

Results of exporting

When you export with HTML, Fireworks generates the following files to help you recreate your image on a Web page:

- It generates an HTML file with the necessary JavaScript and tables to reassemble a sliced image or to create rollover functionality. Fireworks-generated HTML always contains a link to the exported image and sets the Web page background color to the canvas or matte color of the graphic. For more information about using the HTML generated with Fireworks, see "Fireworks HTML" on page 403.

- It generates one or more image files, depending on how many slices you created in your document and how many states you included in buttons or rollovers.

- It generates, if necessary, a file called Spacer.gif, a transparent, 1-pixel by 1-pixel GIF that Fireworks uses to fix spacing problems when the sliced images are reassembled in an HTML table. You may choose whether Fireworks exports a spacer. For more information, see "Using spacers or nested tables when slicing" on page 337.

Many export options are available that affect the way Fireworks exports files. For example, options are available for exporting your files to other Macromedia applications, like Flash. See succeeding sections of this chapter for more on these options.

Exporting with the Export Wizard

Use the Export Wizard to go step by step through the export process. Answer questions about the file destination and intended use, and the Export Wizard suggests file type and optimization settings.

If you prefer to optimize to a target file size, the Export Wizard optimizes the exported file to fit within the size constraint you set.

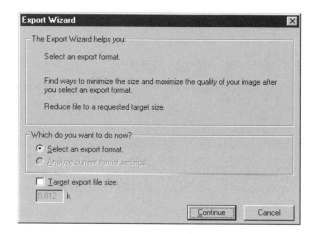

Export Wizard

To export a graphic using the Export Wizard:

1   Choose File > Export Wizard.

2   Answer the questions on each panel, clicking Continue to go to the next.

The Analysis Results screen appears with recommendations about file formats.

Note: Choose Target export file size in the first panel to optimize to a maximum file size.

3   Click Exit.

In the Export Preview window, the 2-Up Preview window shows two recommended export options.

4   Click the preview area that contains the file format you want to use.

5   Make further changes to the optimization settings if needed.

6   Click Export.

7   In the Export dialog box, type a name for the file, choose slicing options and the destination, and click Save.

Optimizing and previewing during export

The Export Preview dialog box displays most Fireworks optimization controls, as well as up to four previews of the exported image. The Options tab contains all the optimization controls found in the Optimize panel and Color Table panel. For more information on optimizing images, see "Optimizing in the workspace" on page 308. Options in Export Preview's Animation panel are also found in the Frames panel. For more information on animating, see "Working with frames" on page 295.

The Export Preview optimizes an unsliced image or all slices to the same setting. To optimize slices to individual settings, use the Optimize panel. The Export Preview also lets you export an image to a target size limit by clicking on the Optimize to Size wizard. This option is also available in the Optimize panel Options pop-up menu.

In addition to optimization controls, Export Preview has unique uses. For example, it appears when setting custom optimization settings during a batch process or when launching Fireworks from within Dreamweaver to optimize an image placed there.

To export a graphic using Export Preview:

1 Choose File > Export Preview.

2 Choose export and optimization settings.

3 Click Export.

4 In the Export dialog box, type a name for the file, choose a Save as type format and the destination, and click Save.

Previewing optimization in the Export Preview

The preview area displays the graphic exactly as it will be exported and estimates file size and download time with the current export settings.

File size and download time estimates

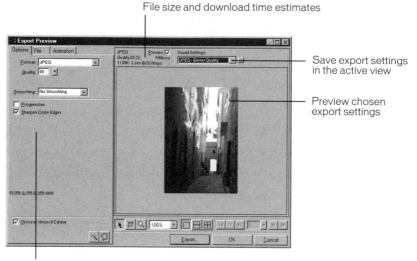

Save export settings in the active view

Preview chosen export settings

Saved set of options for the selected export

You can use split views to compare various settings to find the smallest file size that maintains an acceptable level of quality. You can also constrain the file size using the Optimize to Size wizard.

When exporting animated GIFs or JavaScript rollovers, the estimated file size is a total across all frames.

Note: To increase redraw speed of the Export Preview, deselect Preview. To stop the redraw of the preview area when changing settings, press Esc.

To preview optimization in the Export Preview dialog box:

1 Choose File > Export Preview.

2 To zoom in or zoom out in the preview, choose the Zoom tool. Click to magnify the preview. Alt-click (Windows) or Option-click (Macintosh) to zoom out.

3 To pan the preview area, choose the Pointer tool and drag in a preview, or hold down the Spacebar and drag in a preview.

When multiple views are open, all previews are magnified to the same level. All previews pan simultaneously to display the same portion of the image.

4 To compare optimization settings in the Export Preview, click a split-view button to divide the preview area into two or four previews.

Each preview window can display a preview of the graphic with different export settings.

 5 To optimize a graphic based on a target file size, click the Optimize to Size wizard. Enter a file size in kilobytes.

The Optimize to Size wizard attempts to match the requested file size using these methods:

- Adjusting JPEG quality

- Modifying JPEG smoothing

- Altering the number of colors in 8-bit images

- Changing dither settings in 8-bit images

- Enabling or disabling optimization settings

Exporting frames or layers as multiple files

Fireworks can export all layers or all frames in a document as separate image files using a single export command. Each frame or layer exports as a separate image using the optimization settings specified in the Optimize panel. The name of the layer or frame determines the file name of each exported file.

To export frames or layers as multiple files:

1 Choose File > Export.

2 Choose one the following:

- To export frames as multiple files, choose Frames to Files.

- To export layers as multiple files, choose Layers to Files.

    Note: This exports all layers on the current frame.

3 Select Trim Images to automatically crop the exported images to fit the objects on each frame.

If you want to export frames or layers the same size as the document, deselect Trim Images.

4 Choose a destination and click Save.

Exporting an area

Use the Export Area tool to export a portion of a Fireworks graphic.

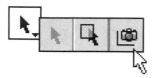

To export a portion of a document:

1 Choose the Export Area tool from the Tools panel.

2 Drag a marquee defining the portion of the document to export.

   When you release the mouse button, the export area remains selected.

3 Resize the export area as required:

• Hold down Shift and drag a handle to resize the export area marquee proportionally.

• Hold down Alt (Windows) or Option (Macintosh) and drag a handle to resize the marquee from the center.

• Hold down Alt+Shift (Windows) or Option+Shift (Macintosh) and drag a handle to constrain the proportions and resize from the center.

• Use the arrow keys to move the marquee. Hold down Shift while using the arrow keys to resize the marquee.

4 Double-click inside the export area marquee to go to Export Preview.

5 Adjust settings in the Export Preview and click Export.

6 In the Save as pop-up menu, choose Images Only.

7 In the Export dialog box, type a file name, choose a destination folder, and click Save.

   Note: To cancel without exporting, double-click outside the export area marquee, press Esc, or choose another tool.

Exporting a slice

Some Web designers create a graphic and then cut it into pieces known as slices. This process is called *slicing*. Slicing is useful if, for example, you want to export some parts of an image as GIF and some as JPEG, to take advantage of both formats. The pieces are then reassembled on a Web page using an HTML table. For more information on slicing, see "Creating slices" on page 256.

Using Export Preview allows you to optimize slices during export. However, optimizing in Export Preview only lets you optimize all slices to the same new setting. You can, however, optimize individual slices in the workspace (see "Optimizing in the workspace" on page 308).

To export selected slices:

1 Finalize the slices' optimization:

• Choose File > Export to export without additional optimization.

• Choose File > Export Preview to change optimization settings and click Export.

2 Choose a slicing method:

• None prevents slicing when exporting, even if you drew slice objects in the document.

• Export Slices exports slices defined by slice objects. Select Include Areas without Slices to export the slices and the graphic. If you have selected individual slices before export, choose Selected Slices Only to export only the slices you have chosen.

• Slice Along Guides exports slices defined by existing guides.

3 In the Export dialog box, type a file name, choose a destination folder, and click Save.

Each slice is exported with unique optimization settings as defined for each slice in the Optimize panel.

Note: To export an individual selected slice, right-click (Windows) or Control-click (Macintosh) and choose Export Selected Slice.

Using spacers or nested tables when slicing

When Fireworks exports HTML for a sliced image, the slices are reassembled in a table. You can export the table for sliced documents using spacers or nested tables:

• Spacers are images that cause table cells to align properly when viewed in a browser.

• A nested table is a table within a table. The nested table does not use spacers. The table may load more slowly in a browser, but because there are no spacers it is easier to edit the HTML.

You can specify unique table export settings for sliced objects for each document. If desired, you can use the Set Defaults button in the HTML Setup dialog box to apply defaults for all new documents.

To define how Fireworks exports HTML tables:

1 Choose File > HTML Setup, or click the Options button in the Export dialog box.

2 Go to the Table tab and choose settings.

3 Choose a setting for Space with:

Nested Tables - no Spacers creates a nested table with no spacers.

Single Table - no Spacers creates a single table with no spacers. This option can cause tables to display incorrectly in some cases.

1-Pixel Transparent Spacer uses a 1-pixel by 1-pixel transparent GIF as a spacer that is resized as needed in the HTML.

4 Select a cell color for text slices:

• Select Use Canvas Color to give cells the same background color as the document canvas.

• Deselect Use Canvas Color to choose a color from the color box pop-up window.

5 From the Contents pop-up menu, choose what to place in empty cells:

None causes empty cells to remain blank.

Spacer Image places a small transparent image called spacer.gif in empty cells.

Non-breaking Space places a space HTML tag in empty cells. The cell appears hollow.

Note: Empty cells only occur if Include Areas without Slices is deselected in the Export dialog box.

6 Click OK.

Exporting vector paths

You can export vector paths to be opened in other vector applications, including Macromedia FreeHand, Adobe Illustrator 7 or later, or Flash 3 or later. In addition, you can copy and paste a vector path into other vector programs.

When you export to FreeHand or Illustrator, the appearance of objects may differ, depending on whether that application supports a given Fireworks feature.

These features are not supported in FreeHand and Illustrator, and do not appear in the exported file:

- Live Effects
- Blending modes
- Texture, pattern, Web dither fills, and all gradient fills (FreeHand)
- Slice objects and image maps
- Many text formatting options
- Guides, grids, and canvas color
- Bitmap images (FreeHand)

In addition, object edges are set to hard and vertical text becomes horizontal.

Exporting to FreeHand and Illustrator

You can export paths from Fireworks to FreeHand or Illustrator to use in your print graphics or to edit with more complex path-editing tools.

To export a graphic for FreeHand or Illustrator:

1 Choose File > Export.

2 Choose Illustrator 7 from the Save as pop-up menu.

3 Click the Options button.

4 In the Illustrator Export Options dialog box choose one of the following:

Export Current Frame Only preserves layer names.

Convert Frames to Layers exports each Fireworks frame as a layer.

5 Select FreeHand Compatible to export the file for use in FreeHand.

Choosing FreeHand Compatible omits images and converts gradient fills to solid fills.

6 Click OK.

7 In the Export dialog box, type a file name, choose a destination folder, and click Save.

Exporting to Macromedia Flash

You can export Fireworks paths to Macromedia Flash for use in Flash graphics or animations on your Web site.

Note: To export a Fireworks path that contains no bitmap characteristics, copy and paste the vector path into Flash using Edit > Copy as Vectors.

Some formatting is lost unless you choose Maintain Appearance in the Flash SWF Export Options dialog box. Stroke size and stroke color are maintained.

Formatting lost during export includes:

- Live Effects

- Opacity and blending modes (objects with opacity become symbols with an alpha channel).

- Masks

- Slice objects, image maps, and behaviors (for example, rollovers are lost).

- Some text formatting options, such as kerning and bitmap strokes

- Feather edges

- Layers

- Anti-aliasing on objects (the Flash player applies anti-aliasing at the document level. Therefore, anti-aliasing is applied to the document when you export).

When exporting to Flash, you can make several choices about how objects are exported.

To export a graphic to Flash:

1 Choose File > Export.

2 Choose Flash SWF from the Save as pop-up menu.

3 Click the Options button.

4 To maintain the document's appearance, choose either or both of these options:

   Choose Objects: Maintain Appearance converts vector objects to bitmap objects and preserves the appearance of applied strokes and fills. Editability is lost.

   Choose Text: Convert to Paths converts text to paths, preserving any custom kerning or spacing you entered in Fireworks.

5 To main path editability, choose Objects: Maintain Paths and Text: Maintain Editability. Effects and formatting are lost.

6 Set the quality of JPEG images using the JPEG quality pop-up slider.

7 Select the frames to be exported and the frame rate in seconds.

8 Click OK.

9 In the Export dialog box, type a file name, choose a destination folder, and click Save.

Copying and pasting selected paths

Use Copy as Vectors to copy selected Fireworks paths to other applications such as FreeHand, Flash, Adobe Photoshop, Illustrator, or CorelDRAW.

Copy as Vectors copies only Fireworks paths.

To copy selected Fireworks paths:

1 Choose Edit > Copy as Vectors.

2 Switch to an open document in another application.

3 Paste the paths into the other application.

Exporting to Dreamweaver libraries

Dreamweaver library items simplify the process of editing and updating a frequently used Web site component, such as a navigation bar. A library item is a portion of an HTML file located in a folder named library at your root site. Library items appear in the Dreamweaver Library palette. You can then drag a copy to any page in your Web site.

You cannot edit a library item directly in the Dreamweaver document; you can only edit the master library item. Then, you can have Dreamweaver update every copy of that item as it is placed throughout your Web site.

You can also export Dreamweaver HTML from Fireworks. For more information on working with Dreamweaver files, see "Getting Fireworks files into Dreamweaver" on page 349.

To export a graphic to Dreamweaver:

1 Choose File > Export.

2 Choose Dreamweaver Library from the Save as pop-up menu.

3 Choose a library folder in your Dreamweaver site in which to place the files. If this is not a library folder, the Select Folder dialog box appears where you can create or locate the folder. Select the folder and click Open.

4 If your image contains slices, choose slicing options. For more information, see "Exporting a slice" on page 336.

5 Select Put Images in Subfolder to choose a separate folder for saving images.

6 Click Save.

Exporting to Director

Combine the power of Fireworks and Director. Fireworks now lets you export graphics into Director 7 and 8 and reimport Director graphics into Fireworks. The export process preserves the behaviors and slices of the graphic. You can safely export sliced images with rollovers and even layered images. This lets Director users take advantage of the optimization and graphic design tools of Fireworks without compromising quality.

To export a graphic to Director:

1 Choose File > Export.

2 Choose Director from the Save as pop-up menu.

3 Choose an option from the Source pop-up menu:

  Fireworks Layers exports each layer in the document.

  Fireworks Slices exports the slices in the document.

4 Select Trim Images to automatically crop the exported images to fit the objects on each frame.

5 Select Put Images in Subfolder to choose a folder for images.

6 In the Export dialog box, type a file name, choose a destination folder, and click Save.

  Note: If your version of Director does not include support for importing Fireworks Director files, install Fireworks Import Xtra for Director before importing Fireworks files into Director. Go to http://www.macromedia.com to download the free Fireworks Import Xtra for Director.

Exporting to Photoshop

A Fireworks image exported into Photoshop maintains the same editability when reopened in Fireworks as other Photoshop graphics. Export options regarding editability, appearance, and file size let you determine the best possible export procedure for your particular graphic. Photoshop users can work with their graphic in Fireworks and then continue editing in Photoshop.

To export a graphic to Photoshop:

1 Choose File > Export.

2 Choose Photoshop PSD from the Save as pop-up menu.

3 In the Settings pop-up menu choose one of the following:

Maintain Editability over Appearance converts objects to layers, keeps effects editable, and converts the text to editable Photoshop text layers.

Maintain Fireworks Appearance converts each object into an individual Photoshop layer, turns effects into objects, and turns text into images.

Smaller Photoshop File flattens each layer into a fully rendered image.

Custom allows you to choose specific settings for objects, effects, and text. For more information, see "Customizing files for export to Photoshop" on page 343.

4 In the Export dialog box, type a file name, choose a destination folder, and click Save.

Note: Photoshop 5.5 and earlier cannot open files with more than 100 layers. You must delete or merge layers if the Fireworks document you are exporting contains more than 100 objects.

Customizing files for export to Photoshop

When you export a file to Photoshop, you can choose customized settings for exporting objects, effects, and text.

To customize settings for export to Photoshop:

1 In the Export dialog box, choose Custom from the Settings pop-up menu.

2 In the Objects pop-up menu choose one of the following:

Convert to Photoshop Layers converts individual Fireworks objects to Photoshop layers.

Flatten Each Fireworks Layer flattens each Fireworks layer into a Photoshop layer.

3 In the Effects pop-up menu choose one of the following:

Maintain Editability converts Fireworks Live Effects to their equivalent in Photoshop. If the effects do not exist in Photoshop they are discarded.

Render Effects flattens effects into their objects. They are not editable in Photoshop.

4 In the Text pop-up menu choose one of the following:

Maintain Editability converts text to an editable Photoshop layer. Text formatting that is not supported by Photoshop will be lost.

Render Text turns text into an image object.

Exporting in WBMP format

Wireless Bitmap (WBMP) is a graphic format used for mobile computing devices. This format is specifically used on Wireless Application Protocol (WAP) pages.

To export a graphic in WBMP format:

1   In the Optimize panel, choose WBMP from the format type pop-up menu.

    Note: As this is a 1-bit format, only two colors are visible: black and white.

2   Choose File > Export.

3   Choose a format from the Save as type pop-up menu. This is usually Images Only or HTML and Images.

4   In the Export dialog box, type a file name, choose a destination folder, and click Save.

Exporting CSS layers

Cascading Style Sheets (CSS) allow you to make smaller, faster Web pages. CSS layers let you create style sheets that define how different elements, such as headers and links, appear. These are normally used by expert users so they can further manipulate the HTML after export. CSS layers can overlap and be stacked on top of one another. In Fireworks, normal HTML output does not overlap.

To export a graphic in CSS layers:

1   Choose File > Export.

2   Choose CSS Layers from the Save as type pop-up menu.

3   In the Source pop-up menu choose one of the following:

    Fireworks Layers exports all layers as CSS layers.

    Fireworks Frames exports all frames as CSS layers.

    Fireworks Slices exports the slices in the document as CSS layers.

4   Select Trim Images to automatically crop the exported images and layers to fit the objects.

5   Select Put Images in Subfolder to choose a folder for images.

6   In the Export dialog box, type a file name, choose a destination folder, and click Save.

Exporting to Lotus Domino Designer

Exporting images to Domino Designer results in a single image file. This file is in either GIF or JPEG format, depending on the optimization settings you choose before exporting.

To export a graphic to Domino Designer:

1 Choose File > Export.

2 Choose Lotus Domino Designer from the Save as type pop-up menu.

3 In the Source pop-up menu choose one of the following:

Fireworks Frames exports the top four frames into a file.

Fireworks Layers exports the top four layers into a file.

Fireworks Slices exports the first four frames of each slice as a separate file.

4 Select Trim Images to automatically crop the exported images to fit the objects on each frame.

5 In the Export dialog box, type a file name, choose a destination folder, and click Save.

Using the Update HTML command

The Update HTML command updates either Fireworks-generated HTML and images or images only. Use Launch and Edit from Dreamweaver when updating HTML to preserve the changes you have made to an HTML file that is being edited in Dreamweaver. For more information, see "Fireworks HTML" on page 403.

To update HTML:

1 Choose File > Update HTML.

2 Select the file to update in the Locate HTML File dialog box.

3 Click Open.

4 If no Fireworks-generated HTML is found, click OK to insert new HTML at the end of the document.

5 If Fireworks-generated HTML is found, choose one of the following and click OK:

Replace Images and their HTML replaces the previous Fireworks HTML.

Update Images Only overwrites only the images.

6 The Select Images Folder opens. Choose a folder to place the images into and click Open.

Editing Fireworks images placed in Dreamweaver

Edit Fireworks images placed in Dreamweaver by launching and editing graphics from Dreamweaver. Edit GIFs and JPEGs from within Dreamweaver using a Fireworks source file, or optimize the image without affecting the source.

Before you launch and edit, be sure to set Fireworks as an external editor in Dreamweaver. For more information on working with Fireworks images in Dreamweaver, see "Editing Fireworks files placed in Dreamweaver" on page 356.

In Dreamweaver, choose Edit and Launch Fireworks to update Fireworks graphics. In other HTML editors, edit the original Fireworks source file and choose File > Update HTML from within Fireworks to update the HTML and images.

HTML Setup

HTML Setup lets you define how Fireworks exports HTML. These settings can be document specific or used as your default setting for all HTML exports. Changes made in the Document Specific tab affect the current document only. General and Table settings are global preferences.

To define how Fireworks exports HTML:

1 Choose File > HTML Setup or click the Options button in the Export dialog box.

2 In the General tab choose from the following options:

• Choose an HTML Style to set the style for exported HTML.

• Choose a file extension name from the Extension pop-up menu or enter a new one.

• Select Include HTML Comments to include comments regarding where to cut and paste in the HTML.

• Select Lowercase File Name to make the name of the HTML file, including the extension and image files, lowercase on export.

• Choose an associated application from the File Creator pop-up menu (Macintosh). When you open the exported HTML file, it automatically opens in the application you have specified.

3 In the Table tab, choose settings for your HTML tables. For information on how to define HTML tables for export, see "HTML Setup" on page 346.

4 In the Document Specific tab, choose from the following options:

- Choose a formula for auto-naming slices in the Slice Auto-naming pop-up menus.

- Enter text into the Alternate Image Description text box. This alt text appears on the image placeholder while the image is downloading from the Web or in place of an image if it fails to download. In some browsers it may also appear as a tooltip when the mouse passes over the image. This is also an aid for vision-impaired Web users.

- Select Multiple Nav Bar HTML Pages when using an HTML document with no frames.

5 Click Set Defaults to save these settings as your global default settings.

6 Click OK.

19

CHAPTER 19
Using Dreamweaver and Fireworks Together

Unique integration features make it easy to work on files interchangeably in Macromedia Dreamweaver 4 and Macromedia Fireworks 4. Dreamweaver and Fireworks recognize and share many of the same file edits, including changes to links, image maps, table slices, and more. Together, the two applications provide a streamlined workflow for editing, optimizing, and placing Web graphics files in HTML pages.

If you want to modify Fireworks images and tables placed in a Dreamweaver document, you can launch Fireworks to make edits and then return to the updated document in Dreamweaver. If you want to make quick optimization edits to placed Fireworks images and animations, you can launch the Fireworks optimization dialog box and enter updated settings. In either case, updates are made to the placed files in Dreamweaver, as well as to the source Fireworks files, if those source files were launched.

Getting Fireworks files into Dreamweaver

You can place Fireworks images and HTML code in Dreamweaver in a number of different ways. In Dreamweaver, you can use the insert features to place Fireworks files into documents. From Fireworks, you can export files directly to a Dreamweaver site folder or you can copy and paste HTML code into a Dreamweaver document.

Placing Fireworks images in Dreamweaver

You can place Fireworks-generated GIF, JPEG, or PNG images directly in a Dreamweaver document.

To insert a Fireworks image into a Dreamweaver document:

1   Place the insertion point where you want the image to appear in the Dreamweaver Document window.

2   Do one of the following:

*   Choose Insert > Image.

*   Click the Insert Image button in the Common category of the Objects panel.

3   Navigate to the desired Fireworks file, and click Open.

If the Fireworks file is not in the current Dreamweaver site, a message appears, asking whether you want to copy the file to the root folder.

Inserting Fireworks HTML code into Dreamweaver

Dreamweaver lets you insert Fireworks-generated HTML code, complete with associated images, slices, and JavaScript, into a document. This insertion feature makes it easy for you add tables or image maps created in Fireworks to a Dreamweaver document.

To insert Fireworks HTML into a Dreamweaver document:

1   In Dreamweaver, save your document in a defined site.

2   Place the insertion point in the document where you want the inserted HTML code to begin.

3   Do one of the following:

*   Choose Insert > Interactive Images > Fireworks HTML.

*   Click the Insert Fireworks HTML button in the Common category of the Objects panel.

4   In the dialog box that appears, click Browse to choose the desired Fireworks HTML file.

5   Select the Delete File After Insertion option to move the HTML file to the Recycle Bin (Windows) or Trash (Macintosh) when the operation is complete.

Use this option if you no longer need the Fireworks HTML file after inserting it. This option does not affect the source PNG file associated with the HTML file.

Note: If the HTML file is on a network drive, it is permanently deleted, not moved to the Recycle Bin or Trash.

6   Click OK to insert the HTML code, along with its associated images, slices, and JavaScript, into the Dreamweaver document.

Copying and pasting Fireworks HTML into Dreamweaver

A fast way to place Fireworks-generated images and tables in Dreamweaver is to copy and paste Fireworks HTML code directly into a Dreamweaver document.

To copy and paste Fireworks HTML into Dreamweaver:

1 In Fireworks, choose Edit > Copy HTML Code.

2 Follow the wizard as it guides you through the settings for exporting your HTML and images. When prompted, specify your Dreamweaver site folder as the destination for the exported images.

The wizard exports the images to the specified destination and copies the HTML code to the Clipboard.

3 In Dreamweaver, place the insertion point in the document where you want to paste the HTML code, and choose Edit > Paste.

All HTML and JavaScript code associated with the Fireworks files you exported is copied into the Dreamweaver document, and all links to images are updated.

To export and paste Fireworks HTML into Dreamweaver:

1 In Fireworks, choose File > Export.

2 In the Export dialog box, specify your Dreamweaver site folder as the destination for the exported images.

3 Choose HTML and Images from the Save as type pop-up menu.

4 Choose Copy to Clipboard from the HTML pop-up menu, and click Save.

5 In Dreamweaver, place the insertion point in the document where you want to paste the HTML code, and choose Edit > Paste.

All HTML and JavaScript code associated with the Fireworks files you exported is copied into the Dreamweaver document, and all links to images are updated.

Exporting Fireworks files to Dreamweaver

The File > Export command in Fireworks lets you export and save optimized images and HTML files to a location inside the desired Dreamweaver site folder. You can then open the files for editing in Dreamweaver.

Alternatively, you can export Fireworks files as Cascading Style Sheet (CSS) layers or Dreamweaver library items. Dreamweaver library items simplify the process of editing and updating a frequently used Web site component, such as a series of footer links or a navigation bar. A library item is a portion of an HTML file located in a folder named Library at your site root. You can drag copies of a library item to any page in your Web site.

To export Fireworks images and HTML to Dreamweaver:

1 In Fireworks, choose File > Export.

2 Choose HTML and Images from the Save as type pop-up menu.

3 Choose Export HTML File from the HTML pop-up menu.

4 Specify a destination folder inside your Dreamweaver site folder.

5 Click Save to export your files.

To export Fireworks files as CSS layers:

1 In Fireworks, choose File > Export.

2 Choose CSS Layers (.htm) from the Save as type pop-up menu.

3 Specify a destination folder inside your Dreamweaver site folder.

4 Click Save to export your files.

To export a Fireworks file as a Dreamweaver library item:

1 In Fireworks, choose File > Export.

2 Choose Dreamweaver Library (.lbi) from the Save as type pop-up menu.

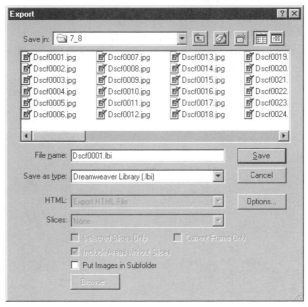

3 Name the file, and specify a destination folder named Library located at the Dreamweaver site root.

If necessary, Fireworks prompts you to create this folder.

4 Click Save to export your file.

Launching Fireworks from within Dreamweaver

You can launch Fireworks directly from a Dreamweaver document by targeting a placed Fireworks image, table slice, or table for either editing or optimization. In order for these launch-and-edit features to work properly, you must designate Fireworks as the primary external image editor in Dreamweaver.

Designating Fireworks as the primary external image editor for Dreamweaver

Dreamweaver 4 provides preferences for automatically launching specific applications to edit specific file types. To use the Fireworks launch-and-edit features, make sure that Fireworks 4 is set as the primary editor for GIF, JPEG, and PNG files in Dreamweaver.

Although you can use earlier versions of Fireworks as external image editors, these versions offer limited launch-and-edit capabilities. Fireworks 3 does not fully support the launch and edit of placed tables and slices within tables, while Fireworks 2 does not support the launch and edit of source PNG files for placed images.

To set Fireworks 4 as the primary external image editor for Dreamweaver 4:

1 In Dreamweaver, choose Edit > Preferences and select File Types/Editors.

2 In the Extensions list, select a Web file extension (.gif, .jpg, or .png).

3 In the Editors list, select Fireworks 4 and click Make Primary.

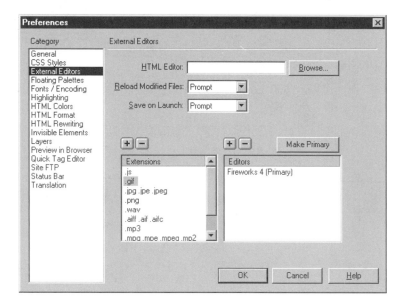

4 Repeat steps 2 and 3 to set Fireworks 4 as the primary editor for other Web file extensions.

About Design Notes and source files

Whenever you export a Fireworks file from a saved PNG source to a Dreamweaver site, Fireworks writes a Design Note that contains information about the file. For example, when you export a Fireworks table, Fireworks writes a Design Note for each exported slice file and for the HTML file that assembles the table slices. These Design Notes contain references to the source PNG file that spawned the exported files.

When you launch and edit a Fireworks image from within Dreamweaver, Dreamweaver uses the Design Note to locate a source PNG for that file. For best results, always save your Fireworks source PNG file and exported files in a Dreamweaver site. This ensures that any user sharing the site will be able to locate the source PNG when launching Fireworks from within Dreamweaver.

Specifying launch-and-edit preferences for Fireworks source files

The Fireworks launch-and-edit preferences let you specify how to handle source PNG files when launching Fireworks files from another application, such as Macromedia Director or Dreamweaver.

Dreamweaver recognizes the Fireworks launch-and-edit preferences only in certain cases where you launch and optimize a Fireworks image. Specifically, you must be launching and optimizing an image that is not part of a Fireworks table and that does not contain a correct Design Note path to a source PNG file. In all other cases, including all launch-and-edit cases of Fireworks images, Dreamweaver automatically launches the source PNG file, prompting you to locate the source file if it cannot be found.

To specify launch-and-edit preferences for Fireworks:

1 In Fireworks, choose Edit > Preferences, and click the Launch and Edit tab (Windows) or choose Launch and Edit from the pop-up menu (Macintosh).

2 Specify the preference options to use when editing or optimizing Fireworks images placed in an external application:

Always Use Source PNG automatically launches the Fireworks PNG file that is defined in the Design Note as the source for the placed image. Updates are made to both the source PNG and its corresponding placed image.

Never Use Source PNG automatically launches the placed Fireworks image, whether or not a source PNG file exists. Updates are made to the placed image only.

Ask When Launching lets you specify each time whether or not to launch the source PNG file. When you edit or optimize a placed image, Fireworks displays a message prompting you to make a launch-and-edit decision. You can also specify global launch-and-edit preferences from this message.

Editing Fireworks files placed in Dreamweaver

Launch-and-edit integration lets you use Fireworks to edit Fireworks-generated images and tables placed in a Dreamweaver document. Dreamweaver automatically launches Fireworks, letting you make the desired Fireworks edits to the image. The updates you make in Fireworks are automatically applied to the placed image in Dreamweaver.

Fireworks recognizes and preserves many edits made to the document in Dreamweaver, including changed links, edited image maps, and edited text in text slices. The Property inspector in Dreamweaver helps you identify Fireworks-generated images, table slices, and tables in a document.

Editing Fireworks images

You can launch Fireworks to edit individual images placed in a Dreamweaver document.

To launch and edit a Fireworks image placed in Dreamweaver:

1 In Dreamweaver, choose Window > Properties to open the Property inspector, if needed.

2 Do one of the following:

• Select the desired image. (The Property inspector identifies the selection as a Fireworks image and displays the name of the known PNG source file for the image.) Then click Edit in the Property inspector.

- Hold down Control (Windows) or Command (Macintosh), and double-click the image you want to edit.

- Right-click (Windows) or Control-click (Macintosh) the desired image, and choose Edit With Fireworks 4 from the context menu.

  Dreamweaver launches Fireworks, if it is not already open.

3 If prompted, specify whether to launch a source Fireworks file for the placed image.

4 In Fireworks, edit the image. The document window indicates that you are modifying an image from Dreamweaver.

   Dreamweaver recognizes and preserves all edits applied to the image in Fireworks.

5 When you are finished making edits, click Done in the document window.

   Clicking Done exports the image using the current optimization settings for the source PNG file, updates the GIF or JPEG used by Dreamweaver, and saves the PNG source file if a source file was selected.

   Note: When you open an image from the Dreamweaver Site window, the Fireworks integration features described above are not in effect; Fireworks does not open the original PNG file. To use the Fireworks integration features, open images from within the Dreamweaver Document window.

Editing Fireworks tables

When you launch and edit an image slice that is part of a placed Fireworks table, Dreamweaver automatically launches the source PNG file for the entire table.

To launch and edit a Fireworks table placed in Dreamweaver:

1 In Dreamweaver, choose Window > Properties to open the Property inspector if needed.

2 Do one of the following:

• Click inside the table, and click the TABLE tag in the status bar to select the entire table. (The Property inspector identifies the selection as a Fireworks table and displays the name of the known PNG source file for the table.) Then click Edit in the Property inspector.

• Click the top left corner of the table to select it, and then click Edit in the Property inspector.

• Select the desired table slice, and click Edit in the Property inspector.

• Hold down Control (Windows) or Command (Macintosh), and double-click the image you want to edit.

• Right-click (Windows) or Control-click (Macintosh) the desired table slice, and choose Edit With Fireworks 4 from the context menu.

   Dreamweaver launches Fireworks, if it is not already open. The source PNG file for the entire table appears in the document window.

3 In Fireworks, edit the table image.

   Dreamweaver recognizes and preserves all edits applied to the image in Fireworks.

4 When you are finished making edits, click Done in the document window.

   Clicking Done exports HTML and image slice files for the table using the current optimization settings, updates the table placed in Dreamweaver, and saves the PNG source file. Fireworks exports and replaces only those HTML and image slice files that are needed to update the table in Dreamweaver.

Optimizing Fireworks images and animations placed in Dreamweaver

You can launch Fireworks from Dreamweaver to make quick export changes, such as resampling or changing the file type, to placed Fireworks images and animations. Fireworks lets you make changes to optimization settings, animation settings, and the size and area of the exported image.

To change optimization settings for a Fireworks image placed in Dreamweaver:

1 In Dreamweaver, select the desired image and choose Commands > Optimize Image in Fireworks.

2 If prompted, specify whether to launch a source Fireworks file for the placed image.

3 In Fireworks, make the desired edits in the optimization dialog box:

- To edit optimization settings, click the Options tab. For more information, see "Optimizing and previewing during export" on page 333.

- To edit the size and area of the exported image, click the File tab. For more information, see "Resizing placed Fireworks images" on page 360.

- To edit animation settings for the image, click the Animation tab. For more information, see "Editing placed Fireworks animations" on page 360.

4 When you are finished editing the image, click Update.

Clicking Update exports the image using the new optimization settings, updates the GIF or JPEG placed in Dreamweaver, and saves the PNG source file if a source file was selected.

If you changed the format of the image, Dreamweaver's link checker prompts you to update references to the image. For example, if you changed the format of an image called my_image from GIF to JPEG, clicking OK at this prompt changes all references to my_image.gif in your site to my_image.jpg.

Resizing placed Fireworks images

When launching and optimizing a Fireworks image from Dreamweaver, you can resize the image and select a specific image area to be exported.

To specify exported image dimensions:

1 In Fireworks, in the optimization dialog box, click the File tab.

2 To scale the image as it is exported, specify a scale percentage or enter the desired width and height in pixels. Select Constrain to scale the width and height proportionally.

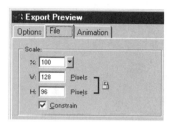

3 To export a selected area of the image, select the Export Area option and specify the export area:

• Drag the dotted border that appears around the preview until it encloses the desired export area. (Drag inside the preview to move hidden areas into view.)

• Enter pixel coordinates for the boundaries of the export area.

Editing placed Fireworks animations

If you are launching and optimizing a placed Fireworks animation, you can also edit the animation settings. The animation options in the optimization dialog box are similar to those available in the Fireworks Frames panel.

To edit an animated image:

1 In Fireworks, in the optimization dialog box, click the Animation tab.

2 Use the following techniques to preview animation frames at any time:

• To display a single frame, select the desired frame in the list on the left side of the dialog box, or use the frame controls in the lower right area of the dialog box.

• To play the animation, click the Play/Stop control in the lower right area of the dialog box.

3 Make edits to the animation:

• To specify the frame disposal method, select the desired frame in the list and choose an option from the pop-up menu (indicated by the trash icon).

• To set the frame delay, select the desired frame in the list and enter the delay time in hundredths of a second.

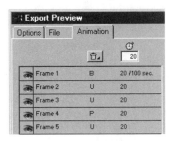

• To set the animation to play repeatedly, click the Looping button and choose the desired number of repetitions from the pop-up menu.

• Select the Auto-Crop option to crop each frame as a rectangular area, so that only the image area that differs between frames is output. Selecting this option reduces file size.

• Select the Auto-Difference option to output only pixels that change between frames. Selecting this option reduces file size.

Updating Fireworks HTML placed in Dreamweaver

The File > Update HTML command in Fireworks provides an alternative to the launch-and-edit technique for updating Fireworks files placed in Dreamweaver. With Update HTML, you can edit a source PNG image in Fireworks and then automatically update any exported HTML code and image files placed in a Dreamweaver document. This command lets you update Dreamweaver files even when Dreamweaver is not running.

To update Fireworks HTML placed in Dreamweaver:

1 In Fireworks, choose File > Update HTML.

2 Navigate to the Dreamweaver file containing the HTML you wish to update, and click Open.

3 Navigate to the folder destination where you want to place the updated image files, and click Choose.

   Fireworks updates the HTML and JavaScript code in the Dreamweaver document. Fireworks also exports updated images associated with the HTML and places the images in the specified destination folder.

   If Fireworks cannot find matching HTML code to update, it gives you the option of inserting new HTML code into the Dreamweaver document. Fireworks places the JavaScript section of the new code at the beginning of the document and places the HTML table or link to the image at the end.

Creating Web photo albums

The Create Web Photo Album command in Dreamweaver lets you automatically generate a Web site that showcases an album of images from a given folder. This command uses JavaScript to call Fireworks, which creates a thumbnail and a larger version for each of the images in the folder. Dreamweaver then creates a Web page containing all the thumbnails, and links to the larger images. To use the Create Web Photo Album, you must have both Dreamweaver and Fireworks installed on your system.

Before you begin, place all the images for your photo album in a single folder. (The folder is not required to be in a site.) In addition, make sure that the image file names end in extensions recognized by the Create Web Photo Album command (.gif, .jpg, .jpeg, .png, .psd, .tif, or .tiff). Images with unrecognized file extensions are not included in the photo album.

To create a Web photo album:

1 In Dreamweaver, choose Commands > Create Web Photo Album.

2 In the Photo Album Title text field, enter a title. The title will be displayed in a gray rectangle at the top of the page containing the thumbnails.

If desired, you may enter up to two lines of additional text to appear directly beneath the title, in the Subheading Info and Other Info text fields.

3 Choose the folder containing source images by clicking the Browse button next to the Source Images Folder text field. Then choose (or create) a destination folder in which to place all the exported images and HTML files by clicking the Browse button next to the Destination Folder text field.

The destination folder should not already contain a photo album; if it does, and if any new images have the same names as previously used images, you may overwrite existing thumbnail and image files.

4 Specify display options for the thumbnail images:

• Choose a size for the thumbnail images from the Thumbnail Size pop-up menu. Images are scaled proportionally to create thumbnails that fit within a square that has the indicated pixel dimensions.

• To display the file name of each original image below the corresponding thumbnail, select Show Filenames.

• Enter the number of columns for the table that displays the thumbnails.

5 Choose a format for the thumbnail images from the Thumbnail Format pop-up menu:

GIF WebSnap 128 creates GIF thumbnails that use a Web adaptive palette of up to 128 colors.

GIF WebSnap 256 creates GIF thumbnails that use a Web adaptive palette of up to 256 colors.

JPEG - Better Quality creates JPEG thumbnails with relatively higher quality and larger file sizes.

JPEG - Smaller File creates JPEG thumbnails with relatively lower quality and smaller file sizes.

6 Choose a format for the large-size images from the Photo Format pop-up menu. A large-size image of the specified format is created for each of your original images. You may specify a format for the large-size images that differs from the format you specified for the thumbnails.

Note: The Create Web Photo Album command does not let you use your original image files as the large-size images because original image formats other than GIF and JPEG might not display properly on all browsers. Note that if your original images are JPEG files, the large-size images generated may have larger file sizes or lower quality than the original files.

7 Choose a Scale percentage for the large-size images.

Setting Scale to 100% creates large-size images the same size as the originals. Note that the scale percentage is applied to all of the images; if your original images aren't all the same size, scaling them by the same percentage may not produce the desired results.

8 Select Create Navigation Page for Each Photo to create an individual Web page for each source image, containing navigation links labeled Back, Home, and Next.

If you select this option, the thumbnails link to the navigation pages. If you don't select this option, the thumbnails link directly to the large-size images.

9 Click OK to create the HTML and image files for the Web photo album.

Fireworks launches (if it's not already running) and creates the thumbnails and large-size images. This may take several minutes if you've included a large number of image files. When the processing is complete, Dreamweaver becomes active again and creates the page containing the thumbnails.

10 When a dialog box appears that says "Album Created," click OK. You may have to wait a few seconds for your photo album page to appear. The thumbnails are shown in alphabetical order by file name.

Note: Clicking the Cancel button in the Dreamweaver dialog box after processing has begun does not stop the process of creating the photo album; it merely prevents Dreamweaver from displaying the main photo album page.

CHAPTER 20
Automating Repetitive Tasks

Web designers often get bogged down in repetitive tasks, such as optimizing images or converting images to fit within certain constraints. Part of the power of Fireworks is its capability to automate and simplify many tedious drawing, editing, and file conversion tasks.

To speed up your editing process, use Find and Replace to search for and replace elements within a file or elements from multiple files. Find and replace elements such as URLs, fonts, color, text, and commands created in the History panel.

Use Batch Process to convert entire groups of image files into other formats or to change their color palettes. Batch Process can apply custom optimization settings to groups of files. You can also resize a group of files, making Batch Process an ideal tool for creating thumbnails.

Use the History panel to create commands that are shortcuts for commonly used features or to create a script that can perform a complex series of steps. Fireworks can understand and execute JavaScript, so advanced users can automate very complex tasks by writing JavaScript commands and then executing them within Fireworks. You can control nearly every Fireworks command or setting through JavaScript using special JavaScript commands that Fireworks can interpret.

Finding and replacing

Use Find and Replace to search for and replace elements in a document, such as text, URLs, fonts, and colors. Find and Replace can search the current document or multiple files.

As you use Find and Replace, Fireworks can track and store a log of the changes in the Project Log panel. Find and Replace only works in Fireworks PNG files or in files containing vector objects, such as FreeHand, uncompressed CorelDRAW, and Illustrator files.

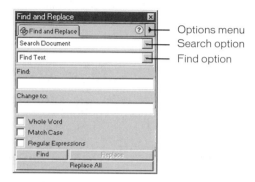

Find and Replace panel

To find and replace elements of a document:

1 Open the document.

2 Open the Find and Replace panel:

• Choose Edit > Find and Replace

• Choose Window> Find and Replace

• Press Control-F (Windows) or Command-F (Macintosh).

3 From the Search pop-up menu, choose a source for the search.

4 From the Find pop-up menu, choose an attribute to search for.

5 Set Find and Change To options.

6 Choose the type of find-and-replace operation you want to conduct:

• Find locates the next instance of the element. Found elements appear selected in the document.

• Replace changes a found element with the contents of the Change To option.

• Replace All finds and replaces every occasion of a found element throughout the search range.

   Note: Replacing objects in multiple files saves those files; you cannot reverse the change using Edit › Undo.

Selecting the source for the search

Fireworks can perform a find and replace in any of five locations. Choose an option from the Search pop-up menu to select the range of content you want to find and replace:

- Search Selection finds and replaces elements only among the currently selected objects and text.

- Search Frame finds and replaces elements only within the current frame.

- Search Document finds and replaces elements in the active document.

- Search Project Log finds and replaces elements in files listed in the Project Log. For more information, see "Managing searches with the Project Log" on page 379.

- Search Files finds and replaces elements across multiple files. If you choose Search Files, navigate to a file you want to search, and then click Add to include that file in the find and replace list. Click Add All to add all files in the current folder to the find and replace list.

Finding and replacing in multiple files

When finding and replacing among multiple files, choose Replace Options from the Options pop-up menu to set how multiple open files are handled after the search.

To save and close each file after it is searched:

1 Choose Replace Options from the Options pop-up menu of the Find and Replace panel.

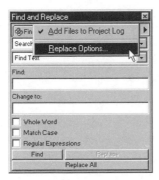

2 Check Save and Close Files in the Replace Options dialog box and click OK.

Each file is saved and closed after the find and replace. Only the originally active documents remain open.

Note: If Save and Close is disabled and you are batch processing a large number of files, Fireworks may run out of memory and abort the batch process.

3 Choose one of the following from the Backups pop-up menu:

- To find and replace without backing up the original files, choose No Backups. The changed files replace the original files.

- To create and store only one backup copy of each file changed during a find and replace, choose Overwrite Existing Backups.

  If you perform additional find-and-replace operations, the previous original file always replaces the backup copy. The backup copies are stored in a subfolder called Original Files.

- To save all backup copies of files changed during a find and replace, choose Incremental Backups.

The original files are moved to an Original Files subfolder within their current folder, and an incremental number is appended to each file name.

If you perform additional find-and-replace operations, the original file is copied to the Original Files folder, and the next higher number is added to its file name.

For example, for a file named Drawing.png, the first time you find and replace, the backup file is named Drawing-1.png. The second time you find and replace, the backup file is named Drawing-2.png, and so on.

Finding and replacing text

Choose Find Text from the Find pop-up menu of the Find and Replace panel to search for and replace words, phrases, or text strings in Fireworks documents. In the Find option, enter the text to search for. Enter the replacement text in the Change To option.

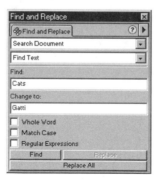

You can also choose options that further define the search:

- Whole Word finds the text only in the same form in which it appears in the Find option, not as part of any other word.

- Match Case distinguishes between uppercase and lowercase letters when searching text.

- Regular Expressions matches parts of words or numbers conditionally during a search.

Finding and replacing fonts

Choose Find Font from the Find pop-up menu of the Find and Replace panel to search for and replace fonts in one or more Fireworks documents.

Specify the font or font characteristics in the Find and Change To areas. Specify the font or font characteristics to use instead in the Change To area:

- Min sets the minimum point size of the selected font to find.

- Max sets the maximum point size of the selected font to find.

Finding and replacing colors

Choose Find Color from the Find pop-up menu to search for and replace colors in Fireworks documents.

Choose an item from the Apply to pop-up menu to determine how the colors found in the find and replace are applied:

- Fills finds and replaces a fill color, except within pattern fills.

- Strokes finds and replaces stroke colors only.

- Fills & Strokes finds and replaces both fill and stroke colors.

- Effects finds and replaces effect colors only.

- All Properties finds and replaces fill, stroke, and effect colors.

Finding and replacing URLs

Choose Find URL from the Find pop-up menu of the Find and Replace panel to search for and replace URLs assigned to Web objects in Fireworks documents.

You can also choose options that further define the search:

- Whole Word finds the text only in the same form in which it appears in the Find option, not as part of any other word.
- Match Case distinguishes between uppercase and lowercase letters when searching text.
- Regular Expressions matches parts of words or numbers conditionally during a search.

Finding and replacing non-Websafe colors

A non-Websafe color is a color not included in the Web216 color palette. A color is non-Websafe if it is not common to both Macintosh and Windows platforms. Choose Find Non-Web216 from the Find pop-up menu of the Find and Replace panel to search for all non-Websafe colors and replace them with Websafe colors.

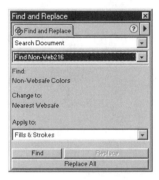

Note: Find Non-Web216 does not find or replace pixels within image objects.

Batch processing

Batch processing is a convenient way to automatically convert a group of graphic files. When batch processing, choose from these options:

- Convert a selection of files to another format.
- Convert a selection of files to the same format with different optimization settings.
- Scale exported files.
- Find and replace text, colors, URLs, fonts, and non-Web216 colors.
- Rename groups of files by adding a prefix or suffix.
- Perform commands on a selection of files.

To batch process files:

1 Choose File > Batch Process.

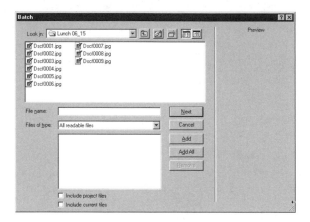

2 Choose the files to process. Select files from different folders, or group them by file type.

    Add adds selected files and folders to the list of files to batch process. If a folder is selected, all valid, readable files within the folder are added to the batch process.

    Note: Valid files are files that have been created, named, and saved. If the latest file version is not saved, you are asked to save it, and you can then continue the batch process. If you don't save the file, the entire batch process ends.

    Add All adds all valid files in the currently selected folder to the list of files to batch process.

    Remove removes selected files from the list of files to batch process.

3 Select Add Files from Project Log to add all files from the Project Log. These files will not appear in the list of files to batch process, but they are included in the process.

4 Select Add Current Open Files to add all currently open files. These files will not appear in the list of files to batch process, but they are included in the process.

5 Click Next.

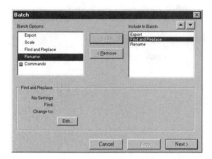

6 To add a task to the batch, select it in the Batch Options list and click Add.

Each task may be added only once, except commands.

 7 To reorder the list, select the task in the Include in Batch list and click the up and down order buttons.

Note: The order in which tasks appear in the Include in Batch list is the order in which the tasks will be performed during the batch process.

8 Select a task in the Include in Batch list to view extra options for that task. Choose settings for each option as required.

9 To remove a task from the batch, select the task in the Include in Batch list and click Remove.

10 Click Next.

11 Choose options for saving processed files:

Same Location as Original File saves the file in the same location as its source file and overwrites the source file if the file names are the same and in the same format.

Custom Location lets you choose a location in which to save the processed files.

12 Select Backups to choose backup options for the original files. It is always safer to back up files. For more information, see "Backing up batch-processed files" on page 377.

13 Click Save Script to save as a script. For more information, see "Saving batch processes as scripts" on page 377.

14 Click Batch to save your batch process.

Changing optimization settings with a batch process

Add Export in the Batch Process dialog box to change file optimization settings

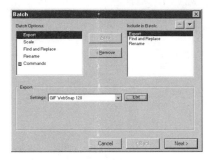

To set export settings to apply to files during a batch process:

1   From the Settings pop-up menu, choose an option:

   Use Settings from Each File keeps each file's previous export settings during the batch process. For example, when batch processing a folder of GIFs and JPEGs, the resulting files remain GIFs and JPEGs and the original palette and compression settings are used when exporting each file.

   Custom lets you enter custom export settings for the batch process. Or you can click Edit to enter settings in the Export Preview dialog box. Click OK.

2   Choose a preset export setting such as GIF Web 216 or JPEG - Better Quality. All files will be converted to this setting.

3   Click Next to continue the batch process.

Scaling graphics with a batch process

Add the Scale option in the Batch Process dialog box to alter the height and width of the images being exported.

To set scaling options for batch-processed files.

1   In the Scale pop-up menu choose an option:

• Choose No Scaling to export the files unaltered.

• Choose Scale to Size and enter a width and height to scale images to an exact width and height.

• Choose Scale to Fit Area and enter maximum width and height values to make images fit proportionally within the specified width and height range.

   Note: Choose Scale to Fit Area to convert a group of images to thumbnail images.

• Choose Scale to Percentage to scale images by a percentage.

2 Click Next to continue the batch process.

Finding and replacing during a batch process

Add Find and Replace in the Batch Process dialog box to find and replace text, fonts, colors, or URLs within buttons, hotspots, or slices when batch processing.

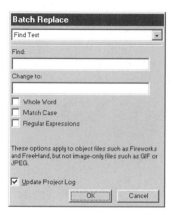

Batch Replace affects only the following file formats: Fireworks PNG, Illustrator, FreeHand, and CorelDRAW. Batch Replace does not affect GIFs and JPEGs.

To select attributes to find and replace during a batch process:

1 Click Edit to open the Batch Replace dialog box.

2 Select the type of attribute to find and replace from the Find pop-up menu.

3 In the Find option, enter or choose the specific element to find.

4 In the Change To option, enter or choose the specific element to replace found items.

5 To add changed files to the Project Log so they are easy to locate later, choose Update Project Log.

6 Click OK to store Find and Replace settings.

7 Click Next to continue the batch process.

For more information about Find and Replace options, see "Finding and replacing" on page 365.

Note: While you can find and replace URLs during a batch process, no new HTML files are generated.

Changing file names with a batch process

Add Rename in the Batch Process dialog box to change the names of the files being processed.

To set naming options for batch-processed files:

1 Choose an option from the Rename pop-up menu.

Original Name leaves file names unchanged.

Add Prefix lets you enter text to add to the beginning of the file name. For example, if you enter "night_", then the file Sunrise.gif is renamed night_Sunrise.gif when it is batch processed.

Add Suffix lets you enter text to add to the end of the file name before the file extension. For example, if you enter "_day", then the file Sunset.gif is renamed Sunset_day.gif when it is batch processed.

2 Click Next to continue the batch process.

Performing commands with a batch process

Add the Commands option to enable JavaScript commands to be performed on files.

To set command options for batch-processed files:

1 Click the plus sign (Windows) or the triangle (Macintosh) beside the Commands option to view the available commands.

2 Select a command and click Add to add it to the Include in Batch list.

These commands cannot be edited.

For more information on commands, see "Creating command scripts using the History panel" on page 380.

Note: Some commands do not work during a batch process. Choose commands that work within the document without requiring any object to be selected.

Backing up batch-processed files

You can save backup copies of the original files from a batch process. Backup copies of files are placed in an Original Files subfolder in the same folder as each original file.

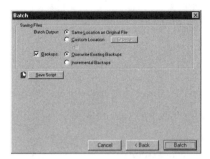

To back up batch-processed files:

1 Select Backups in the Batch Process dialog box.

2 Choose how you want to back up the files:

Overwrite Existing Backups overwrites the previous backup file.

Incremental Backups keeps copies of all the backup files. When you run a new batch process, a number is appended to the end of the file name of the new backup copy.

Note: If Backup is deselected, batch processing in the same file format overwrites the original file if the name is the same. However, batch processing in a different file format creates a new file and does not move or delete the original file.

3 Click Batch to finish the batch process, or check Back to return to the Batch Process dialog box.

Saving batch processes as scripts

Save batch process settings as cross-platform Scriptlets™ to easily recreate the batch process in the future.

To create a batch script:

1 In the Batch Process dialog box, click Save Script.

2 Enter a name and destination for the script and click Save.

Note: If you save your script in the Fireworks 4\Configuration\Commands folder, it appears in the Commands menu.

To run a batch script:

1 Do one of the following:

• Choose File > Run Script.

• Double-click the script file name on the desktop.

2 Select a script and click Open.

3 Choose the files to process with the script:

   Current Open Files processes all open documents.

   Project Log (All Files) processes all files listed in the Project Log panel.

   Project Log (Selected Files) processes the files currently selected in the Project Log panel.

   Custom lets you select files to process.

   Note: Click on the button beside the Files to Process pop-up menu to select files to process.

4 Click OK.

For more information on choosing files, see "Batch processing" on page 371.

Running scripts by dragging and dropping

If you have a batch process that you repeat frequently, save it as a script, then drag that script from your hard drive to the Fireworks icon on your desktop to run the batch process.

• Dragging a script file to the Fireworks application launches Fireworks and immediately run that script. You can also drag a script file plus readable files or folders to the Fireworks application to immediately process those files.

• Dragging multiple script files and multiple graphic files onto Fireworks processes the graphics files multiple times, once for each script.

Project Log

The Project Log helps track and control changes you make in multiple files when using Find and Replace or when batch processing. Any documents changed by Find and Replace are recorded in the Project Log.

Managing searches with the Project Log

Use the Project Log to navigate through selected files, export selected files using their last export settings, or select files to be batch processed.

The Project Log records each changed document and displays the frame of the document that contains the change, as well as the date and time of the change.

Manually add files to the Project Log to track files that you plan to edit frequently.

To manually add files to the Project Log:

1 Choose Window > Project Log.

2 Choose Add Files from the Project Log Options pop-up menu and navigate to the file you want to add.

3 Select the file and click Add.

To open files listed in the Project Log:

Double-click a file named in the Project Log.

To remove an entry from the Project Log:

Choose one or more entries and choose Clear Selection from the Project Log Options pop-up menu.

To remove all entries from the Project Log:

Choose Clear All from the Project Log Options pop-up menu.

To export a file listed in the Project Log using its last export settings:

Select the file and choose Export Again from the Project Log Options pop-up menu.

Viewing and printing the Project Log

The latest version of the Project Log is stored as an HTML file in the Fireworks 4\Settings folder. Open the Project_Log.htm file in a browser to view or print the Project Log.

Scripting

You can reduce the tedium of some repetitive tasks by creating macro scripts in Fireworks. Just perform the steps in Fireworks that you want to include in the script, then use the History panel to save them as one command. Or write your own JavaScript code in a text editor to run within Fireworks.

Use scripts for tasks such as making changes to text; applying colors, strokes, and fills; changing document size and resolution; setting a specific canvas color; or applying multiple effects or distortions to several objects. You can control nearly every command or setting in Fireworks through JavaScript using special JavaScript commands that Fireworks can interpret.

Extending Fireworks

Macromedia Dreamweaver also uses JavaScript. You can write scripts that control Fireworks from within Dreamweaver. For documentation on the JavaScript API, visit http://www.macromedia.com/support/fireworks/extend.html.

Creating command scripts using the History panel

The History panel records a list of the steps you have performed while working in Fireworks. Each step is stored on a separate line of the History panel, starting with the most recent. By default, the panel remembers 20 steps. However you can change this value at any time.

To change the number of actions stored in the History panel, select Preferences from the Edit menu and enter the new value in the Undo Steps field. The History panel stores the information in memory, so be aware that a large number may impede computer performance.

Save groups of steps in the History panel as a command that you can reuse. Saved commands are stored as JSF files in the Fireworks 4\Configuration\Commands folder.

You can execute saved commands in any Fireworks documents. They are not document specific.

To undo or redo steps using the History panel:

- Drag the Undo Marker up the panel until you reach the last step you want to undo or redo.

- Click along the Undo Marker track on the left of the History panel.

  Undone steps remain in the History panel highlighted in gray.

To change the number of steps the History panel remembers:

1 Choose Edit > Preferences.

2 Change Undo Steps to the number of steps you want the History panel to record.

   Note: Additional steps require more computer memory.

To clear all steps from the History panel:

Choose Clear History from the History panel Options pop-up menu in order to free memory and disk space.

Clearing actions from the History panel removes your ability to Undo edits.

To save steps as a command:

1 Choose the steps to save as a command:

- Click a step, then Shift-click another to select a range of steps to save as a command.

- Control-click (Windows) or Command-click (Macintosh) to select noncontiguous steps.

2 Click the Save button at the bottom of the History panel.

3 Enter a name for the command and click OK.

   The command appears on the Commands menu.

Playing steps or commands

You can execute recorded commands or a selection of actions in the History panel at any time.

To play back a saved command:

1　If necessary, select one or more objects.

2　Choose the command from the Commands menu.

To replay a selection of steps:

1　Select one or more objects.

2　Choose the steps in the History panel.

3　Click the Replay button at the bottom of the History panel.

Steps marked with an X are nonrepeatable and cannot be played back.

Separator lines indicate that a different object has become selected. Commands created from steps that cross a separator line can produce unpredictable results.

To apply selected steps to objects in many documents:

1　Select a range of steps.

2　Click the Copy button at the bottom of the History panel.

3　Select one or more objects in any Fireworks document.

4　Choose Edit > Paste.

To repeat the last step:

Choose Edit > Repeat.

Renaming and deleting commands

You can rename or delete commands that appear in the Commands menu.

To rename a command:

1　Choose Commands > Edit Command List.

2　Select a command.

3　Click Rename, enter a new name, and click OK.

To delete a command from within Fireworks:

1 Choose Commands > Edit Command List.

2 Select a command and click Delete.

To delete a command from outside of Fireworks:

Delete the JSF file for the command from the
Fireworks 4\Configuration\Commands folder.

Editing or customizing a script

Command scripts are saved as JavaScript. You can open and edit them in any text
editor, such as NotePad (Windows) or SimpleText (Macintosh).

You can write scripts in JavaScript and use Fireworks-specific commands to
control Fireworks commands and settings. For more on using JavaScript with
Fireworks, see "Extending Fireworks" on page 380.

To edit selected actions as JavaScript in a text editor:

1 Select a range of steps.

2 Click the Copy button at the bottom of the History panel.

3 Switch to a text editing application.

4 Paste the steps.

CHAPTER 21
Fireworks for Photoshop Users

If you are an Adobe Photoshop user new to Macromedia Fireworks, you'll notice some commonalities between the two applications. Like Photoshop 5.5, Fireworks offers flexible tools and features for creating, modifying, and optimizing images in Web format. Other Fireworks features, such as the Layers panel and the History panel, have Photoshop counterparts that appear similar, with some functional differences.

This chapter discusses the main differences between Photoshop 5.5 and Fireworks 4. If you are a Photoshop user who wants to learn Fireworks, then this chapter is for you.

Using Photoshop shortcuts in Fireworks

To make your transition between the two applications easier, you can set up Fireworks to use the same keyboard shortcuts for menu commands as Photoshop.

To use Photoshop keyboard shortcuts for Fireworks menu commands:

1 In Fireworks, choose Edit > Keyboard Shortcuts.

2 Choose Photoshop from the Current Set pop-up menu.

3 If desired, customize shortcut keys for specific menu commands. For more information, see "Changing keyboard shortcut sets" on page 57.

4 Click OK.

Importing Photoshop files into Fireworks

Fireworks provides excellent support for importing native Photoshop (PSD) files, with options for retaining many aspects of the imported files, including layers, masks, and editable text. As a result, you can bring Photoshop images into Fireworks for further editing and Web optimization without losing the ability to export the images back into Photoshop.

Specifying Photoshop file import options

The import preference options in Fireworks let you specify how to handle layers and text in imported Photoshop files. Depending on the options that you choose, you can control the degree of appearance and editability retained in imported files.

To specify import options for Photoshop files:

1 Choose Edit > Preferences, and then click the Import tab (Windows) or choose Import from the pop-up menu (Macintosh).

2 Specify import options:

Layers: Convert to Fireworks Objects imports each layer in the Photoshop file as a separate bitmap object on a single layer in Fireworks.

Layers: Share Layer Between Frames copies the imported layer structure across all frames in the Fireworks file.

Layers: Convert to Frames imports each layer in the Photoshop file as an object on a separate frame in Fireworks. This option is useful for importing files that you want to use as animations.

Text: Editable converts text in the Photoshop file to editable Fireworks text. This option lets you edit imported text using the Fireworks text tools. The converted text may vary slightly in appearance from the original.

Text: Maintain Appearance converts text in the Photoshop file to a bitmap object in Fireworks. This option maintains the original appearance of the text but does not allow you to edit it using the Fireworks text tools.

Use Flat Composite Image imports the Photoshop file as a flattened image without layers. This option works only if a composite image is included in the Photoshop file.

3 Click OK.

Importing or opening Photoshop files

When you import or open a Photoshop file in Fireworks, it converts to a PNG file using the import preferences that you have specified. In addition to preserving layers and text as specified by the import options, Fireworks preserves and converts the following Photoshop features:

• Layer masks convert to Fireworks object masks.

• Layer effects convert to Fireworks Live Effects, if a corresponding Live Effect exists. For example, the Drop Shadow layer effect converts to a Drop Shadow Live Effect in Fireworks.

• Blending modes for layers convert to Fireworks blending modes for corresponding objects, if those blending modes are supported by Fireworks.

• The first alpha channel in the Channels palette converts to transparent areas in the Fireworks image. Fireworks does not support additional Photoshop alpha channels.

Photoshop adjustment layers, clipping groups, and paths are not supported by Fireworks. Fireworks ignores these features when importing Photoshop files.

To import a Photoshop file into Fireworks:

1 Choose File > Import or File > Open and navigate to a Photoshop (PSD) file.

2 Click Open. The Photoshop file is converted to PNG and opened in Fireworks.

Bitmap and vector editing

In Photoshop 5.5, you create and edit images by modifying groups of *pixels,* the building blocks of bitmap images. Fireworks provides comparable support for editing bitmap images, but also offers extensive vector-editing capabilities usually associated with drawing programs like Macromedia FreeHand or Adobe Illustrator.

Fireworks lets you work with both bitmap and vector objects in the same file. Each type of graphic has a different editing mode associated with it.

Vector mode

Vector mode is the default editing mode in Fireworks. In vector mode, you can use various drawing tools to create *vector objects*. Also known as *path objects*, vector objects consist of adjustable points connected with path segments. Unlike bitmap objects, vector objects consist of discrete elements that you can easily select and edit.

For example, you can draw a vector object shaped like a rectangle and paint it by adding a stroke color to its outline and a fill color to its interior. You can then select the rectangle at any time to apply flexible edits, such as changing its stroke color or stretching or resizing its shape, all without affecting other objects in the file.

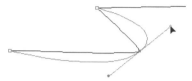

Bitmap mode

You can create new bitmap objects in Fireworks by importing files saved in a bitmap image format, such as Photoshop (PSD). You can also convert vector objects to bitmap objects by choosing Modify > Convert to Bitmap.

When you double-click a bitmap object, you enter bitmap mode, as indicated by the striped border around the document window or the bitmap itself. In bitmap mode, you can use various tools to select, move, paint, and modify pixels, much as you do in Photoshop. You exit bitmap mode by clicking the Stop button on the Status bar (Windows) or at the bottom of the document window (Macintosh).

Gradients

Fireworks and Photoshop 5.5 both let you fill an area with a gradient—a fill consisting of a smooth blend between two or more colors. However, differences in the bitmap and vector characteristics of each application affect how gradients are applied and edited.

Creating gradients

In Photoshop 5.5, you drag with the gradient tool to apply a gradient to a selection of pixels or to an entire layer.

In Fireworks, you can apply gradients as a type of fill to vector objects. After selecting the desired object, you choose a gradient type from the Fill Category pop-up menu in the Fill panel. (Gradient fills are listed below the line division in the pop-up menu.) Fireworks applies the gradient to the interior of the object, just as with any other type of fill.

Fireworks also lets you paint with bitmap gradients as in Photoshop. In bitmap mode you can make a pixel selection using the Lasso, Marquee, or Magic Wand tool, and choose a gradient type from the Fill panel. Then select the Paint Bucket tool, and click or drag inside the pixel selection to fill it.

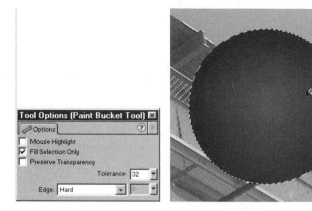

Editing gradients

In Photoshop 5.5, you must specify the colors and shape of a gradient before applying it to an image.

In Fireworks, you can edit gradient fills inside vector objects at any time. Simply select the object containing the gradient and change the settings for the gradient on the Fill panel. You can even drag the fill handles that appear inside the object to adjust the position, angle, and width of the gradient. The old gradient fill is immediately updated to reflect the new gradient settings.

Layers

Although the Fireworks Layers panel resembles the Photoshop 5.5 Layers palette in appearance, layers in Fireworks can behave quite differently, depending on which editing mode you are in.

Layers in vector mode

In vector mode, Fireworks handles layers much as drawing applications like Macromedia FreeHand or Adobe Illustrator do. You can think of a Fireworks layer as a container holding as many objects as you want to put in it. When you draw a vector object, it becomes a new object on the current layer. The Layers panel lists each object, complete with the object name and thumbnail, as a separate item under its container layer.

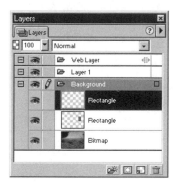

You can easily drag objects up or down in the Layers panel to change their stacking order within a layer or to move them to another layer entirely. You can also edit and delete objects without affecting other objects on the same layer.

Layers in bitmap mode

When you create or import a new bitmap image, it becomes a bitmap object on the current layer. This bitmap object behaves like a Photoshop layer when you enter bitmap mode.

For instance, when you paint on a bitmap object in bitmap mode, you replace any pixels already on that object, whether they are transparent or colored. Once an element is created, it becomes a permanent part of the bitmap object. To create an element separate from the bitmap object, you must first exit bitmap mode.

Groups

With Photoshop 5.5 clipping groups, you can use one layer as a mask for other layers in the group. Although Fireworks does not offer an exact counterpart to clipping groups, you can accomplish a variety of masking effects by using vector masks and bitmap masks in conjunction with the Layers panel.

In Fireworks, the Modify > Group command lets you group together selected objects so that they behave like a single entity. If you move, transform, or change attributes of the group, all the objects in the group change. Grouping objects in Fireworks is most similar to linking layers together in Photoshop.

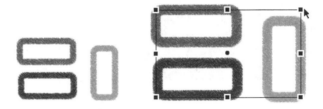

Masks

Fireworks provides masking features that are similar to layer masks in Photoshop 5.5.

To add an empty mask to an object in Fireworks, you select the object and click the New Mask button at the bottom of the Layers panel. A mask thumbnail appears next to the object thumbnail in the Layers panel, in much the same way that layer mask thumbnails appear next to layer thumbnails in Photoshop. You can then paint in the document window, as you do in Photoshop, to create a bitmap mask.

In addition to bitmap masks, you can create vector masks in Fireworks by pasting a vector or text object as a mask. You can then use vector drawing tools such as the Pen tool to modify the mask.

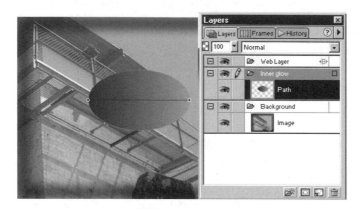

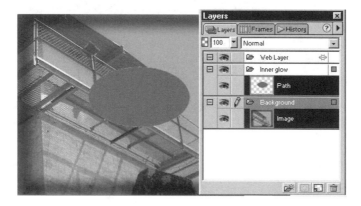

Text

Both Fireworks and Photoshop 5.5 provide support for creating and editing text in documents. You can also export text from one application to the other without losing the ability to make text edits.

In Photoshop, you create text on a type layer and edit its content and attributes using the Type Tool dialog box. Similarly, in Fireworks you create text as a text object on the current layer and edit it using the Text Editor.

Because Fireworks treats text as objects, you can manipulate and modify text in a variety of ways. As in Photoshop, you can select, move, delete, and resize text at any time. Furthermore, you can move text objects to any layer, wrap text automatically inside an area, attach text to a path, and apply transformations, fills, strokes, styles, and Live Effects to text. After any of these edits, text remains fully editable in the Text Editor. The Text Editor also lets you apply attributes such as font, size, and color to individual characters within a text block.

Macromedia Fireworks

Filters and tonal adjustments

Both Fireworks 4 and Photoshop 5.5 offer filters for applying special effects to documents. In Fireworks, you apply filters by selecting an object and then choosing a filter command from the Xtras menu. You can also find filters for color and tonal adjustments, such as Brightness/Contrast or Curves, under the Xtras menu. When you apply a filter to a vector object, Fireworks converts it to a bitmap object.

Fireworks lets you add Photoshop filters and other plug-in filters to the Xtras menu. In addition, you can apply many filters, including Photoshop plug-ins, as editable Live Effects.

Effects

Fireworks 4 and Photoshop 5.5 provide an array of graphical effects, such as shadows and glows, which you can apply to elements in your document and change at any time.

In Photoshop, you use layer effects to add enhancements to a selected layer. In Fireworks, you use the Effect panel to add one or more Live Effects to a selected object. Once you apply a Live Effect, it appears listed in the Effect panel for the selected object, making it easy for you to adjust the effect settings, turn it off, on, or remove the effect altogether.

Furthermore, the Effect panel lets you apply many filters, including most Photoshop plug-in filters, as Live Effects. This feature gives you the ability to apply filters to vector and bitmap objects alike, with the flexibility of changing filter settings at any time.

Task automation

You can automate repetitive tasks in both Fireworks 4 and Photoshop 5.5. The File > Batch Process command in Fireworks lets you apply automated tasks to a batch of documents, much as in Photoshop. Like the Actions palette and File > Automate menu in Photoshop, the Commands menu in Fireworks lets you run automated command scripts on your document. You can choose from a variety of built-in commands or create your own commands.

To record and create your own command script in Fireworks, you use the History panel, which displays recently performed tasks just like the History palette in Photoshop. Simply highlight the desired range of tasks and choose Save as Command from the History panel Options pop-up menu. Fireworks adds your new command to the Commands menu.

Fireworks commands are saved as JavaScript files in your Fireworks application folder. Because Fireworks is capable of interpreting JavaScript, you can edit the commands you save or write your own JavaScripts to perform many Fireworks tasks.

Animation

Like Photoshop 5.5, Fireworks 4 lets you create Animated GIF files. In addition, Fireworks provides the ability to use symbols to copy and tween animation elements easily.

Creating and previewing animations

In the ImageReady application included with Photoshop 5.5, you use the Animation palette to create and preview animation frames.

In Fireworks, you use the Frames panel to create animation frames. Like the ImageReady Animation palette, the Frames panel lets you specify options such as frame delay and looping. To preview your animation in Fireworks, you use the frame controls that appear at the bottom of the document window.

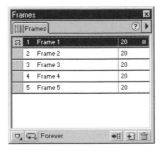

Creating and tweening symbols

In Fireworks, you can create special objects called *symbols.* Because symbol objects can be copied throughout a document as updatable *instances,* they are especially useful for creating animations. For example, you can place instances of the same symbol on separate frames and then update the contents of all instances simultaneously.

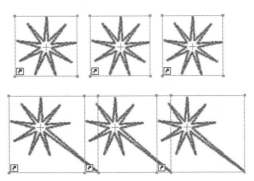

Symbols also provide a way for you to create animation frames using tweening. In Fireworks, you tween between two or more instances of the same symbol to generate intermediate instances, which you can then distribute to separate frames. Fireworks recognizes many attributes when tweening instances, including location, transformation, opacity, and Live Effects.

Web optimization

With respect to optimizing files for Web output, Fireworks 4 is very similar to the ImageReady application included with Photoshop 5.5.

Like ImageReady, Fireworks provides tabbed panels in the document window for previewing both the original and optimized versions of the document. The Optimize panel in Fireworks corresponds to the Optimize palette in ImageReady, letting you choose preset or custom optimization options. In addition to GIF, JPEG, and PNG, Fireworks supports optimization in other image formats such as TIFF, PICT, and BMP.

Once you have set optimization options in Fireworks, you use the File > Export command to save and export the optimized version of your file. As with ImageReady, exporting an optimized file from Fireworks does not affect your original source file.

Exporting Fireworks files to Photoshop

Fireworks provides extensive support for exporting files in Photoshop (PSD) format. Export settings let you control which elements in the file remain editable when you reopen it in Photoshop.

To export a file in Photoshop format:

1   Choose File > Export.

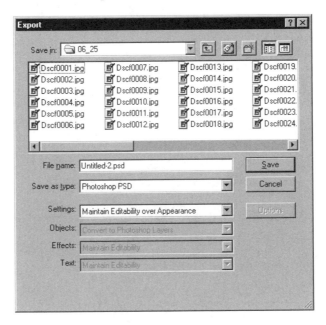

2   In the Export dialog box, name your file and choose Photoshop PSD from the Save As menu.

3   To specify grouped export settings, choose an option from the Settings menu. These settings provide preset combinations of individual export options for objects, effects, and text in the Fireworks file. Individual export options are described in detail in step 4.

Maintain Editability over Appearance sets objects to Convert to Photoshop Layers, effects to Maintain Editability, and text to Maintain Editability. Choose this option if you plan to edit the image extensively in Photoshop and do not need to preserve the exact appearance of the Fireworks image.

Maintain Fireworks Appearance sets objects to Convert to Photoshop Layers, effects to Render Effects, and text to Render Text. Choose this option if you want to maintain control over the Fireworks objects in Photoshop but also want to maintain the original appearance of the Fireworks image.

Smaller Photoshop File sets objects to Flatten Each Fireworks Layer, effects to Render Effects, and text to Render Text. Choose this option if you are exporting a file containing a large number of Fireworks objects.

4   To specify individual export settings, choose Custom from the Settings menu, and choose options from the Objects, Effects, and Text menus:

Objects: Convert to Photoshop Layers converts each Fireworks object to a Photoshop layer and each Fireworks mask to a Photoshop layer mask.

Objects: Flatten Each Fireworks Layer flattens and converts each Fireworks layer to a Photoshop layer. When you choose this option, you lose the ability to edit the Fireworks objects in Photoshop. You also lose features, such as blending modes, that are associated with the Fireworks objects.

Effects: Maintain Editability converts Fireworks Live Effects to corresponding layer effects in Photoshop. Duplicate Live Effects and Live Effects without corresponding Photoshop layer effects are discarded from the exported file.

Effects: Render Effects merges Fireworks Live Effects into the objects that contain them. When you choose this option, you preserve the appearance of the effects, at expense of the ability to edit them.

Text: Maintain Editability converts Fireworks text to editable text layers in Photoshop. When you choose this option, you preserve the appearance of the text, at expense of the ability to edit it.

Text: Render Text converts Fireworks text to bitmap images in Photoshop.

5   Click Save to export the Photoshop file.

CHAPTER 22
Fireworks HTML

Fireworks is a graphic design application built specifically for the Web. Many users of Fireworks, such as graphic artists, may come from a nontechnical background, so taking work created in Fireworks and putting it on the Web may seem a daunting task at first. Many users with technical backgrounds, such as Web designers, may also face similar problems, since they may be used to traditional Web design applications that attempt to do everything in one package. The aim of this chapter is to provide you—whatever your background—with a practical understanding of the tasks involved in taking the HTML generated by Fireworks and "doing something" with it.

What are HTML files?

An HTML file is a text file that contains these elements:

- Text that will appear on the Web page.

- HTML tags that define the formatting and structure of that text and of the entire document and links to images and other HTML documents (Web pages).

    HTML tags are enclosed in brackets and look something like this:

    <TAG> affected text </TAG>

    The opening tag tells a browser, for example, to format the text following in a certain way or to include a graphic. The closing tag (</TAG>), when there is one, indicates the end of that formatting.

Fireworks HTML Frequently Asked Questions

The following section lists answers to some of the questions you're likely to ask when working with Fireworks HTML.

What if I don't know much about HTML code?

The code is automatically generated by Fireworks. You do not need to understand it to use it. Once it is generated there is no need to change it to make it work, so long as you do not rename or move files.

How do I insert Fireworks HTML into an HTML file?

There are several options for inserting HTML code into a file:

- Select Edit > Copy HTML Code to copy your HTML from Fireworks to the Clipboard. Open your HTML editor and paste the HTML in the correct location.

- Open the Fireworks-generated HTML in a text editor. Before exporting, select Include HTML Comments in the HTML Setup to include directions for inserting the code into another file. Highlight the necessary code and copy and paste into your HTML file. You do not have to copy the <HTML> and <BODY> tags, as these should already be included in the destination HTML document.

- Use Update HTML. If no matching Fireworks-generated HTML is found, the new HTML is inserted into the file.

What if I want to use some of the Fireworks HTML but not all of it?

Fireworks HTML is well commented, telling you what pieces of code relate to. But first you must select Include HTML Comments in the HTML Setup dialog box. For example if the code is JavaScript it will be placed between <SCRIPT> and </SCRIPT> tags. All HTML comments begin with <! and end with -->. Anything between these two markers is not interpreted as HTML or JavaScript code.

After you have selected Include HTML Comments, the HTML that should be copied is indicated using the following comments:

<!-----BEGIN COPYING THE HTML HERE---->

<!----STOP COPYING THE HTML HERE------>

How do I insert a button into an HTML file?

Buttons are written in JavaScript. In the HTML, look for code between the <SCRIPT> and </SCRIPT> tags and copy and paste this into your target HTML file.

To insert an individual button, you may find it easier to create a separate Fireworks document for a button. When you export the document, the HTML is simpler to follow, as it contains just the code for that button.

How do I insert slices into an HTML file?

Slices are exported as images. The HTML table defines HTML to reassemble the slices.

Paste all of the <TABLE> section, including the tags, where you want the sliced graphic to appear on the page.

Paste any <MAP> sections immediately after the </TABLE> tag for the sliced graphic.

What do I need to know about JavaScript to paste it into an HTML file?

JavaScript appears between <SCRIPT> and </SCRIPT> tags in the exported HTML. Copy the <SCRIPT> and </SCRIPT> tags as well as the code.

Follow the instructions in the comments generated inside the Fireworks HTML. Remember in HTML Setup to select Include HTML Comments.

Paste JavaScript between the <HEAD> and </HEAD> tags. HTML table information should be pasted between the <BODY> and </BODY> tags.

How do I replace an old version of exported HTML with a new version?

You can replace old HTML in several ways:

- Use Update HTML. You have the option to update only the images or the HTML and images.

- Copy the HTML code to the Clipboard and paste it into the older HTML file.

- Export the HTML again and overwrite the older file.

- To completely overwrite the older version, update the HTML and choose Replace images and their HTML.

If I make changes in my Fireworks document, how do I update just the relevant HTML?

When you update HTML exported to Dreamweaver, the changes you have made outside Fireworks are not affected. However, if you change the Fireworks-generated HTML and this needs to be updated, the changes will be overwritten. Use the Update HTML command.

If you are using another HTML editor, the Update HTML command gives you the option to replace just the images so the changes you have made to the HTML are preserved.

Do people usually design entire Web pages using Fireworks?

No, but it can be done.

Fireworks specializes in the visual elements, such as rollovers, graphics, image maps, hotspots, and optimizing graphics. Designers may use Fireworks for one or all of these things.

Designers often work with other applications, such as Photoshop and other graphic design packages, or Web designers such as Dreamweaver and Adobe GoLive.

How do I update Fireworks images that were exported to Dreamweaver?

Launch Fireworks from within Dreamweaver and then Edit the image. The link between Fireworks and Dreamweaver preserves changes made to the HTML. For more information, see "Editing Fireworks files placed in Dreamweaver" on page 356.

What is the recommended way to integrate Fireworks into a work flow with other applications?

The best way to achieve a consistent work flow is to use Fireworks and Dreamweaver together. Typically, you create the graphics or rollovers in Fireworks and then place them in Dreamweaver. Once you have placed those items in Dreamweaver, you can launch and edit them in Fireworks from Dreamweaver.

Using Launch and Edit in Dreamweaver helps to preserve the links within the HTML (see "Launching Fireworks from within Dreamweaver" on page 353). Fireworks uses document relative URLs, so it is necessary to keep the images and HTML file in the same folder structure. For more on relative URLs, see "Entering absolute or relative URLs" on page 233.

What if I don't have Dreamweaver?

Fireworks lets you export in Generic, FrontPage, and GoLive formats. File > HTML Setup lets you set up global preferences for your preferred method of export for HTML.

When pasting code to Microsoft FrontPage 98, why is the code altered and the links broken?

It is important to keep files with images and HTML code in the correct location. If possible, export them to the final location where they will reside on the Web site. Fireworks uses document relative URLs, so if the HTML or images are moved the URL links are broken.

Where do I go for technical help if something isn't working?

You can make use of these resources: Online Help and TechNotes at http://www.macromedia.com/support/fireworks.

INDEX

T